Mastering Cloud Auditing

Comprehensive concepts, best practices, tools, and techniques for auditing modern cloud systems

Venkata Ramana Krothapalli

bpb

www.bpbonline.com

First Edition 2026

Copyright © BPB Publications, India

ISBN: 978-93-65891-225

LIMITS OF LIABILITY AND DISCLAIMER OF WARRANTY

The information contained in this book is true and correct to the best of author's and publisher's knowledge. The author has made every effort to ensure the accuracy of these publications, but the publisher cannot be held responsible for any loss or damage arising from any information in this book.

All trademarks referred to in the book are acknowledged as properties of their respective owners but BPB Publications cannot guarantee the accuracy of this information.

To View Complete
BPB Publications Catalogue
Scan the QR Code:

www.bpbonline.com

Dedicated to

To my mother, Smt Annapoorna
who taught me morals, ethics, resilience, curiosity, and
the value of hard work and for your unwavering love,
sacrifices, and belief in me

About the Author

Venkata Ramana Krothapalli (CISA, CISSP, CCSK, CCZT, PMP, P3O, ITIL) is a seasoned information security professional with more than 3 decades of experience in different industries, across various geographies, performing diverse roles such as consultant, auditor, CISO, trainer, speaker. He is passionate about information security and skilled in balancing between business needs and information security requirements and has helped various organizations through creating and implementing effective security strategies that are effective in protecting the organizations' information.

He is keen in volunteering and associated with professional bodies such as ISACA, ISC2, TRECERT in various activities including representing the boards of local chapters, journal reviewer, exam developer, providing training to membership etc. and he is a recipient of 'Special Recognition Award' from CISO platform and a finalist in the category of 'Lifetime Achievement Award' from Disaster Recovery Institute.

Ramana holds a master's degree in resources development technology and PG diploma in computer applications from Andhra University.

About the Reviewer

Peeyush Maharshi is a seasoned Enterprise Architect and Technology Leader with over two decades of experience driving digital transformation, cloud adoption, and AI-powered solutions. He has architected comprehensive end-to-end solutions leveraging Cloud platforms, AI/ML technologies, Generative AI, Large Language Models (OpenAI, Anthropic, Hugging Face), Natural Language Processing, and Big Data to solve complex business challenges. Throughout his career, Peeyush has led large-scale modernization initiatives including cloud migrations, containerization, monolith-to-microservice transformations, and platform upgrades using factory-based delivery models. He specializes in defining enterprise data strategies that incorporate Data Lakes, Data Fabrics, and Data Marts while establishing robust data governance frameworks to enhance organizational data maturity. With extensive experience in enterprise governance and compliance adherence, Peeyush has successfully established audit controls at the enterprise level across different geographical locations. His expertise spans multiple domains, enabling organizations to achieve both technical excellence and regulatory compliance. As an avid reader of non-fiction and technology literature, Peeyush serves as a Technical Reviewer for various publications, including Java architecture handbooks, microservice adoption guides, and data science references. His passion for continuous learning and knowledge sharing makes him a valuable contributor to the technology community.

Acknowledgement

This book is a testament to the power of shared wisdom and steadfast support. I want to express my deepest gratitude to the vast security professional community. Your innovative spirit, commitment to excellence, and willingness to share expertise have profoundly influenced my understanding of cloud auditing. I am indebted to the many minds that have shaped this critical field.

I extend a heartfelt thanks to my professional colleagues across many chapters of my career in banking, consulting, and auditing. The rich diversity of our shared experiences, the rigorous debates, and the practical lessons learned together have directly influenced the content of this book. Your insights have been, and continue to be, invaluable. I am also sincerely grateful to the employers who provided me with opportunities and environments that nurtured my growth, enriched my journey, and helped cultivate the expertise reflected in these pages.

Above all, I thank my beloved family and friends, your unwavering faith in me has been my anchor. This book is as much a reflection of their faith in me as it is of my own efforts. A special note of gratitude goes to my spouse, Nasreen, who stood beside me through late nights and early mornings, whose critical eye and honest feedback were indispensable to the quality of this book and to my son, Sameer, whose very presence motivates me at attempting and doing something new and varied each time. Thank you for your endless encouragement, understanding, and the sacrifices you made so I could dedicate myself to this work. Your love and support made every word possible.

I am also grateful to BPB Publications for entrusting me with this project and for the guidance and support provided throughout the journey.

I also would like to acknowledge the reviewers, technical experts and editors who helped shape the book into its final form. Your insights and expertise have undoubtedly elevated the quality of this book. In particular, I wish to recognize Peeyush Maharshi, whose insightful technical reviews were instrumental in shaping the final manuscript.

To all who have walked this path with me, a big thank you. This book is a reflection not only of individual effort but of a community, a profession, and a circle of support that made it possible.

Preface

As organizations around the globe continue their accelerated migration to cloud environments, the importance of robust, insightful, and adaptive auditing practices has never been greater. This handbook is designed to be your trusted guide, an essential resource for auditors, IT professionals, and security practitioners who seek to navigate the evolving landscape of cloud technologies with clarity and confidence.

Cloud computing has not merely changed where data resides, it has transformed the very foundations of governance, risk management, security, and compliance. Recognizing these seismic shifts, I set out to create a practical, accessible, and experience-driven guide to cloud auditing. My goal was straightforward, to illuminate the complexities of cloud assurance, offer actionable methodologies, and share lessons drawn from real-world challenges and successes.

Whether you are a seasoned technology auditor, a cybersecurity leader, or someone newly venturing into the world of cloud assurance, this book is structured to meet you where you are and help you go further. Each chapter aims to equip you with both foundational knowledge and practical tools that you can apply directly within your organization.

Thank you for joining me on this journey toward mastering cloud auditing. I invite you not just to read, but to engage and become a proactive advocate for secure, compliant, and strategically aligned cloud adoption. The future of trustworthy cloud computing depends on informed, empowered professionals like you.

Divided into four key sections, the book starts by laying the foundation of auditing and cloud computing fundamentals. Readers will gain a thorough understanding of how traditional auditing principles are adapted to cloud infrastructures.

The second section delves into regulations, critical frameworks and standards, such as the NIST Standards, ISO/IEC 27017/27-18, and the Cloud Security Alliance's Cloud Controls Matrix (CCM) and Consensus Assessments Initiative Questionnaire (CAIQ), which serve as benchmarks for assessing the maturity and effectiveness of cloud security. Each framework is broken down to show its practical applications in real-world audits.

In the third section, the book addresses the specific areas auditors must focus on within cloud environments, including security, data privacy, infrastructure, and third-party cloud service providers. Detailed chapters offer step-by-step guidance on how to audit each of these areas, with insights into the tools, techniques, and methodologies used by experienced auditors.

The final section emphasizes on automation and auditing across complex, multi-cloud environments. It also includes a forward-looking chapter on the future of cloud auditing, highlighting trends like AI-driven audits and the evolving landscape of cloud governance.

By the end of this book, the reader will be able to confidently apply the knowledge and skills gained and assess the cloud controls including security and privacy, allowing them to independently and effectively audit the cloud environments.

Chapter 1: Introduction to Auditing - This chapter provides an overview of auditing, covering its purpose, principles, and importance in risk management and compliance. It introduces key auditing concepts, such as internal vs. external audits, and the role of auditors.

Chapter 2: Fundamentals of Cloud Computing - A primer on cloud computing, focusing on its core models (IaaS, PaaS, SaaS), deployment types (public, private, hybrid), popular cloud platforms, benefits and challenges. It sets the stage for understanding the unique auditing requirements in the cloud.

Chapter 3: Challenges in Cloud Auditing - This chapter covers cloud computing and traditional auditing practices. It explains the new challenges auditors face in a cloud environment, such as shared responsibility models and data governance complexities.

Chapter 4: GRC in Cloud - This chapter discusses Governance, Risk, and Compliance (GRC) in the cloud and how GRC organizations manage risks, comply with regulations, and align their IT with business goals.

Chapter 5: Common Cloud Regulations - An exploration of key regulations relevant to cloud auditing, such as GDPR, HIPAA, and PCI-DSS. It discusses how cloud environments must adhere to these regulations and the role of auditors in ensuring compliance.

Chapter 6: NIST Cloud Computing Standards - A detailed look at the National Institute of Standards and Technology (NIST) Frameworks and how they apply to cloud auditing. This chapter covers controls, risk management, and using the NIST framework in audits.

Chapter 7: ISO/IEC 27017 and ISO/IEC 27018 - Overview of ISO/IEC 27017, the international standard for cloud-specific security controls, and its role in cloud auditing and ISO/IEC 27001 and 27018 for information security and privacy in the cloud.

Chapter 8: CSA – CCM and STAR Program - This chapter introduces the Cloud Security Alliance's Cloud Controls Matrix (CCM), Consensus Assessments Initiative Questionnaire (CAIQ) and how auditors can leverage it for cloud security assessments. It discusses controls related to compliance, risk, and governance and the STAR program of CSA.

Chapter 9: Auditing Cloud Infrastructure - This chapter covers the specifics of auditing the underlying cloud infrastructure, including virtualization, containerization, and multi-tenancy. It discusses tools for auditing resource allocation and usage.

Chapter 10: Auditing Cloud Security - A practical guide to auditing cloud security controls, focusing on identity and access management (IAM), encryption, and network security. It covers the tools and methodologies used to evaluate security in cloud environments.

Chapter 11: Auditing Cloud Governance and Privacy - This chapter focuses on auditing governance and data privacy in the cloud, including data residency, data encryption, and privacy-by-design principles. It emphasizes compliance with national and international regulations.

Chapter 12: Auditing Cloud Service Providers - Guidance on auditing cloud service providers, covering third-party risk management, service level agreements (SLAs), and the shared responsibility model. It includes key metrics to measure CSP compliance and performance.

Chapter 13: Automating Cloud Auditing - This chapter explores the use of automation tools in cloud auditing, such as continuous control monitoring (CCM) and SIEM tools.

Chapter 14: Emerging trends in Cloud Auditing - A forward-looking chapter discussing emerging trends in cloud auditing, such as AI and machine learning-driven audits, cloud supply chain security, and the evolving regulatory landscape.

Coloured Images

Please follow the link to download the
Coloured Images of the book:

https://rebrand.ly/579e8f

We have code bundles from our rich catalogue of books and videos available at https://github.com/bpbpublications. Check them out!

Errata

We take immense pride in our work at BPB Publications and follow best practices to ensure the accuracy of our content to provide with an indulging reading experience to our subscribers. Our readers are our mirrors, and we use their inputs to reflect and improve upon human errors, if any, that may have occurred during the publishing processes involved. To let us maintain the quality and help us reach out to any readers who might be having difficulties due to any unforeseen errors, please write to us at :

errata@bpbonline.com

Your support, suggestions and feedbacks are highly appreciated by the BPB Publications' Family.

At www.bpbonline.com, you can also read a collection of free technical articles, sign up for a range of free newsletters, and receive exclusive discounts and offers on BPB books and eBooks. You can check our social media handles below:

Instagram   *Facebook*   *Linkedin*   *YouTube*

Get in touch with us at: business@bpbonline.com for more details.

Piracy

If you come across any illegal copies of our works in any form on the internet, we would be grateful if you would provide us with the location address or website name. Please contact us at business@bpbonline.com with a link to the material.

If you are interested in becoming an author

If there is a topic that you have expertise in, and you are interested in either writing or contributing to a book, please visit www.bpbonline.com. We have worked with thousands of developers and tech professionals, just like you, to help them share their insights with the global tech community. You can make a general application, apply for a specific hot topic that we are recruiting an author for, or submit your own idea.

Reviews

Please leave a review. Once you have read and used this book, why not leave a review on the site that you purchased it from? Potential readers can then see and use your unbiased opinion to make purchase decisions. We at BPB can understand what you think about our products, and our authors can see your feedback on their book. Thank you!

For more information about BPB, please visit www.bpbonline.com.

Join our Discord space

Join our Discord workspace for latest updates, offers, tech happenings around the world, new releases, and sessions with the authors:

https://discord.bpbonline.com

Table of Contents

CHAPTER 1
Introduction to Auditing

Introduction

This chapter provides an overview of auditing, covering its advantages, principles, and importance in risk management and compliance. It introduces key auditing concepts, types of audits such as internal vs. external audits, auditing standards, auditing process, and the role of auditors.

Structure

This chapter covers the following topics:

- Introduction to auditing
- Types of audits
- Key auditing concepts
- Auditing standards
- Auditing process
- Ethics in auditing

Objectives

By the end of this chapter, readers will be able to understand the importance of auditing, crucial concepts, and the general process of auditing. Readers will also learn about competence requirements for auditors and relevant standards against which the audits can be planned and performed.

Introduction to auditing

Auditing is the systematic examination of financial records, information systems, business, technical processes, and other relevant documentation. This is done to assess their accuracy, completeness, and adherence to established standards or regulations. It serves as a critical mechanism for ensuring transparency, accountability, and the efficient management of resources. Auditing is often performed by internal or external auditors who are tasked with verifying that financial reports or organizational processes, either business or technical, comply with applicable laws, regulations, and standards.

The importance of auditing cannot be overstated in today's complex business environment. Audits help organizations maintain integrity in financial reporting, prevent fraud, ensure compliance with laws, and improve operational efficiency. For external stakeholders such as investors, creditors, and regulatory bodies, auditing provides a reasonable assurance that an organization's financial statements present a true and fair view of its financial position and processes, indicating whether they are reliable and robust. For internal stakeholders, such as management and board members, audits serve as a tool for improving governance and internal controls, helping organizations achieve their objectives more effectively.

Evolution and history of auditing

The practice of auditing has a long history, dating back to ancient civilizations. Early forms of auditing were used primarily to verify the records of government officials and treasurers, ensuring that public funds were properly accounted for. In the medieval period, auditors were employed by monarchies and religious institutions to oversee financial activities and safeguard assets.

Modern auditing, as we know it today, began to take shape during the Industrial Revolution, when the growth of large-scale businesses and corporate structures made it necessary to establish more formalized auditing processes. By the early 20th century, the need for greater corporate transparency led to the development of auditing standards and regulatory frameworks. Auditing has become an integral part of corporate governance, with many professional bodies, such as the **Institute of Internal Auditors (IIA)** and the **Information Systems Audit and Control Association (ISACA)**, playing a pivotal role in shaping the profession.

Scope and relevance of auditing

While auditing has been traditionally associated with the verification of financial statements, it has expanded significantly over the years. Auditors today may conduct a variety of audits, depending on the specific needs of the organization or industry. In addition to financial audits, which focus on the accuracy of financial records, there are internal audits that examine an organization's internal controls and risk management systems, compliance audits that ensure adherence to laws and regulations, information system audits to evaluate how an organization safeguards its information assets, and operational audits that evaluate the efficiency and effectiveness of business processes.

Moreover, as business environments have grown more complex, specialized forms of auditing have emerged. Forensic audits, for example, are used to investigate financial crimes such as embezzlement or fraud, while environmental audits assess compliance with environmental regulations and the impact of business activities on the environment. These diverse applications demonstrate the adaptability of auditing to meet a wide range of organizational needs.

In essence, auditing acts as a safeguard for both organizations and their stakeholders, promoting trust and confidence in financial reporting, governance, and compliance with regulations.

Key requirements for auditors

The following quote sums up what makes you a good auditor:

> *To be a good auditor, you have to be better at business than your client*

-Ron Weber

Competent auditors are integral to the effectiveness of an audit process. Their personal traits, technical knowledge, skills, and ongoing professional development all contribute to the reliability and quality of the audit outcomes. Here are some traits that competent auditors must display:

- **Professional behavior**: Auditors must demonstrate ethical behavior, be open-minded, observant, diplomatic, perceptive, decisive, adaptable, and maintain confidentiality and integrity. They should also exhibit sound judgment, demonstrate respect for others, and be committed to impartiality.

- **Knowledge and skills**: Auditors should understand audit principles, procedures, and methods. This includes being familiar with auditing techniques, sampling methods, and relevant terminology.

- **Knowledge of regulations and legal requirements**: Auditors must understand the standards, legal and regulatory requirements against which audits are conducted, as well as the organizational context. They should be knowledgeable about the specific industry or sector they are auditing, technologies, as well as its unique risks, practices, and terminology.

- **Technical and interpersonal skills:**
  - o **Analytical and critical thinking**: Auditors should be capable of analyzing complex information and drawing reasonable conclusions.

  - o **Communication skills**: Effective verbal and written communication is essential for clearly conveying audit findings and observations.

  - o **Interpersonal skills**: Auditors should build and maintain relationships with stakeholders, exhibit respect, and engage effectively with auditees.

- **Experience and continuous learning**: Auditors should focus on continuous professional development to expand their knowledge and skills over time to maintain their competence and keep pace with changes in relevant standards, technologies, and practices.

Various roles of an auditor

The role of an auditor is to provide independent, objective evaluations of an organization's financial statements, business and technical processes, and compliance with laws and standards. Auditors are expected to play a critical part in ensuring transparency, accountability, and trust for all stakeholders. They help stakeholders such as management, shareholders, and regulatory bodies understand the accuracy and reliability of an organization's reporting and operations. Here are some key roles of an auditor that may vary depending on the degree of independence:

- Assessing financial accuracy
- Evaluating internal controls
- Compliance checks
- Reporting findings
- Promoting ethical conduct
- Supporting corporate governance
- Identifying and mitigating risks
- Advising on process improvements
- Supporting strategic decision-making

The last four roles listed above are more applicable to internal auditors. In summary, auditors are critical in ensuring accuracy, efficiency, compliance, and ethical conduct within organizations. Their role adds value by verifying information and identifying risks and improvement areas that support long-term organizational success.

Types of audits

Auditing is not a one-size-fits-all approach. Audits can be categorized into several distinct types, each serving a specific purpose. However, the way these types are defined or grouped may differ across various sources, depending on the criteria or context used for classification. Several different types of audits exist based on various factors such as objectives and scope of the audit, organizational structure, degree of independence, and audit location. In the following sub-sections, we will be exploring in detail the main types of audits commonly conducted in organizations.

Financial audits

Financial audits are the most common type of audit, primarily focused on verifying the accuracy and fairness of an organization's financial statements. These audits ensure that financial reports are prepared according to accepted accounting principles. External auditors, typically from accounting firms, carry out financial audits to provide stakeholders (such as investors and regulators) with an independent assessment of the financial health and performance of the organization.

Key aspects of financial audits are as follows:

- Verification of assets, liabilities, income, and expenses
- Ensuring compliance with accounting standards
- Detecting errors, misstatements, or fraudulent activities

Internal audits

Internal audits are conducted by employees of an organization or an in-house internal audit department. Unlike external audits, which focus on a specific scope as part of the engagement, internal audits examine an organization's internal controls, risk management processes, and governance. The goal is to assess operational efficiency, ensure compliance with laws and internal policies, and identify areas for improvement. Internal auditors report their findings directly to management and the board of directors. At times, internal auditors also participate in internal organizational improvement activities while ensuring that their independence and objectivity are maintained.

Some key objectives of internal audits are as follows:

- Evaluating the effectiveness of internal controls
- Ensuring regulatory compliance
- Identifying areas for cost reduction or process improvement
- Monitoring risk management strategies

External audits

External audits are performed by independent auditing firms that are external to the organization, and their main goal is to provide an objective evaluation of the financial statements or specific business processes and practices, and vary in nature for different engagements based on the scope. Unlike internal audits, which are ongoing and driven by management's needs, external audits occur periodically and are generally required by law or regulation (e.g., for public companies or non-profits), or client mandates. External auditors are independent of the organization, which enhances the credibility and objectivity of their reports.

External audits also serve to:

- Provide assurance to external stakeholders such as investors, creditors, and regulators
- Detect fraud or mismanagement
- Validate adherence to financial reporting standards

Operational audits

Operational audits focus on evaluating the efficiency and effectiveness of an organization's operational processes. The goal is to identify inefficiencies, assess resource utilization, and recommend improvements that can enhance performance. Operational audits often go beyond financial matters to include areas such as production processes, supply chain management, and customer service operations.

Key objectives of operational audits are as follows:

- Improving operational efficiency and effectiveness
- Evaluating resource management
- Enhancing the organization's ability to achieve its strategic goals

Information system audits

Information system audits examine the management controls of an organization's information assets, including technical infrastructure and business applications, to evaluate whether the information assets are safeguarded adequately. Information system audits specifically focus on confidentiality, integrity, and availability:

In addition, information system audits cover the following aspects:

- Adherence to relevant legal and regulatory requirements
- Organizational strategies, policies, and procedures
- Verification of information protection mechanisms
- Review of technical and managerial controls implementation

Compliance audits

Compliance audits assess whether an organization adheres to external laws, regulations, and internal policies. These audits are particularly common in industries such as healthcare, finance, and environmental management, where regulatory requirements are strict. Compliance audits may be conducted by internal teams or external auditors, and failure to meet regulatory standards can result in penalties or legal consequences.

Compliance audits typically cover the following:

- Adherence to specific legal and regulatory requirements
- Implementation of internal policies and procedures
- Reporting on areas of non-compliance and recommending corrective actions

Forensic audits

Forensic audits are specialized investigations aimed at uncovering financial fraud, embezzlement, or other forms of misconduct. These audits are often used in legal proceedings to gather evidence related to financial crimes. Forensic auditors employ advanced techniques to trace illicit activities and produce findings that can withstand scrutiny in court.

Key areas covered by forensic audits include the following:

- Detecting and investigating fraud or financial crimes
- Analyzing financial data for suspicious activities
- Assisting in legal actions by providing expert witness testimony or reports

Audits vs. assessments

An audit, usually conducted annually, is a standardized, more focused, in-depth, and systematic examination that verifies compliance with regulations and standards, while an assessment can be performed regularly and is flexible, a broader evaluation that aims to identify areas for improvement. An audit is generally conducted by a qualified auditor and is used to express an opinion, while an assessment can be performed by any subject matter expert and is used to evaluate a system, process, or individual aiming for improvements.

Key auditing concepts

Understanding key auditing concepts is critical for appreciating the nuances of the audit process. These concepts form the foundation for conducting effective audits and ensuring that the results are reliable, objective, and beneficial for the organization and its stakeholders. We will be looking at key auditing concepts in the following sub-sections.

Audit evidence

Audit evidence refers to the information collected by the auditor to support their findings and conclusions. This evidence can be obtained through various methods, such as physical inspections, document reviews, and interviews. The quality of audit evidence is essential to determine the accuracy of the auditor's opinion.

Types of audit evidence include the following:

- Documentary evidence (e.g., invoices, contracts)
- Physical evidence (e.g., inventory count, physical assets)
- Testimonial evidence (e.g., statements from employees or third parties)

Materiality

Materiality is a key concept in auditing that refers to the significance of financial information or misstatements that could influence the decision-making process of users of the financial statements. Auditors assess materiality during the planning phase to determine which areas of the audit require the most attention.

Factors that determine materiality include the following:

- The size of the misstatement
- The nature of the misstatement (e.g., fraud vs. clerical error)
- The potential impact on stakeholders

Risk assessment

Risk assessment involves identifying and evaluating risks that may affect the accuracy and reliability of financial statements or other audited processes. Auditors focus on areas with a higher risk of material misstatements, fraud, or inefficiencies. Understanding risk helps auditors prioritize their efforts and allocate resources more effectively.

Key elements of risk assessment are as follows:

- **Inherent risk**: The susceptibility of an account or process to material misstatement, before considering controls
- **Control risk**: The risk that internal controls will not prevent or detect material misstatements
- **Detection risk**: The risk that auditors fail to detect a material misstatement

Control environment

The control environment refers to the overall attitude, awareness, and actions of management regarding the importance of internal controls. A strong control environment reflects the commitment of the organization to ethical behavior, compliance with laws, and accurate financial reporting. It forms the basis for effective risk management and operational efficiency.

Elements of a strong control environment include the following factors:

- **Tone at the top**: The commitment of senior management to ethics and compliance
- **Segregation of duties**: Ensuring no single individual controls an entire process
- **Monitoring controls**: Ongoing evaluation of internal controls for effectiveness

Independence and objectivity

The concepts of independence and objectivity are fundamental to the credibility of auditors. Auditors must be free from any conflicts of interest that could compromise their ability to deliver an impartial and unbiased opinion. Independence can be categorized into:

- **Independence of mind**: Being able to form an unbiased opinion
- **Independence in appearance**: Avoiding situations that may appear to compromise independence

Auditing standards

Auditing standards provide a framework for auditors to perform their work in a systematic, consistent, and reliable manner. These standards ensure that audits are conducted with a high degree of professionalism and that the findings are comparable and trustworthy across organizations and industries. Different bodies have developed standards depending on the type of audit being performed. In the following sub-sections, we will explore key global and regional auditing standards.

International Standards on Auditing

The **International Standards on Auditing (ISAs)** are a set of principles issued by the **International Auditing and Assurance Standards Board (IAASB)**. ISAs provide a globally recognized framework for auditing financial statements and are widely used across many countries.

The primary objectives of ISAs are as follows:

- Ensuring high-quality audits
- Promoting consistency in the auditing process
- Providing clear guidance on how audits should be performed

Key principles of ISAs are listed here:

- **Planning the audit**: Auditors are required to develop a plan that defines the scope and objectives of the audit.

- **Risk assessment**: ISAs emphasize the identification of significant risks that could lead to material misstatements.

- **Gathering evidence**: Auditors must obtain sufficient and appropriate audit evidence to support their conclusions.

- **Reporting**: The auditor's report should provide a clear and objective assessment of the financial statements' fairness.

Countries that have adopted ISAs often customize the standards to align with their local regulations or accounting principles.

Generally Accepted Auditing Standards

In the *United States*, **Generally Accepted Auditing Standards (GAAS)** are established by the **American Institute of Certified Public Accountants (AICPA)**. GAAS are designed to provide a comprehensive set of guidelines for conducting audits of both private and public entities. GAAS shares many similarities with ISAs, but they also reflect the unique legal and regulatory environment of the *U.S.*

The GAAS framework is built around three categories:

- **General standards**: Address the qualifications and ethical standards required of auditors (e.g., competence, independence, and due professional care).

- **Standards of fieldwork**: Guide how audits should be conducted, including planning, internal control assessment, and evidence collection.

- **Standards of reporting**: Define how audit results should be communicated, emphasizing fairness and the disclosure of any identified issues.

GAAS is applied primarily in the U.S., though elements of it are integrated into other international auditing standards.

ISO 19011:2018

ISO 19011:2018 is a globally recognized standard that provides guidelines for auditing management systems, including quality management, environmental management, and other areas such as occupational health and safety or energy management. Unlike ISAs and GAAS, which focus on financial audits, ISO 19011 offers a comprehensive approach to auditing various management systems within organizations.

Key features of ISO 19011 are as follows:

- **Applicability**: The standard applies to audits of different types of management systems, making it highly versatile.

- **Principles of auditing**: ISO 19011 outlines the principles of auditing, such as integrity, fair presentation, due professional care, confidentiality, and independence.

- **Audit program management**: It emphasizes the importance of establishing an effective audit program that aligns with an organization's goals and risks.

- **Competence of auditors**: The standard provides guidance on the necessary competencies for auditors, particularly in areas relevant to the systems being audited.

ISO 19011 is widely used by organizations that operate internationally or those with complex operational processes that span multiple domains (e.g., technology, information security, quality, and environment). The standard ensures that audits in these areas are conducted with consistency and thoroughness.

IIA standards

The IIA sets the professional standards for internal auditors through its **international professional practices framework (IPPF)**, which includes the **international standards for the professional practice of internal auditing (ISPPIA)**. These standards are essential for guiding internal auditors on how to perform their duties effectively and maintain objectivity and professionalism.

Core elements of the IIA standards include:

- **Attribute standards**: These standards address the characteristics of the internal audit function, such as independence, objectivity, and the professional competence of internal auditors.

- **Performance standards**: These standards focus on the performance of individual audit engagements, covering areas such as risk assessment, engagement planning, and audit reporting.

- **Implementation standards**: The IIA also provides implementation standards that offer practical guidance on how to apply the attribute and performance standards in different contexts (e.g., public sector, consulting, or assurance engagements).

The IIA standards are critical for ensuring that internal audits add value to the organization by improving its risk management, control, and governance processes. The internal audit profession, guided by these standards, plays a vital role in safeguarding organizational integrity.

ISACA ITAF

ISACA is a global association that provides **information technology (IT)** professionals with knowledge, credentials, training, and community in audit, security, governance, risk, and privacy. ISACA provides a framework titled **Information Technology Audit Framework (ITAF)** that consists of multiple levels of guidance. The ITAF defines standards and best practices aligned with the sequence of the auditing process in assessing the operational effectiveness of an enterprise and ensuring compliance.

IT audit and assurance standards

The standards are divided into three categories:

- General standards (1000 series) are the guiding principles under which the IT assurance profession operates. These apply to the conduct of all assignments dealing with IT audit and assurance, professional ethics, independence, and objectivity. These general standards also assess due care as well as knowledge, competency, and skills. These standards comprise general aspects of IT audit, such as audit charter, organizational independence, auditor objectivity, reasonable expectation, due professional care, proficiency, assertions, and criteria.

- Performance standards (1200 series) deal with the conduct of the assignments, including planning, supervision, scoping, risk and materiality, resource mobilization, and supervision. Additionally, these standards also include assignment management, audit and assurance evidence, the exercise of professional judgment, and due care. Performance standards comprise aspects related to the planning and execution of IT audits, such as risk assessment, audit scheduling, engagement planning, performance and supervision, evidence, engaging experts, irregularities, and illegal acts.

- Reporting standards (1400 series) address the types of reports, means of communication, and the information communicated. The reporting standards comprise reporting and follow-up activities. The follow-up actions help strengthen the organization's internal control mechanisms, ensuring continuous improvement and accountability.

IT audit and assurance guidelines

These guidelines are designed to support the standards directly and help practitioners achieve alignment with them. They follow the same categorization as the standards, which include general guidelines (2000 series), performance guidelines (2200 series), and reporting guidelines (2400 series).

IT audit and assurance tools and techniques

These documents provide additional guidance for IT audit and assurance professionals and consist of white papers, IT audit/assurance programs, reference books, etc.

Other regional or country-specific standards

In addition to global standards like ISAs and ISO 19011, many countries have developed their own auditing frameworks tailored to local laws and regulations. Some notable examples of regional and country-specific organizations include:

- **Auditing and assurance standards**: The **Institute of Chartered Accountants of India (ICAI)** issues these standards through its **Auditing and Assurance Standards Board (AASB)**. They are largely based on international auditing standards.

- **UK's Financial Reporting Council (FRC)**: In the UK, the FRC issues auditing standards based on ISAs but adapted for *UK*-specific requirements. The *UK* **Corporate Governance Code and Ethical Standards** are particularly significant for audits in the *UK*.

- **Public Company Accounting Oversight Board (PCAOB)**: In the U.S, PCAOB oversees the audits of public companies and establishes auditing standards that apply to these audits. PCAOB standards focus on enhancing the quality and reliability of audits, particularly in the context of public company reporting.

- **Canada's auditing standards**: Canadian auditing standards are governed by the Canadian **Auditing and Assurance Standards Board** (**AASB**), which adopts ISAs with modifications for the Canadian legal environment.

These regional standards reflect the diverse regulatory and legal environments in which audits are conducted, ensuring that auditing practices are aligned with local expectations while adhering to global principles.

Auditing process

The auditing process involves several structured steps designed to ensure the thorough examination and verification of financial records, operational procedures, and other critical aspects of an organization. Each phase of the audit contributes to the overall goal of delivering an accurate, objective, and actionable audit report. The following sub-sections provide a detailed look at the key stages of the audit process.

Planning and scoping the audit

The first step in any audit is to plan the process carefully. Planning involves defining the objectives, scope, and approach for the audit, ensuring that the auditor understands the entity being audited and the potential risks involved.

Key activities in the planning phase are as follows:

- **Understanding the entity**: Auditors begin by gaining a deep understanding of the organization's business model, its operating environment, and any external factors that may influence the audit. This includes reviewing the organization's industry, regulatory landscape, and internal controls.

- **Defining the scope**: The scope of the audit determines which areas of the organization will be reviewed. The scope is often influenced by factors such as the entity's size, complexity, and prior audit results. Audits may focus solely on financial statements or expand to include compliance, operational efficiency, or internal control systems.

- **Setting the audit objective**: The audit objective defines what the audit intends to achieve. For financial audits, the objective might be to verify that the financial statements present a true and fair view of the organization's financial position.

- **Developing the audit strategy**: The audit strategy outlines how the auditor plans to achieve the objectives within the defined scope. This includes selecting specific areas of focus, determining audit techniques (e.g., sampling, testing), and allocating resources (such as personnel and technology).

Risk assessment and control evaluation

Once the audit plan is in place, the auditor assesses risks that may affect the accuracy of financial records or the effectiveness of operations. Risk assessment is a critical step as it helps auditors focus on high-risk areas where material misstatements or irregularities are most likely to occur.

Key activities in risk assessment include the following:

- **Identifying inherent risks**: Inherent risk refers to the likelihood of material misstatement in the financial statements, before considering the effectiveness of internal controls. These risks could stem from complex transactions, industry-specific challenges, or other external factors.

- **Evaluating control risk**: Control risk arises when an organization's internal controls fail to detect or prevent material misstatements. Auditors assess the design and operational effectiveness of internal controls to determine whether they mitigate inherent risks.

- **Conducting a risk-based approach**: Auditors use the results of the risk assessment to adopt a risk-based approach, focusing their attention and resources on the areas that pose the highest risk of misstatement or non-compliance. This ensures the audit is both efficient and effective.

Gathering evidence and sampling

After identifying the key risks, auditors move on to gathering sufficient and appropriate audit evidence. The purpose of gathering evidence is to support the auditor's opinion on whether the financial statements are free from material misstatement and whether the organization's internal controls are operating effectively.

Methods used for gathering audit evidence are as follows:

- **Inspection of documents and records**: Auditors review documents such as invoices, contracts, and bank statements to verify the accuracy and completeness of financial records.

- **Observation**: Auditors may observe processes, such as physical inventory counts or production operations, to ensure they are conducted as reported.

- **Inquiries**: Interviews with management, employees, and third parties can provide additional insight into the organization's processes, controls, and any potential risks.

- **Confirmation**: Auditors may request confirmations from third parties, such as banks or suppliers, to verify the existence and accuracy of certain transactions or balances.

- **Analytical procedures**: Auditors use analytical procedures to identify any unusual trends, variances, or inconsistencies in financial data that may warrant further investigation.

Sampling plays a crucial role during this phase. Given the volume of transactions in most organizations, it is not practical to audit every transaction. Auditors use statistical and judgmental sampling techniques to select representative samples of transactions for detailed testing. The results of these tests are extrapolated to form conclusions about the overall population.

Performing audit tests

Audit tests is the process of evaluating the accuracy of the organization's records and the effectiveness of its internal controls. There are two main types of audit tests:

- **Substantive tests**: These tests focus on verifying the accuracy of financial statement balances and transactions. Substantive tests include detailed procedures such as confirming account balances, recalculating figures, and verifying the existence of assets.

- **Tests of controls**: These tests assess whether the organization's internal controls are functioning as intended. For example, an auditor may test the approval process for large expenditures to ensure that only authorized individuals can approve payments.

The results of audit tests help auditors determine whether they can rely on the organization's internal controls or whether further substantive testing is required.

Audit report writing and presentation

Once the audit is complete, the findings are compiled into an audit report. The audit report is the formal document that communicates the results of the audit to management, the board of directors, or external stakeholders. The content and structure of the report vary depending on the type of audit, but all audit reports follow certain general principles.

Key components of an audit report are as follows:

- **Introduction**: The introduction outlines the scope, objectives, and methodology of the audit.

- **Executive summary**: This section provides a high-level overview of the key findings and recommendations, particularly for senior management or the board.

- **Detailed findings**: This is the core of the audit report, where auditors present their observations, supported by evidence. Findings may include errors, inefficiencies, or instances of non-compliance with regulations or internal policies.

- **Recommendations**: For each finding, auditors provide practical recommendations for corrective actions. These recommendations aim to improve the organization's financial reporting, controls, or operational efficiency.

- **Conclusion**: The conclusion provides the auditor's overall opinion on the fairness of the financial statements (in the case of financial audits) or the effectiveness of the processes and controls (for other types of audits).

Follow-up on audit recommendations

An audit does not end with the issuance of the audit report. It is equally important for auditors to follow up on their recommendations to ensure that corrective actions have been taken and that the organization has addressed the identified risks or issues. This follow-up process typically involves the following:

- **Tracking the implementation of recommendations**: Auditors work with management to develop an action plan and timeline for implementing the audit recommendations.

- **Conducting a follow-up audit**: In some cases, auditors may conduct a follow-up audit to verify that corrective actions have been successfully implemented and are functioning as intended.

- **Ongoing monitoring**: For internal audits, auditors often integrate the follow-up process into the organization's broader risk management and governance processes, ensuring continuous improvement.

Ethics in auditing

Ethics are a cornerstone of the auditing profession. Since audits involve verifying financial information, processes, and systems, auditors are placed in positions of great responsibility. Stakeholders rely on auditors to provide honest, unbiased, and thorough assessments. Ethical behavior ensures that auditors can perform their duties with integrity, objectivity, and professionalism while safeguarding public trust in financial reporting and governance. This section will look into the core principles of ethics in auditing, the codes of conduct auditors must follow, common ethical dilemmas, and the consequences of unethical behavior.

Importance of ethics in auditing

Ethics in auditing is vital for maintaining the trust and confidence of stakeholders such as investors, management, regulators, and the general public. Ethical auditors provide assurance that an organization's financial statements or internal processes are accurate, reliable, and free from material misstatements or fraud. Unethical behavior, on the other hand, can lead to significant financial and reputational damage, as seen in various corporate scandals.

Here are some key reasons that elaborate on why ethics are critical in auditing:

- **Protecting the public interest**: Auditors have a duty to act in the best interest of the public, rather than serving the needs of any particular individual or organization.

- **Promoting transparency**: Ethical auditors help ensure that financial reporting is transparent and reflects the true financial health of an organization.

- **Preventing conflicts of interest**: Auditors must avoid situations where their personal or financial interests could compromise their objectivity or independence.

- **Ensuring accountability**: Ethical auditing practices hold management accountable for their actions and help promote good governance within organizations.

Core principles of auditing ethics

The ethical framework for auditors is grounded in several core principles, which are defined by professional bodies such as IIA, ISACA, and national auditing bodies. Here are some core principles of auditing:

- **Integrity**: Integrity is the foundational principle of auditing ethics. Auditors must conduct their work with honesty and truthfulness. They are expected to be straightforward in their dealings, ensuring that they do not mislead, conceal, or misrepresent information. Integrity also means that auditors should not allow personal interests or relationships to influence their professional judgment.

- **Objectivity**: Objectivity refers to auditors' requirement to maintain impartiality and neutrality in their work. They must avoid biases, conflicts of interest, and undue influence from management or other stakeholders. Objectivity is critical in ensuring that the auditor's findings and conclusions are based solely on the evidence gathered and not influenced by external pressures.

- **Confidentiality**: Auditors often have access to sensitive and confidential information about the organization they are auditing. The principle of confidentiality ensures that auditors do not misuse or disclose this information without proper authorization, except in cases where disclosure is required by law or to prevent illegal activities. Respecting confidentiality helps protect the client's privacy and maintains trust between the auditor and the organization.

- **Professional competence and due care**: Auditors are expected to maintain a high level of professional competence, continually updating their knowledge and skills to keep up with changes in accounting standards, auditing techniques, and regulatory requirements. Due care refers to the diligence with which auditors must carry out their work, ensuring that they meet the required standards of the profession. Auditors should not undertake audits if they lack the necessary expertise or resources to perform them effectively.

- **Professional behavior**: Auditors must comply with all relevant laws, regulations, and professional standards, and must avoid any actions that could discredit the auditing profession. This includes avoiding actions that may create the perception of impropriety or lack of professionalism.

- **Codes of conduct and ethical guidelines**: Various professional bodies have established codes of conduct and ethical guidelines that auditors must adhere to. These guidelines provide clear expectations regarding behavior and help auditors navigate complex ethical issues that may arise during the audit process.

Common ethical dilemmas in auditing

Despite clear ethical standards, auditors often encounter ethical dilemmas in their work. These situations can be challenging, requiring auditors to make difficult decisions while balancing their professional obligations with other pressures. Some common ethical dilemmas include the following:

- **Conflicts of interest**: A common ethical dilemma auditors usually face is the issue of conflict of interest. This occurs when the auditor's objectivity is compromised by a relationship with the client or personal interests. For example, if an auditor has a financial stake in the organization being audited, they may be tempted to overlook discrepancies in the financial statements. To mitigate this risk, auditors must disclose any potential conflicts of interest and, if necessary, recuse themselves from the audit.

- **Pressure from management**: Auditors may face pressure from senior management to present a more favorable picture of the organization's financial position than is warranted. This could involve manipulating financial statements, downplaying risks, or ignoring internal control deficiencies. Ethical auditors must resist such pressures and adhere to their duty to report the facts accurately.

- **Acceptance of gifts or hospitality**: Auditors may be offered gifts, entertainment, or other forms of hospitality from clients, which can compromise their independence or create the appearance of impropriety. Ethical standards typically prohibit auditors from accepting any gifts or benefits that could influence their professional judgment. To avoid these situations, many auditing firms have strict policies on gifts and hospitality.

Consequences of unethical behavior in auditing

The consequences of unethical behavior in auditing can be severe, both for the auditor and the organization being audited. Unethical actions can lead to financial penalties, legal liabilities, loss of reputation, and in some cases, criminal prosecution. High-profile corporate scandals such as Enron and WorldCom demonstrate the devastating effects that unethical auditing practices can have on stakeholders and the broader economy.

Key consequences include the following:

- **Loss of professional accreditation**: Auditors found to have violated ethical standards may lose their licenses or certifications, effectively ending their professional careers.

- **Legal penalties**: Unethical auditors may face civil or criminal charges, depending on the severity of their misconduct.

- **Reputational damage**: Both auditors and the organizations they audit can suffer significant reputational harm if unethical practices are uncovered. This can lead to a loss of business, trust, and investor confidence.

Upholding ethics in the auditing profession

To promote ethical behavior in auditing, ongoing education, and strong governance structures are essential. Global professional bodies require auditors to undergo continuous ethics training and to follow rigorous standards in their work. Additionally, organizational culture plays a crucial role in fostering an ethical audit environment. Management should set the right tone at the top, emphasizing integrity, transparency, and accountability throughout the organization.

To sum up, the ethical responsibilities of auditors are essential for ensuring the reliability and integrity of financial reporting, governance, and compliance processes. Auditors must adhere to established ethical principles and codes of conduct, resist pressures that could compromise their independence, and navigate ethical dilemmas with professionalism and integrity. Failure to uphold these standards can lead to significant financial, legal, and reputational consequences, underscoring the critical role that ethics play in the auditing profession.

Conclusion

In summary, this chapter covered how auditing plays a vital role in ensuring the accuracy, transparency, and accountability of organizational practices. From the foundational types of audits to the key auditing concepts of evidence, materiality, and risk, each element contributes to a systematic approach to review and validation. Auditing standards such as ISO 19011, the IIA, and ISACA standards provide essential frameworks, guiding auditors through the auditing process and enabling them to deliver reliable results. Finally, ethical principles serve as the backbone of the auditing profession, demanding integrity, objectivity, and confidentiality. Together, these elements underscore the importance of auditing in promoting trust and sound governance across organizations.

In the next chapter, we will focus on the fundamentals of cloud computing, providing a foundation for auditors to conduct effective audits by building on the knowledge and skills acquired in this chapter.

Multiple choice questions

1. **What is auditing?**
    a. Auditing is the examination of financial records, information systems, business, and technical processes
    b. Auditing is the systematic examination of financial records, information systems, business, and technical processes
    c. None of these

2. **Which of the following is not a competence requirement for auditors?**

   a. Friendly behaviour

   b. Knowledge and skills

   c. Technical and interpersonal skills

   d. Continuous learning

3. **Which of the following is not an auditing standard?**

   a. ISO 19011

   b. ISO 9001

   c. GAAS

   d. ISACA ITAF

4. **Which of the following is not one of the key reasons why ethics are critical in auditing?**

   a. Protecting the public interest

   b. Detecting fraud

   c. Ensuring accountability

   d. Promoting transparency

5. **The methods for gathering audit evidence include all of the following except:**

   a. Inspection of documents

   b. Observation

   c. Confirmation

   d. Auditor opinion

Answers

1	c
2	a
3	b
4	b
5	d

CHAPTER 2

Fundamentals of Cloud Computing

Introduction

This chapter offers an overview of the fundamentals of cloud computing, including core cloud models, deployment models, popular platforms, and cloud architecture and design. Additionally, it addresses essential risks and considerations associated with cloud adoption.

Structure

The chapter covers the following topics:

- Introduction to cloud computing
- Core cloud models
- Cloud deployment models
- Popular cloud platforms
- Cloud architecture and design
- Key risks and considerations in cloud adoption

Objectives

By the end of this chapter, readers will gain the essential knowledge needed to conduct cloud audits effectively. This foundational understanding of cloud computing enables auditors to confidently assess cloud environments, identify risks, evaluate controls, and ensure compliance efficiently within the dynamic and intricate landscape of cloud computing.

Introduction to cloud computing

Cloud computing is a model of delivering **information technology** (**IT**) resources over the internet as needed. Rather than managing on-premises servers or personal data centers, businesses and individuals can access storage, computing power, and applications through remote servers hosted by third-party providers. These resources are accessed via a network connection, allowing users to work from virtually any device and location.

Historically, computing required costly infrastructure, localized storage, and direct management of IT resources, which limited scalability and flexibility. Over time, advancements in virtualization technology, faster internet speeds, and reduced storage costs led to the development of cloud computing. This evolution has redefined how organizations deploy and manage software, enabling a more dynamic, flexible approach to IT management.

Brief history and rise of cloud computing

The roots of cloud computing can be traced to the 1960s, when computing pioneers like *John McCarthy* theorized that computing could be organized as a public utility. However, the technological landscape at that time lacked the infrastructure to make this a reality.

Cloud computing as we know it began in the late 1990s and early 2000s, with the introduction of services like *Salesforce* (the first significant SaaS offering) and **Amazon Web Services** (**AWS**), which launched in 2006 and offered storage and computation as scalable services. The introduction of these platforms was groundbreaking, providing scalable resources that businesses could adapt to demand, ultimately leading to the widespread adoption of cloud technologies.

Core benefits of cloud computing

Cloud computing offers several compelling advantages that contribute to its rapid adoption across industries. These benefits include the following:

- **Scalability**: Cloud platforms allow businesses to scale their resources up or down based on demand. This elasticity ensures they only pay for the resources they need at any given time.

- **Cost savings**: By using cloud resources, organizations can avoid the high upfront costs of purchasing and maintaining on-premises hardware. Instead, they can pay for services on a subscription or usage-based model, converting capital expenses into operational expenses.

- **Flexibility and accessibility**: Cloud computing provides access to applications and data from any location, enhancing remote work capabilities and enabling real-time collaboration.

- **Efficient resource utilization**: Cloud providers manage large-scale data centers optimized for performance and resource allocation. This allows businesses to benefit from economies of scale without the complexity of managing their own data centers.

Key terminologies in cloud computing

Understanding cloud computing requires familiarity with a set of core terms. Here are a few of the most frequently encountered concepts:

- **Virtualization**: A technology that allows multiple virtual machines to run on a single physical server, enabling efficient resource use and isolation of workloads.

- **Elasticity**: The ability of a cloud platform to dynamically allocate and reallocate resources to meet changing demand.

- **Multi-tenancy**: A single cloud environment can support multiple users (or tenants) who share the underlying infrastructure but operate independently.

- **On-demand self-service**: The user can provision cloud resources with minimal provider interaction, allowing for near-instant resource allocation.

- **Resource pooling**: Cloud providers pool resources to serve multiple customers, increasing efficiency and lowering costs.

These terms form the foundation of cloud computing and help users understand how cloud systems are structured and managed.

Core cloud models

Auditors must thoroughly understand core cloud models, as they offer the necessary context to evaluate risks, controls, and compliance measures accurately. The core cloud models are outlined in the upcoming subsections. The following figure depicts the core cloud models:

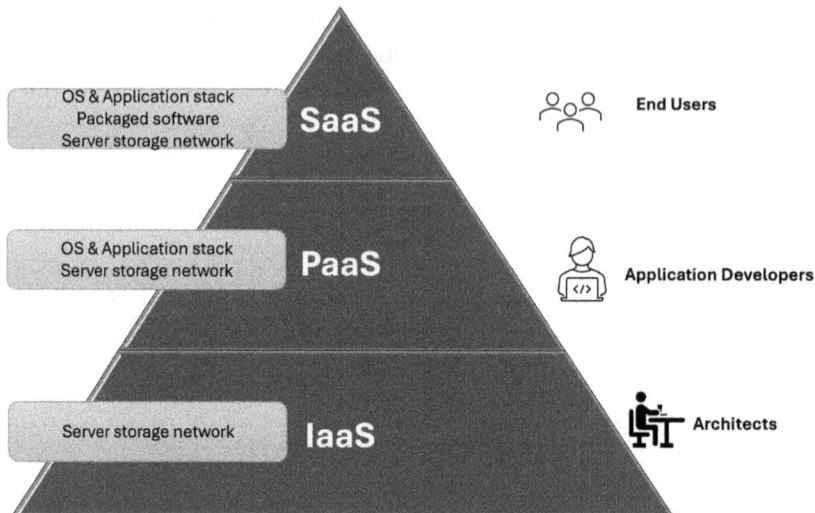

Figure 2.1: *Core cloud models*

Infrastructure as a Service

Infrastructure as a Service (**IaaS**) provides essential computing resources such as virtual machines, storage, and networks. It is the foundation upon which users can deploy and manage their operating systems, applications, and other software. IaaS providers handle the hardware maintenance, including server storage and networking infrastructure, while users manage the higher layers like OS, middleware, and applications.

Here are some features of IaaS:

- **On-demand resources**: IaaS enables users to rent processing power, memory, and storage as needed.
- **High scalability**: Users can scale their resources up or down based on real-time requirements.
- **Cost-effectiveness**: IaaS reduces the need for capital investment in physical infrastructure.

Example providers:

- AWS EC2
- Microsoft Azure Virtual Machines
- **Google Compute Engine** (**GCE**)

Use cases are as follows:

- Ideal for organizations requiring flexible scaling, like tech startups.
- Supports disaster recovery setups and large-scale data storage needs.

Platform as a Service

Platform as a Service (PaaS) offers a complete development and deployment environment in the cloud. PaaS allows developers to focus on building applications without worrying about underlying infrastructure, operating systems, or storage.

Here are some features of PaaS:

- **Built-in development tools**: PaaS environments come with tools for application development, testing, and deployment.

- **Automated scalability**: PaaS platforms often provide automatic scalability, adapting to the app's needs.

- **Integrated databases and middleware**: Many PaaS services include options for databases and middleware integration, enabling faster and more cohesive development.

Example providers:

- **Google App Engine**: Offers a platform for web application development and hosting.

- **Microsoft Azure App Service**: Supports multiple languages and provides integrated database and deployment options.

- **Heroku**: Known for ease of use, popular with developers for quickly deploying web applications.

Use cases are as follows:

- Web and mobile app development where rapid deployment and scalability are required.

- Projects that benefit from integrated databases and automated back-end maintenance.

Software as a Service

Software as a Service (SaaS) delivers fully functional software applications over the internet, typically accessed through a web browser. SaaS allows users to connect and use cloud-based applications without the need to install, maintain, or upgrade the software locally.

Here are some features of SaaS:

- **Subscription-based access**: Most SaaS offerings operate on a subscription model, reducing upfront costs.

- **Automatic updates**: Providers handle maintenance and updates, ensuring users have the latest features and security patches.

- **Accessibility**: SaaS applications can be accessed from any device with an internet connection.

Example providers:

- **Microsoft 365**: A suite of productivity tools accessible online.

- **Salesforce**: A popular **customer relationship management** (CRM) platform enabling companies to manage customer relationships.

- **Google Workspace**: A collection of collaboration and productivity tools.

Use cases are as follows:

- CRM systems, email services, and office applications that need high accessibility and minimal setup.

- Ideal for businesses seeking flexible, pay-as-you-go access to applications without the need for heavy IT management.

Comparing IaaS, PaaS, and SaaS

Table 2.1 provides comparisons at the feature level for each model:

Feature	IaaS	PaaS	SaaS
Control level	High; users manage OS, apps	Moderate; users focus on apps	Low; users access the software
Flexibility	High; custom configurations	Moderate; some flexibility	Low; fixed configurations
Setup complexity	High; customizable but complex	Medium; less complex	Low; ready-to-use
Maintenance	Self-maintained (Operating Systems and apps)	Minimal (platform only)	None (provider maintained)
Cost	Pay-as-you-go, varied costs	Subscription/usage model	Subscription

Table 2.1: Comparison of cloud models

Let us look at when to use each model:

- **IaaS**: Best for organizations with skilled IT staff who need control over the environment or need a custom solution.

- **PaaS**: Suited for developers who want to focus on application development without managing infrastructure.

- **SaaS**: Ideal for end-users who require quick and easy access to applications, such as office suites, CRM, and **enterprise resource planning** (ERP) tools.

Here are some real-world applications:

- A tech startup may choose IaaS for developing a highly customized software product.

- Enterprises building mobile apps might use PaaS to accelerate development.

- Small to medium businesses may rely on SaaS for CRM or collaboration tools to streamline operations without technical management.

Cloud deployment models

Understanding cloud deployment models (public, private, hybrid, and multi-cloud) is crucial for auditors, as it enables them to customize their evaluation based on the unique features and risks of each environment. In the upcoming subsections, we will be looking at the explanations of the different cloud deployment models that are depicted in *Figure 2.2*:

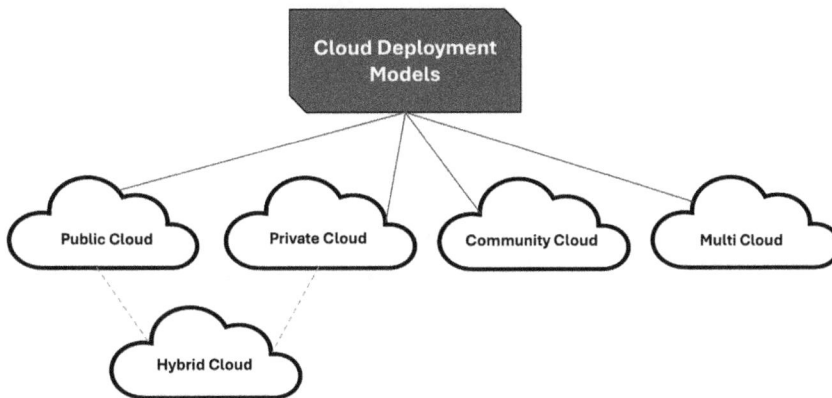

Figure 2.2: Cloud deployment models

Public cloud

The public cloud model involves cloud resources delivered over the internet and shared across multiple clients. Public cloud providers own and manage the infrastructure, offering services on a pay-as-you-go basis. Resources are hosted on the provider's premises, and clients access them via secure internet connections. Public clouds are highly scalable, cost-effective, and require minimal maintenance by users.

Here are some advantages:

- **Cost efficiency**: No need for organizations to purchase or maintain physical infrastructure.

- **High scalability**: Easily accommodates increases in demand.

- **Accessibility**: Accessible from any internet-connected device, supporting global collaboration.

Here are some limitations:

- **Security concerns**: Multi-tenancy and internet-based access may raise security and privacy concerns.

- **Compliance issues**: Certain industries with strict regulatory requirements may face challenges with public cloud storage.

Example providers:

- AWS
- Microsoft Azure
- **Google Cloud Platform (GCP)**

Use cases are as follows:

- Ideal for companies with limited IT resources or those that require large-scale data processing.
- Often used for non-sensitive applications, collaborative projects, and web hosting.

Private cloud

In a private cloud, resources are exclusively used by a single organization. The infrastructure can be hosted either on-premises or at a third-party data center, but is reserved solely for the organization's use, offering higher levels of control and security.

Here are some advantages:

- **Enhanced security**: Isolated infrastructure reduces the risk of unauthorized access and data breaches.
- **Greater customization**: Allows customization of hardware, storage, and networking for specific needs.
- **Compliance**: Easier to meet regulatory requirements, as data remains within organizational boundaries.

Here are some limitations:

- **Cost**: Higher initial investment and ongoing maintenance costs compared to public cloud.
- **Limited scalability**: Scaling may require purchasing additional hardware, unlike the rapid scalability of the public cloud.

Example providers:

- VMware private cloud
- OpenStack

Use case:

- Private cloud is preferred by large organizations with sensitive data, such as financial institutions and healthcare organizations, which require enhanced data privacy and regulatory compliance.

Hybrid cloud

Hybrid cloud models combine public and private cloud environments, allowing data and applications to be shared between them. This model gives organizations greater flexibility to move workloads between environments based on changing requirements, security needs, and costs.

Here are some advantages:

- **Flexibility and control**: Allows organizations to retain control over sensitive data in a private cloud while leveraging the scalability of the public cloud.

- **Cost optimization**: Businesses can run high-demand workloads in the public cloud and maintain critical operations in a private cloud, balancing costs and performance.

- **Business continuity**: Hybrid setups offer redundancy and failover options, enhancing resilience against downtime.

Here are some limitations:

- **Complex management**: Managing a hybrid environment can be challenging, as it requires synchronization between private and public systems.

- **Potential security risks**: Data transferred between public and private clouds must be secured to avoid breaches.

Use cases are as follows:

- **Disaster recovery**: Organizations can store backup data in the public cloud while operating primary applications in the private cloud.

- **Data bursting**: During peak demand periods, companies can use public cloud resources to supplement their private cloud infrastructure.

Community cloud

A community cloud is a collaborative model where multiple organizations with similar requirements share the same cloud infrastructure. This model is often used by organizations within the same industry or geographic region that need to adhere to similar compliance standards or security protocols.

Here are some advantages:

- **Cost sharing**: Community members can share the costs of infrastructure, reducing expenses.

- **Enhanced collaboration**: Provides a unified environment that fosters collaboration among members with shared goals.

- **Compliance and security**: Tailored for industries with specific compliance requirements, like government and healthcare.

Here are some limitations:

- **Limited customization**: Since infrastructure is shared, customization options are limited compared to a private cloud.

- **Access restrictions**: Membership requirements can restrict access and require shared governance.

Use cases are as follows:

- Government agencies or educational institutions collaborating on joint projects.

- Healthcare providers sharing a community cloud to manage sensitive health data in compliance with healthcare regulations.

Multi-cloud

Multi-cloud involves using multiple cloud services from different providers for different tasks within a single architecture. Unlike a hybrid cloud that integrates private and public environments, multi-cloud leverages multiple public clouds to avoid dependency on a single vendor, providing redundancy, flexibility, and enhanced disaster recovery options.

Here are some advantages:

- **Reduced vendor lock-in**: By using multiple providers, organizations avoid dependency on a single vendor, increasing bargaining power.

- **Enhanced resilience**: Multi-cloud setups reduce downtime risks, as failure in one provider's services can be mitigated by another.

- **Optimized performance**: Organizations can select specific providers based on their strengths (e.g., one for AI capabilities and another for storage).

Here are some limitations:

- **Complex management**: Managing multiple cloud environments requires skilled personnel and sophisticated tools for seamless integration.

- **Higher costs**: Using multiple providers can sometimes increase costs and create billing complexities.

Use cases:

- Large corporations are diversifying their cloud infrastructure across providers to reduce risk.

- Companies needing access to specialized services from different providers for optimized performance (e.g., using GCP for machine learning and AWS for data storage).

Popular cloud platforms

Gaining knowledge of popular cloud platforms is invaluable for auditors conducting cloud audits because it enhances their ability to evaluate the environment effectively. Let us discuss the popular cloud platforms.

Amazon Web Services

AWS is the world's leading cloud platform, offering a broad suite of cloud services that include computing power, storage options, machine learning, analytics, and more. AWS is known for its extensive range of services and infrastructure designed to accommodate startups, large enterprises, and government agencies alike. Since its launch in 2006, AWS has set the industry standard for cloud offerings.

Here are some major services:

- **Compute**: Amazon **Elastic Compute Cloud (EC2)** offers scalable virtual servers.

- **Storage**: Amazon **Simple Storage Service (S3)** is highly durable, scalable storage for files and data.

- **Database**: Amazon RDS provides managed relational databases, and DynamoDB supports NoSQL.

- **Machine learning and AI**: Services like Amazon SageMaker enable developers to build and train machine learning models.

- **Networking**: Amazon VPC and AWS VPN for creating isolated cloud networks with secure, encrypted connectivity to on-premises or remote users, Route 53 for domain management and centralized network routing, and Transit Gateway for multiple VPCs and hybrid cloud setups.

- **Security & compliance**: GuardDuty is an intelligent threat detection service, Amazon Inspector scans for vulnerabilities and unintended network exposure, and AWS Security Hub provides you with a comprehensive view of security state in AWS.

Unique features of AWS:

- **Global infrastructure**: AWS has a broad global presence, with data centers across multiple regions and availability zones, ensuring redundancy and low latency.

- **Comprehensive ecosystem**: AWS Marketplace offers third-party integrations and tools, enhancing AWS's versatility.

- **Security**: AWS provides security services like AWS Shield for DDoS protection and AWS **Identity and Access Management (IAM)** for access control.

Use cases:

- Hosting high-traffic websites and applications
- Running data-intensive applications with storage and analytics needs
- Supporting artificial intelligence and machine learning workloads

Microsoft Azure

Microsoft Azure is the second-largest cloud provider, known for its close integration with Microsoft's ecosystem and software, such as Windows Server, Office 365, and SQL Server. Azure provides extensive cloud capabilities, with a strong focus on hybrid cloud solutions, making it an appealing option for enterprises transitioning from on-premises to cloud environments.

Major services:

- **Compute**: Azure Virtual Machines offer scalable compute resources.
- **Storage**: Azure Blob Storage is optimized for large volumes of unstructured data.
- **Database**: Azure SQL Database is a managed relational database service.
- **AI and analytics**: Azure Machine Learning and Azure Synapse Analytics support data science and advanced analytics.

Unique features:

- **Hybrid cloud capabilities**: Azure offers strong support for hybrid models, allowing seamless integration with on-premises systems through *Azure Arc* and *Azure Stack*.
- **Integration with Microsoft tools**: Direct integration with tools like *Active Directory* and *Office 365* enables organizations to adopt a cloud model while maintaining existing software investments.
- **Enterprise security**: Azure's compliance certifications and security features make it suitable for highly regulated industries.

Use cases are as follows:

- Deploying and managing enterprise applications with Microsoft integrations
- Supporting **Internet of Things (IoT)** applications with services like *Azure IoT Hub*
- Hosting virtual desktops and enabling remote work environments with *Windows Virtual Desktop*

Google Cloud Platform

GCP is widely recognized for its strengths in data analytics, machine learning, and containerization. While not as extensive in offerings as AWS or Azure, GCP has a reputation for high-performance infrastructure, particularly with big data processing and artificial intelligence capabilities. Google's leadership in Kubernetes (an open-source container orchestration platform) also makes GCP a preferred choice for developers focused on containerized applications.

Major services are as follows:

- **Compute**: *Google Compute Engine* provides scalable virtual machines.

- **Storage**: *Google Cloud Storage* offers durable object storage for various data types.

- **Big data and analytics**: *BigQuery* is a powerful managed data warehouse for fast SQL-based analytics.

- **Machine learning**: *Google AI Platform* and *TensorFlow* support end-to-end machine learning workflows.

Unique features of GCP:

- **Data and analytics strengths**: GCP's BigQuery is a high-speed analytics platform optimized for processing large datasets.

- **AI and machine learning capabilities**: Google's expertise in AI extends to specialized services like *AutoML*, allowing users to build custom machine learning models without deep expertise.

- **Open-source and developer support**: GCP is highly supportive of open-source projects, especially in containerization (Kubernetes) and data processing.

Use cases are as follows:

- Data-intensive analytics for industries like finance and retail

- Machine learning applications, leveraging Google's AI services and expertise

- Managing containerized applications and microservices with GKE

Other cloud platforms

While AWS, Azure, and GCP dominate the market, other cloud providers also offer valuable and specialized cloud services. These platforms may focus on niche requirements or cater to specific industries.

- **IBM Cloud**: Known for its emphasis on hybrid cloud and AI solutions, IBM Cloud integrates with Watson AI for machine learning applications and offers a robust environment for enterprises needing a hybrid approach. IBM Cloud is also popular in sectors such as banking and finance, which require advanced compliance and security.

- **Oracle Cloud**: Particularly strong in enterprise applications, Oracle Cloud is suited for organizations using Oracle's suite of applications and databases. It provides a robust environment for running ERP, CRM, and database-driven applications.

- **Alibaba Cloud**: A leading cloud provider in Asia, Alibaba Cloud offers a wide array of services similar to AWS and is optimized for businesses operating in the Asia-Pacific region. Its strength lies in e-commerce solutions and scalability, making it popular among digital businesses.

The following table provides a comparative overview of popular cloud platforms:

Platform	Strengths	Primary use cases
AWS	Broad service range, global infrastructure	Web hosting, data processing, AI/ML
Microsoft Azure	Hybrid integration, Microsoft ecosystem	Enterprise apps, IoT, hybrid solutions
Google Cloud Platform	Data analytics, machine learning	Big data, containerized applications
IBM Cloud	Hybrid focus, enterprise-grade AI	Financial services, hybrid cloud deployments
Oracle Cloud	Enterprise applications, database management	ERP, CRM, database-driven apps
Alibaba Cloud	Asia-Pacific dominance, e-commerce focus	Regional e-commerce, digital businesses

Table 2.2: Comparative overview of popular cloud platforms

Cloud architecture and design

Cloud architecture and design refers to the structure and organization of a cloud computing environment, including how the various components (e.g., servers, storage, networks, and applications) are configured, deployed, and integrated to meet business and technical requirements. Understanding cloud architecture and design equips auditors to evaluate whether the cloud environment is secure, resilient, and compliant with organizational and regulatory standards. The key considerations that are considered while creating a design are discussed in the upcoming sub-sections.

Cloud-native architecture

Cloud-native architecture refers to the design and building of applications specifically optimized to run in cloud environments. Unlike traditional software that is built for on-premises infrastructure, cloud-native applications are designed to leverage cloud capabilities such as scalability, resiliency, and flexibility. This architecture, which is depicted in *figure 2.3* typically employs technologies like *microservices, containerization,* and *serverless computing* to maximize efficiency and adaptability:

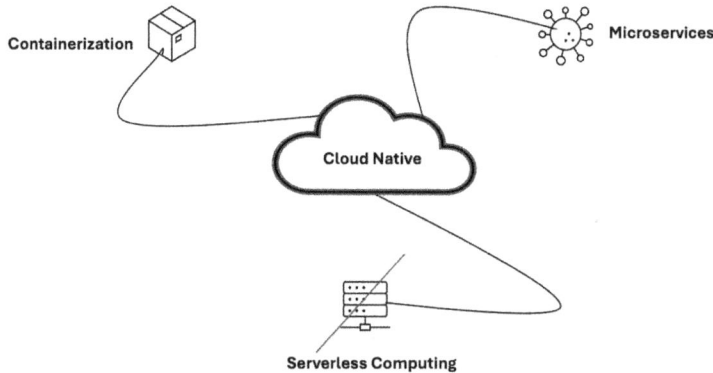

***Figure 2.3:** Cloud-native architecture*

Key concepts in cloud-native architecture:

- **Microservices**: Cloud-native applications often adopt a microservices architecture, breaking applications into smaller, independent services. Each service performs a specific function, allowing faster development, testing, and deployment.

- **Containerization**: Containers package applications and their dependencies, making them lightweight, portable, and consistent across environments. *Docker* and *Kubernetes* are popular tools used for managing containerized applications in cloud-native environments.

- **Serverless computing**: In serverless architectures, cloud providers manage the servers, dynamically allocate resources, and charge only for the compute time consumed by the application. *AWS Lambda* and *Azure Functions* are examples of serverless offerings that allow developers to focus solely on code without managing infrastructure.

Advantages of cloud-native architecture:

- **Scalability**: Microservices and containers make it easier to scale specific parts of an application independently.

- **Resilience**: The failure of one microservice does not necessarily disrupt the entire application.

- **Faster deployment**: Developers can deploy and update individual services without impacting the entire system.

Multi-tenancy and virtualization

Multi-tenancy is a key aspect of cloud computing, allowing multiple users (or tenants) to share the same underlying infrastructure while keeping data isolated. Each tenant can access a customized view of shared resources, making it possible for a single instance of software to serve multiple customers without compromising privacy.

Virtualization underpins cloud infrastructure, allowing physical servers to be partitioned into multiple **virtual machines** (**VMs**), each functioning as an independent server. Virtualization maximizes resource utilization, enabling providers to support more tenants with fewer physical servers.

Advantages of virtualization:

- **Resource optimization**: Virtual machines allow efficient use of hardware, reducing costs and energy consumption.

- **Isolation and security**: Each VM operates in its own environment, preventing interference between workloads.

- **Flexibility**: VMs can be easily scaled, replicated, or moved across different physical servers, adapting to changing demands.

Scalability and load balancing

Scalability in cloud computing refers to the ability to adjust resources based on demand. This can be done *vertically* (adding more resources to a single VM, like random access memory or central processing unit) or *horizontally* (adding more instances to handle increased load).

- **Vertical scaling**: Adding resources to a single instance (e.g., increasing memory) to handle additional load. It is simple to implement, but it has limits on how much a single server can scale.

- **Horizontal scaling**: Adding more instances of a server to distribute load, common in applications with fluctuating traffic. It offers nearly unlimited scalability, especially for stateless applications.

Load balancers distribute incoming traffic across multiple servers to optimize performance and prevent any single server from becoming overwhelmed. Load balancing is essential for applications with high availability requirements, ensuring seamless user experiences even under heavy traffic.

Types of load balancing are listed here:

- **DNS load balancing**: Distributes traffic based on domain name system configurations, directing users to the closest or least-loaded server.

- **Application load balancing**: Uses algorithms like round-robin or weighted distribution to intelligently manage requests.

Benefits are as follows:

- **Improved reliability**: Ensures no single point of failure.

- **Enhanced performance**: Distributes workloads, reducing response times for users.

Networking in cloud

Networking is the backbone of cloud infrastructure, connecting resources, data, and users across vast geographical locations. Cloud networking encompasses virtual networks, IP management, and connectivity solutions tailored to cloud environments.

Key components of networking in cloud:

- **Virtual private cloud (VPC)**: A VPC is a logically isolated section within a public cloud where users can define IP ranges, subnets, and access control settings, simulating an on-premises network.

- **Direct connectivity**: Services like AWS Direct Connect and Azure ExpressRoute provide dedicated connections between on-premises infrastructure and the cloud, ensuring low latency and high security.

- **Firewall and security groups**: These are configured to allow or block specific traffic, safeguarding cloud resources from unauthorized access.

Networking considerations for networking in cloud:

- **Latency and performance**: Choosing data centers and network configurations close to the end-users can help reduce latency and improve user experience.

- **Security and access control**: Implementing firewall rules, encryption, and private networks helps prevent unauthorized access.

Storage in cloud

Storage is a critical aspect of cloud architecture, as it underpins data availability, redundancy, and access. Cloud storage is highly flexible, with options for structured, semi-structured, and unstructured data.

Types of cloud storage are listed here:

- **Object storage**: Designed for storing unstructured data, object storage (e.g., *AWS S3, Azure Blob Storage*) organizes data as objects with unique identifiers. It is highly scalable and ideal for large files like media or backups.

- **File storage**: File storage solutions (e.g., *Amazon EFS, Azure Files*) allow data to be stored in a hierarchical structure. It is commonly used for applications requiring shared file systems.

- **Block storage**: Block storage (e.g., *AWS EBS, Google Persistent Disk*) breaks data into fixed-sized blocks, making it fast and suitable for databases or transactional data.

- **Redundancy and backup**: Cloud providers offer built-in redundancy options, like *replication across multiple data centers* or *snapshots*, to ensure data is safe and recoverable. Here are some of the redundancy options:

- **Automatic replication**: Data is replicated across different servers or regions to ensure high availability.

- **Backup and recovery**: Cloud providers offer regular backups, snapshots, and data restoration options to mitigate data loss during incidents.

The benefits of cloud storage are listed as follows:

- **Scalability**: Storage can be easily expanded as data needs grow.

- **Accessibility**: Data can be accessed from anywhere, making it ideal for remote and distributed teams.

- **Cost efficiency**: Pay-as-you-go models allow organizations to avoid large upfront investments.

Key risks and considerations in cloud adoption

Adopting cloud computing offers many benefits, such as scalability, cost savings, and flexibility. However, it also comes with key risks and considerations that organizations must address to ensure a smooth transition. Let us discuss some of the most important ones.

Security risks

While cloud providers implement strong security controls, moving data and applications to the cloud can introduce specific risks. Security concerns are often amplified due to the multi-tenant nature of public cloud environments, where multiple users share infrastructure.

Primary security risks are as follows:

- **Data breaches**: Unauthorized access to sensitive data stored in the cloud can lead to data breaches, which can be financially and reputationally damaging.

- **Insider threats**: Employees or individuals with access to sensitive data may intentionally or unintentionally compromise data security.

- **Insecure APIs and interfaces**: Cloud services are accessed through APIs that, if not adequately secured, can be vulnerable to attacks.

- **Misconfigured cloud settings**: Misconfiguration is one of the most common cloud security issues, such as leaving storage buckets publicly accessible or mismanaging permissions.

Here are some mitigation strategies:

- **Encryption**: Encrypting data both at rest and in transit can protect data from unauthorized access.

- Access control: Using **role-based access controls (RBAC)** and **multi-factor authentication (MFA)** helps restrict access to authorized users.

- **Regular security audits**: Periodic security assessments, including vulnerability scans, can help identify and resolve security issues early.

Cost management

One of the initial attractions of cloud computing is the potential for cost savings, but cloud costs can quickly escalate without careful management. Usage-based pricing models may lead to unexpected costs if resources are not adequately monitored and managed.

Cost challenges are as follows:

- **Unexpected usage spikes**: In cloud environments, costs can spike due to unforeseen demand or resource usage, impacting budgets.
- **Orphaned resources**: Unused resources, such as idle virtual machines or unused storage volumes, can continue to accrue costs if not removed.
- **Complex billing structures**: Cloud providers offer diverse services with different pricing models, making it challenging to track and optimize costs.

Cost optimization tips are as follows:

- **Rightsizing resources**: Periodically review and adjust resource allocation to avoid overprovisioning.
- **Implementing budget alerts**: Many cloud providers offer budget tracking and alerts, helping organizations monitor spending.
- **Using reserved instances**: For predictable workloads, purchasing reserved instances at discounted rates can significantly reduce costs.
- **Leveraging automation**: Automated tools can help manage and scale resources based on actual usage, preventing resource wastage.

Performance and downtime risks

While cloud providers generally offer high uptime guarantees, unexpected outages or network latency can impact service performance, especially for applications that require high availability and low latency. The distributed nature of cloud infrastructure can also introduce latency for users accessing data across different regions.

Potential performance issues are as follows:

- **Latency**: Data centers located far from the end-users may introduce latency, especially for real-time applications.
- **Network downtime**: Cloud providers occasionally experience outages due to hardware failures, network issues, or software updates, potentially impacting users globally.
- **Service limits**: Cloud providers impose limits on resources (such as compute instances and storage), which may affect performance if not accounted for in advance.

Here are some strategies to mitigate performance risks:

- **Content delivery networks (CDNs)**: Using CDNs can improve latency by caching content closer to end-users.

- **Multi-region deployment**: Deploying applications across multiple regions can reduce latency and improve resilience in case of regional outages.

- **Load testing**: Regularly perform load testing to ensure applications can handle varying loads and identify potential bottlenecks.

Vendor lock-in

Vendor lock-in refers to the difficulty of moving workloads, data, or applications from one cloud provider to another. Each cloud provider has unique APIs, architectures, and services that may not easily transfer across platforms, creating a dependency on that specific provider. Vendor lock-in limits an organization's flexibility and negotiating power.

Key issues with vendor lock-in are as follows:

- **Compatibility challenges**: Services and applications built with one provider's APIs or services may not be compatible with others, requiring extensive rework to migrate.

- **Data transfer costs**: Providers often charge for data transfer, which can be costly when moving large volumes of data out of a platform.

- **Dependency on proprietary tools**: Cloud providers offer specialized tools and services that, while valuable, may restrict an organization's ability to switch providers.

Here are some mitigation strategies:

- **Using open standards**: Employ open-source tools, programming languages, and standards that are compatible across providers.

- **Adopting a multi-cloud strategy**: Leveraging multiple providers reduces dependency on any single platform and provides flexibility.

- **Containerization**: Using containers (like Docker) and orchestration tools (like Kubernetes) can make it easier to migrate applications across different environments.

Legal and compliance considerations

As organizations store and process data in the cloud, they must comply with regulations specific to their industry and geography. Legal and compliance considerations often relate to data privacy, residency, and handling, especially when dealing with **Personally Identifiable Information (PII)** or sensitive information.

Here are some regulatory challenges:

- **Data residency requirements**: Some regions require that data remain within specific geographic boundaries (e.g., the **General Data Protection Regulation (GDPR)** in *Europe*).

- **Industry-specific regulations**: Industries like finance and healthcare have strict data protection regulations, such as the **Health Insurance Portability and Accountability Act (HIPAA)** for healthcare in the *U.S.*, which mandate specific controls for data handling.

  Data sovereignty: In some cases, local governments mandate that data stored within their borders be subject to local laws, which could impact data stored on global cloud platforms.

Best practices for compliance:

- **Data classification**: Classify data based on sensitivity, ensuring proper protection for high-risk data.

- **Encryption and access control**: Implement encryption, access restrictions, and audit trails to meet compliance requirements.

- **Regular compliance audits**: Conduct periodic compliance audits to ensure the cloud environment meets relevant regulatory standards.

- **Choosing providers with compliance certifications**: Opt for providers certified in standards like ISO 27001, SOC 2, and PCI DSS, which demonstrate adherence to industry standards.

Conclusion

The field of cloud computing has rapidly evolved to become an integral part of modern IT infrastructure, offering organizations across industries the flexibility, scalability, and cost savings they need to thrive in a competitive landscape. This chapter has provided a foundational overview of the fundamental aspects of cloud computing, covering the essential cloud models, deployment options, popular platforms, architectural principles, and considerations for adoption.

The upcoming chapter will focus on the challenges in cloud computing from the auditor's perspective. It explains the new challenges auditors face in a cloud environment, such as shared responsibility models and data governance complexities, and provides general recommendations for the auditors to wade through these challenges to ensure the audits are more effective.

Points to remember

- **Overview of cloud computing**: Cloud computing is a model that allows users to access IT resources over the internet, shifting organizations from traditional, on-premises systems to flexible, scalable infrastructure. Cloud computing has redefined IT with key advantages like scalability, flexibility, and cost-efficiency, allowing organizations to innovate faster and reduce operational burdens.

- **Core cloud models**: The three core service models—**Infrastructure as a Service (IaaS)**, **Platform as a Service (PaaS)**, and **Software as a Service (SaaS)**—each provide different levels of control and management, enabling organizations to choose the model that best suits their needs. While IaaS offers more control over infrastructure, PaaS allows developers to focus on application development, and SaaS provides ready-to-use software over the internet.

- **Deployment models**: Organizations can select from various deployment models, including public, private, hybrid, community, and multi-cloud. These deployment models offer unique benefits and address specific needs related to security, compliance, cost, and operational flexibility. The choice of deployment model depends on factors like data sensitivity, regulatory requirements, and the organization's long-term goals.

- **Popular cloud platforms**: AWS, Microsoft Azure, and GCP are among the leading cloud providers, each offering extensive services and tools to support diverse application needs. Each platform has unique strengths, making them suitable for various use cases, from machine learning and big data processing to web hosting and IoT applications. Other platforms, such as IBM Cloud and Oracle Cloud, also provide specialized offerings catering to specific industry requirements.

- **Cloud architecture and design**: Cloud-native design principles, such as microservices, containerization, and serverless computing, enable scalable and resilient applications. Multi-tenancy, virtualization, and networking are essential components of cloud architecture, supporting efficient resource allocation and high availability. Storage options like object, file, and block storage meet diverse data needs, ensuring flexibility and accessibility.

- **Key risks and considerations**: Adopting cloud computing requires an awareness of potential risks, including security, cost management, performance, vendor lock-in, and compliance. By implementing security best practices, managing costs, optimizing performance, and ensuring regulatory compliance, organizations can mitigate risks and maximize cloud benefits.

By understanding these core principles, auditors can provide valuable insights when evaluating an organization's adoption and implementation of cloud solutions. As cloud computing continues to drive the evolution of IT, it presents opportunities to foster innovation, growth, and adaptability in a rapidly evolving digital landscape. This foundational knowledge equips auditors to assess and advise on building resilient, scalable, and future-ready systems, ensuring organizations effectively leverage the potential of the cloud.

Multiple choice questions

1. **Core benefits of cloud computing include all of the following except:**

    a. Scalability

    b. Flexibility and accessibility

    c. Efficient resource utilization

    d. Reliance on the Internet

2. **The ability of provisioning cloud resources by the user with minimal provider interaction, allowing for near-instant resource allocation, is known as:**

    a. Resource pooling

    b. On-demand self-service

    c. Elasticity

    d. Resource provisioning

3. **Which cloud model is best suited for developers who want to focus on application development without managing infrastructure?**

    a. PaaS

    b. IaaS

    c. SaaS

    d. Either PaaS or IaaS

4. **Which cloud deployment model is preferred by large organizations with sensitive data, such as financial institutions and healthcare organizations, that require enhanced data privacy and regulatory compliance?**

    a. Public cloud

    b. Hybrid cloud

    c. Private cloud

    d. Community cloud

5. **Which of the following is not one of the key Risks and Considerations in Cloud Adoption?**

   a. Security risks

   b. Performance and downtime risks

   c. Vendor lock-in

   d. Using open standards

Answers

1	d
2	b
3	a
4	c
5	d

Join our Discord space

Join our Discord workspace for latest updates, offers, tech happenings around the world, new releases, and sessions with the authors:

https://discord.bpbonline.com

CHAPTER 3

Challenges in Cloud Auditing

Introduction

This chapter explores the challenges of cloud computing from an auditor's perspective. It delves into the unique problems auditors encounter in a cloud environment, including shared responsibility models and complexities in data governance. Additionally, it offers general recommendations to help auditors navigate these challenges and enhance the effectiveness of their audits.

Structure

This chapter covers the following topics:

- Evolution of cloud computing
- Lack of visibility and control in cloud
- Multi-tenancy and data isolation issues
- Third-party risks and vendor dependencies
- Trust and transparency issues with CSPs
- Auditability and accountability
- Shared responsibility models
- General recommendations

Objectives

By the end of this chapter, readers will gain a broad understanding of the unique challenges auditors encounter in a cloud-based environment. Readers will also learn about the associated implications of auditing practices and the actionable general recommendations presented, which will help them with strategies needed to navigate these complexities effectively.

Evolution of cloud computing

Cloud computing provides on-demand access to computing resources, such as servers, storage, and applications, over the Internet. This model has rapidly gained popularity due to its cost efficiency, scalability, and flexibility. However, this shift from traditional IT infrastructure to cloud-based environments has significant implications for governance, compliance, and auditing.

Role of auditors in IT environments

Auditors are responsible for evaluating an organization's compliance with legal, regulatory, and internal requirements. In traditional IT setups, auditors could rely on physical access, direct observation, and on-premises controls. In cloud environments, these traditional practices are no longer fully applicable, necessitating the development of new strategies and tools.

Now, let us look at the key challenges faced by auditors in cloud environments:

Figure 3.1: Challenges in cloud auditing

Lack of visibility and control in cloud

Cloud consumers may have limited insight into the inner workings of cloud operations. As a result, they may be unable to verify whether their services are being executed and delivered securely. Different cloud service delivery models offer varying degrees of consumer control and visibility. Nevertheless, it is feasible and already practiced in several non-cloud systems for consumers to request the deployment of additional monitoring mechanisms at the **cloud service provider's (CSP's)** site.

Let us now explore the key challenges associated with the lack of visibility and control in the cloud environment, along with their implications for the auditing process. Key challenges associated with the lack of visibility and control in the cloud environment include:

- **Opaque infrastructure**: In traditional systems, organizations owned and managed their hardware and software. In cloud environments, the infrastructure is managed by the provider, leaving organizations with limited visibility.

- **Dynamic scaling and automation**: Features like auto-scaling and ephemeral instances dynamically modify the infrastructure, complicating the task of monitoring resource configurations and activities.

- **Restricted access**: Cloud providers limit access to their physical data centers and detailed configurations for security and operational reasons, making direct inspections impossible.

Auditors should understand the following implications of auditing cloud environments with respect to the lack of visibility and control in cloud environments:

- **Reliance on provider reports**: Auditors often depend on third-party audit reports, such as **Service Organization Control (SOC)** reports, rather than direct observation.

- **Need for specialized tools**: Organizations must implement cloud-native monitoring solutions (e.g., **Amazon Web Services (AWS)** CloudTrail, Azure Monitor) that can provide audit trails and operational visibility.

- **Control alignment**: Auditors must ensure that the organization's policies align with the cloud provider's controls and that appropriate **service level agreements (SLAs)** are in place.

Multi-tenancy and data isolation issues

Cloud computing achieves substantial economic efficiencies by enabling resource sharing on the CSP's side. For example, multiple **virtual machines (VMs)** may share hardware through a hypervisor, various processes may share an operating system along with supporting data and networking services, and multiple consumers may use the same application or database. However, because these sharing mechanisms rely on sophisticated utilities to maintain the isolation of consumer workloads, there is an inherent risk of isolation failure.

Next, let us examine the core concepts, specific risks, and auditing implications associated with the challenges of multi-tenancy and data isolation.

The core concepts include:

- **Multi-tenancy**: In multi-tenant cloud environments, multiple organizations share the same physical hardware while being logically isolated.

- **Isolation mechanisms**: Virtualization and containerization technologies ensure data separation, but vulnerabilities or misconfigurations can compromise these mechanisms.

The primary risks arising from the challenges of multi-tenancy and data isolation include:

- **Data spillage**: A misconfiguration in access controls or APIs can allow one tenant to inadvertently access another tenant's data.

- **Shared resources**: Common storage, memory, and compute resources can lead to performance and security trade-offs.

- **Cross-VM attacks**: Advanced attacks may exploit side channels or vulnerabilities in hypervisors.

Some of the key implications for auditing in cloud environments comprise:

- **Evaluation of isolation mechanisms**: Auditors must examine the provider's virtualization technologies and data segregation policies.

- **Encryption and key management**: Ensuring tenant data is encrypted and that encryption keys are securely managed is critical.

- **Penetration testing results**: Reviewing the provider's penetration testing and vulnerability assessments helps identify potential weaknesses in multi-tenancy implementations.

Compliance challenges in cloud

When organizational data or processing of such data is transferred to the cloud, the cloud consumer remains ultimately responsible for compliance. However, with direct access to the data, the provider is often better positioned to implement compliance measures. Several challenges can complicate compliance and should be addressed through contractual agreements.

Now, let us explore the key issues, strategies for addressing compliance in such scenarios and implications for auditing in cloud environments.

Compliance challenges in the cloud stem from various issues that organizations must address to meet regulatory and legal requirements effectively, and the key issues include the following:

- **Data localization**: Regulatory frameworks, like GDPR or India's Data Protection Act, require specific types of data to remain within defined geographic regions. Cloud providers' distributed infrastructure complicates this.

- **Standardization gaps**: Providers may offer varying levels of compliance support, making it hard for organizations to standardize controls across multiple providers.

- **Audit trails**: Regulations often require detailed logging of system activity, which can be difficult to access or incomplete in the cloud.

Various strategies for addressing compliance in the cloud environments involve the following:

- **Contractual agreements**: Ensure contracts specify compliance obligations and penalties for breaches.

- **Continuous monitoring**: Use tools that automate compliance checks against industry standards like **Payment Card Industry Data Security Standard (PCI DSS), Health Insurance Portability and Accountability Act (HIPAA)**, or ISO 27001 standard.

- **Regulatory engagement**: Stay updated on changes in laws affecting cloud usage, particularly in jurisdictions where the organization operates.

Auditors need to verify that cloud usage complies with applicable regulations and that organizations regularly update policies to reflect evolving compliance requirements.

Third-party risks and vendor dependencies

Third-party risks and vendor dependencies in a cloud environment refer to potential vulnerabilities, limitations, or challenges that arise from relying on external vendors or service providers for cloud services. These factors can impact the security, availability, and overall performance of cloud solutions.

Let us delve into the core challenges and key audit focus areas associated with third-party risks and vendor dependencies in cloud environments. The core auditing challenges associated with third-party risks and vendor dependencies in the cloud include the following:

- **Service outages**: Even major cloud providers occasionally experience downtime, disrupting critical operations.

- **Vendor lock-in**: Proprietary cloud solutions can make switching providers costly and technically challenging.

- **Supply chain security**: Providers rely on their own third-party vendors, which can introduce additional risks.

Auditors should concentrate on the following key aspects when conducting audits in cloud environments:

- **Third-party assurance**: Assess whether the organization evaluates its cloud providers using certifications (e.g., ISO 27001, SOC reports).

- **Risk mitigation strategies**: Check if the organization has contingency plans, such as multi-cloud strategies or backup arrangements.

- **Vendor management policies**: Review procurement processes to ensure due diligence in selecting and monitoring cloud vendors.

Trust and transparency issues with CSPs

Trust and transparency in a cloud environment refer to the principles and practices that ensure cloud consumers feel confident in cloud services' security, privacy, and reliability. To be precise, trust in a cloud environment means that users believe their data and applications are handled securely and responsibly, involves security, privacy, reliability, compliance, and accountability; and transparency means providing clear, accessible, and honest information about the operations of cloud services that include clear communication, data handling practices, operational visibility, incident reporting, certifications, and audits.

Key trust issues in cloud environments stem from the inherent reliance on third-party service providers and the shared nature of cloud infrastructure. These issues include the following:

- **Limited disclosure**: CSPs may be unwilling to share details about their infrastructure or operational controls due to confidentiality concerns.

- **Incident reporting**: CSPs might delay or withhold reporting security incidents, hindering an organization's ability to respond effectively.

Implications for trust in cloud environments are significant, as they directly affect the relationship between CSPs and their clients, as well as the broader adoption of cloud solutions. Key implications include the following:

- **Blind spots**: Organizations may not fully understand the risks associated with their provider's environment.

- **Lack of verification**: Independent assessments are often limited to what providers allow or report.

In scenarios involving trust and transparency issues in cloud environments, auditors play a critical role in ensuring transparency, mitigating risks, and fostering confidence. Their responsibilities include the following:

- **Demanding transparency**: Review contractual clauses to ensure timely incident reporting and access to audit logs.

- **Industry collaboration**: Advocate for industry standards that promote transparency and build trust, such as STAR certification by the **Cloud Security Alliance (CSA)**.

Auditability and accountability

Auditability and accountability in a cloud environment ensure that cloud providers and users are responsible for their actions and that their activities can be tracked, verified, and reviewed to maintain trust, compliance, and security. Auditability is the capability to track and review operations, processes, and data to ensure compliance and performance. It provides the tools and practices needed to verify that cloud services meet security, regulatory, and operational standards. Accountability refers to the obligation of cloud providers and users to take responsibility for their actions, particularly concerning security, privacy, and compliance. It ensures that stakeholders are answerable for the outcomes of their operations and decisions.

By emphasizing auditability and accountability, organizations can ensure robust governance, enhance security, and maintain compliance in their cloud environments.

Let us now examine the challenges related to auditability, issues of accountability, and the audit practices that should be implemented.

Auditability challenges in cloud environments arise due to the unique nature of cloud computing, including its shared responsibility model, multi-tenancy, and dynamic infrastructure. Key challenges include the following:

- **Dynamic resource allocation**: Resources in cloud environments are allocated and deallocated dynamically, leading to gaps in audit trails.

- **Distributed systems**: Cloud environments often involve distributed architectures, complicating the collection and correlation of logs.

Accountability issues in cloud environments can blur the lines of responsibility, and key accountability issues include:

- **Ownership ambiguity**: Identifying who is responsible for specific controls, whether the CSP or cloud consumer, can be challenging.

- **Layered dependencies**: Application-level issues may stem from underlying platform or infrastructure problems.

To effectively counter auditability and accountability issues in cloud environments, organizations should adopt the following best audit practices:

- **Log integration**: Use tools that aggregate and normalize logs from different layers (e.g., SIEM tools like *Splunk*).

- **Shared responsibility mapping**: Clearly define roles and responsibilities to avoid gaps in accountability.

Shared responsibility models

When using cloud services, security responsibilities vary largely depending on the service delivery model used, while responsibility and accountability for compliance remain entirely with the cloud consumer. Generally, compliance responsibility reflects the degree of control a party has over the architecture stack. The auditor's role is to assess not only a particular service but also the way the service is designed and developed.

The following sections explore the key concepts, implementation challenges, and the auditor's role in relation to shared responsibility models in cloud environments. Key concepts in auditing challenges related to shared responsibility models in cloud environments include the following:

- **CSP's role**: Includes securing the physical infrastructure, hypervisor, and underlying systems.
- **Customer's role**: Involves securing applications, data, user access, and configurations.

Challenges in the implementation of shared responsibility models in cloud environments include:

- **Misalignment**: Organizations may overlook their responsibilities, assuming the provider handles everything.
- **Communication gaps**: Poor coordination between customers and providers can lead to control gaps.

The cloud auditor plays a critical role in addressing the challenges of implementing shared responsibility models in cloud environments. Their responsibilities include:

- **Assess understanding**: Ensure the organization fully understands its responsibilities within the shared model.
- **Verify implementation**: Audit both the customer's and provider's controls to ensure end-to-end security and compliance.

Governance complexities

Cloud computing can significantly complicate an organization's governance approach. While some considerations may differ based on the specific type of cloud service being utilized (e.g., SaaS, IaaS, or PaaS), a comprehensive cloud governance program should address all aspects of the various service models. This is essential because the distinctions between these models are minimal, and a cloud migration initiative may involve workloads across any combination of **Infrastructure as a Service (IaaS), Platform as a Service (PaaS), and Software as a Service (SaaS)**.

Now, let us look at the core challenges arising out of the cloud governance complexities and the auditor's role in such scenarios.

The core challenges related to governance in cloud environments involve managing risks, maintaining oversight, and ensuring compliance amidst a complex and dynamic landscape. These challenges include the following:

- **Decentralization**: Cloud adoption often occurs independently across business units, bypassing central IT governance.

- **Shadow IT**: Employees or teams may procure cloud services without approval, leading to security and compliance risks.

- **Policy enforcement**: Ensuring consistent governance across diverse cloud services and platforms is inherently difficult.

The auditor's role in relation to governance challenges in cloud environments is critical for ensuring that organizations maintain control, visibility, and compliance amidst the complexities of cloud computing, and key responsibilities include:

- **Centralized frameworks**: Evaluate whether the organization has a robust governance framework to oversee all cloud activities.

- **Monitoring tools**: Assess the effectiveness of tools used to discover and manage shadow IT.

- **Training programs**: Verify that employees understand cloud policies and the importance of compliance.

General recommendations

In the context of addressing challenges in cloud auditing, the following are general recommendations for auditors to effectively mitigate these obstacles and ensure audits are conducted efficiently and thoroughly:

- Auditors must ensure that the organization's policies align with the cloud provider's controls and that appropriate SLAs are in place.

- Auditors must examine the provider's virtualization technologies and data segregation policies to ensure proper data isolation mechanisms are in place.

- Ensuring tenant data is encrypted and that encryption keys are securely managed is critical.

- Reviewing the provider's penetration testing and vulnerability assessments helps identify potential weaknesses in multi-tenancy implementations.

- Ensure contracts specify compliance obligations and penalties for breaches.

- Utilize tools that automate compliance checks against industry standards like PCI DSS, HIPAA, or ISO 27001.

- Stay updated on changes in laws affecting cloud usage, particularly in jurisdictions where the organization operates.

- Auditors need to verify that cloud usage complies with applicable regulations and that organizations regularly update policies to reflect evolving compliance requirements.

- Assess whether the organization evaluates its cloud providers using certifications (e.g., ISO 27001, SOC reports).

- Check if the organization has contingency plans, such as multi-cloud strategies or backup arrangements.

- Review procurement processes to ensure due diligence in selecting and monitoring cloud vendors.

- Review contractual clauses to ensure timely incident reporting, access to audit logs, and transparency between the CSP and the cloud consumer.

- Advocate for industry standards that promote transparency and build trust, such as STAR certification by the CSA.

- Use tools that aggregate and normalize logs from different layers (e.g., SIEM tools like Splunk).

- Ensure shared responsibility mapping exists to define roles and responsibilities to avoid gaps in accountability.

- Assess Understanding to ensure the organization fully understands its responsibilities within the shared model.

- Audit both the customer's and provider's controls to verify the implementation of controls and ensure end-to-end security and compliance.

- Evaluate whether the organization has a robust governance framework to oversee all cloud activities.

- Assess the effectiveness of monitoring tools used to discover and manage shadow IT.

- Evaluate training programs to verify that employees understand cloud policies and the importance of compliance.

Conclusion

The transition to cloud computing has revolutionized IT infrastructure but introduced significant challenges for auditors accustomed to traditional environments. This expanded exploration provides a nuanced understanding of the challenges auditors face in the cloud era. Adapting to this shift requires auditors to rethink their approaches, develop new competencies, and adopt cloud-specific tools and frameworks. Organizations and auditors can build a secure and compliant cloud ecosystem by addressing visibility, shared responsibilities, and governance complexities.

The next chapter explores **Governance, Risk, and Compliance (GRC)** in cloud environments, focusing on how GRC organizations manage risks, ensure regulatory compliance, and align IT with business objectives. This understanding will be invaluable for auditors aiming to conduct effective audits in cloud environments.

Points to remember

- **Adaptation to reduced visibility**: Cloud environments inherently limit direct access to infrastructure. Auditors must rely on third-party assurance reports and cloud-native monitoring tools to gain operational visibility.

- **Addressing multi-tenancy risks**: Ensuring data isolation and understanding the provider's virtualization and encryption controls are critical to mitigating risks in shared environments.

- **Navigating compliance complexities**: Rapidly evolving regulations and the global nature of cloud infrastructures require continuous monitoring and regular updates to compliance strategies.

- **Mitigating third-party risks**: Effective vendor management practices, including SLAs and contingency planning, are essential to reducing risks associated with third-party dependencies.

- **Building trust and transparency**: Organizations must advocate for greater transparency from cloud providers, leveraging contractual agreements and independent certifications to ensure accountability.

- **Understanding shared responsibilities**: Clarity in shared responsibility models is crucial to avoid gaps in security and compliance. Auditors play a key role in verifying both provider and customer adherence.

- **Streamlining governance**: Implementing a robust governance framework that addresses shadow IT and standardizes policies across cloud services helps mitigate security and compliance challenges.

- **Focus on auditability**: Ensuring audit trails are comprehensive, accessible, and aligned with regulatory requirements is vital to maintaining accountability in cloud environments.

Multiple choice questions

1. **Which of the following ensures the isolation of organisational data in multi-tenant cloud environments?**

    a. Virtualization and containerisation

    b. Data quarantine

    c. Data encryption

    d. Physical separation of servers

2. **Which of the following is not a risk of hosting data in a multi-tenant cloud environment?**

   a. Data spillage

   b. Cross-VM attacks

   c. Performance and security trade-offs

   d. Higher costs of hosting

3. **Which of the following is not a key issue in relation to compliance challenges in the cloud?**

   a. Data localization

   b. Standardization gaps

   c. Contractual agreements

   d. Audit trails

4. **Which of the following is one of the key trust issues with cloud service providers?**

   a. Data security

   b. Data visibility

   c. Limited exposure

   d. Compliance with industry standards

5. **Who is responsible for securing the physical infrastructure, hypervisor, and underlying systems under the shared responsibility model?**

   a. Cloud consumer

   b. Cloud service provider

   c. Cloud broker

   d. Cloud auditor

Answers

1	a
2	d
3	c
4	c
5	b

CHAPTER 4
GRC in Cloud

Introduction

Governance, Risk, and Compliance (GRC) are crucial components for businesses that leverage cloud technologies. As organizations increasingly migrate to the cloud, they face unique challenges that demand a reimagining of traditional GRC practices. The cloud introduces complexities such as shared responsibilities between service providers and clients, multi-tenant architectures, and dynamic scalability, all of which influence governance structures, risk profiles, and compliance requirements.

The strategic role of GRC in the cloud extends beyond regulatory adherence. It ensures that cloud IT aligns with business goals, minimizes operational disruptions, and builds trust among stakeholders. This chapter examines how organizations can adapt their GRC practices to effectively navigate the cloud environment.

This chapter explores GRC in the cloud, examining how organizations manage risks, comply with regulations, and align their IT strategies with business objectives.

Structure

The chapter covers the following topics:

- Overview of GRC

- GRC frameworks
- Risk management in cloud
- Compliance requirements in cloud
- Integrating cloud with enterprise GRC
- Role of auditors in cloud GRC implementation
- GRC automation and tools for cloud

Objectives

By the end of this chapter, readers will gain an understanding of the fundamental concepts of GRC and its application in cloud environments, focusing on how organizations manage risks, ensure regulatory compliance, and align IT with business objectives. This understanding will be instrumental for auditors seeking to assess GRC in cloud environments.

Overview of GRC

As mentioned at the beginning of the chapter, GRC stands for **Governance, Risk, and Compliance**. Essentially, it is a unified approach to managing these three crucial aspects of an organization. Instead of treating them as separate silos, GRC integrates them to improve efficiency, reduce risks, and ensure alignment with business objectives.

The following figure depicts GRC components:

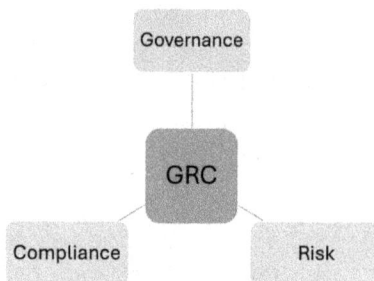

Figure 4.1: Depicting GRC components

Let us understand them in detail:

- **Governance** refers to the framework of rules, policies, and procedures that guide an organization's operations. It establishes clear lines of responsibility, ensures accountability and ethical conduct, and promotes transparency. Effective governance in cloud environments ensures the following:
  - Clear roles and responsibilities in the shared responsibility model.
  - Proper management of cloud resources to avoid cost overruns and inefficiencies.

- **Risk management** involves identifying, assessing, and mitigating potential threats to the organization, such as financial losses, legal liabilities, and reputational damage. Risks in the cloud may include:

  o Data breaches resulting from unsecured data leading to unauthorized access.

  o Compliance violations that result from failure to meet regulatory requirements due to a lack of visibility or control.

  o Operational risks arise from downtime due to cloud provider outages.

- **Compliance** focuses on adhering to all relevant laws, regulations, and industry standards, both internal and external, that apply to cloud environments. Organizations must navigate regional and global standards, often requiring the adaptation of compliance frameworks to cloud realities.

The integration of GRC into cloud strategies empowers organizations to establish trust, mitigate potential disruptions, and achieve operational excellence.

By combining these elements, GRC helps organizations to perform the following:

- **Strategic alignment:** Achieve business goals more effectively by aligning IT with business strategies and mitigating potential roadblocks.

- **Proactive risk management:** Reduce risks by proactively identifying and addressing potential threats.

- **Enhanced compliance:** Ensure compliance by implementing robust processes to adhere to all relevant regulations.

- **Operational efficiency:** Improve efficiency by streamlining operations and minimizing redundancies.

- **Better insights:** Enhance decision-making by providing a comprehensive view of the organization's risks and opportunities.

In simpler terms, imagine a company trying to build a house. Governance would be the blueprint and building codes, ensuring a solid foundation and adherence to safety standards. Risk management is the process of identifying potential hazards, such as earthquakes or floods, and taking steps to prevent damage. Compliance would ensure the house meets all local zoning regulations and obtains the necessary building permits. GRC brings these elements together to ensure the home is built safely, efficiently, and under the plan.

GRC in cloud vis-à-vis traditional GRC

The implementation of GRC in cloud environments presents unique challenges and considerations compared to traditional, on-premises organizations.

Here is a breakdown of the key differences between cloud and traditional on-premises environments across different GRC:

Category	Cloud	On-premises
Responsibilities	Shared responsibility model: provider secures infrastructure; customer secures data, applications, and configurations.	Full control and responsibility over all aspects of IT infrastructure and security.
Operating environment	Highly dynamic: resources are constantly provisioned, scaled, and decommissioned, requiring agile GRC processes.	A more static environment makes it easier to implement and maintain consistent GRC controls.
Data sovereignty and compliance	Must ensure compliance with data sovereignty and privacy regulations (e.g., GDPR, CCPA); may involve choosing specific regions or adding security measures.	Easier to manage compliance within the organization's own data centers.
Visibility and control	Challenging to maintain visibility and control, especially in complex multi-cloud or hybrid deployments.	More direct visibility and control over IT infrastructure.
Third-party risk management	Increased third-party risk from relying on cloud providers; requires assessment, audits, and SLA compliance monitoring.	Limited third-party risk compared to cloud environments.
GRC tools and technologies	Cloud-native GRC tools offer enhanced automation, scalability, and integration with cloud platforms.	Traditional GRC tools may need customization or integration to handle cloud-specific challenges.

Table 4.1: GRC in the cloud vis-à-vis on-premises environments

By understanding these key differences, organizations can develop and implement effective GRC strategies that address the unique risks and challenges associated with cloud computing.

This includes the following:

- **Adopting a cloud-first GRC approach:** Integrating cloud considerations into the overall GRC framework from the outset.

- **Leveraging cloud-native GRC tools and technologies:** Automating and streamlining GRC processes.

- **Establishing clear roles and responsibilities:** Defining who is responsible for which aspects of cloud security and compliance.

- **Conducting regular risk assessments and audits:** Continuously monitoring and evaluating cloud security posture.

- **Staying informed about emerging threats and vulnerabilities**: Adapting GRC controls to address new and evolving risks.

- **Building a strong security culture:** Educating employees about cloud security best practices and their role in protecting organizational assets.

- **Adhering to cloud best practices:** Implementing and establishing cloud-specific standards internally and enforcing consistently within a controlled environment.

- **Enhancing compliance:** Mapping regulatory and industry compliance and continuously monitoring using the GRC tools.

By effectively managing GRC in the cloud, organizations can reap the benefits of cloud computing while mitigating the associated risks and ensuring compliance with relevant regulations.

Cloud GRC should not operate in isolation but should be seamlessly integrated into broader governance framework, including corporate GRC, information technology GRC, and cybersecurity GRC programs within an organization. This ensures that cloud-specific risks and compliance requirements are addressed within the context of the organization's overall governance strategy, aligning cloud operations with corporate policies, IT systems, and cybersecurity measures for a cohesive and comprehensive approach.

Auditing GRC in the cloud requires adapting to the cloud service provider's shared responsibility model, leveraging cloud-native tools, and focusing on automation. Auditors need expertise in cloud platforms, sound knowledge of regulations and standards related to cloud, and a robust understanding of how the organization implements controls within its cloud infrastructure.

The choice between traditional and cloud-based GRC auditing depends on various factors, including the organization's size, budget, technical expertise, and specific needs. Ultimately, the goal is to select an approach that best supports the organization's risk management and compliance objectives.

GRC frameworks

Organizations seeking to establish a robust GRC framework often leverage existing best practices. These best practices are typically outlined in standards or frameworks developed by various reputable organizations. Each standard offers distinct advantages and aligns with different organizational needs and goals. The choice of standards/frameworks to be adopted often depends on the organization's industry, regulatory requirements, and operational environment, and one or a combination of the standards or frameworks may be utilized in building the GRC framework. By adopting these frameworks, organizations can standardize their processes, implement effective control mechanisms, and assess the performance of their GRC initiatives.

Here is a summary of key GRC standards or frameworks that can guide organizations in building their optimal GRC framework.

COSO ICIF

The Committee of Sponsoring Organizations of the Treadway Commission (COSO) publishes the **Internal Control—Integrated Framework (ICIF),** which provides a comprehensive framework for internal control, encompassing financial reporting, operations, and compliance.

This framework is comprised of five key components, namely:

- Control environment
- Risk assessment
- Control activities
- Information and communication
- Monitoring activities

ISO 38500

ISO/IEC 38500:2024, titled Information Technology, Governance of IT for the Organization is published by the **International Organization for Standardization (ISO)** and the **International Electrotechnical Commission (IEC)** and offers guidance on the corporate governance of **information and communication technology (ICT).**

The key principles include:

- Value delivery
- Risk management
- Resource management
- Performance measurement, conformance

COBIT

Control Objectives for Information and Related Technologies (COBIT) framework is published by the **Information Systems Audit and Control Association (ISACA)** and provides a holistic framework for IT governance and management, enabling organizations to maximize the benefits of IT while optimizing IT-related risks.

The key principles of this framework include:

- Meeting stakeholder needs
- Covering the enterprise end-to-end
- Applying a single
- Integrated framework
- Enabling a holistic approach
- Separating governance from management

ITGC

The framework, **IT general controls (ITGC), is** published by ISACA and provides a framework for ITGC, which are the foundational controls that support the effective functioning of IT systems and applications.

The key areas addressed in this framework include:

- Change management
- Access control
- Systems operations
- Application development
- Maintenance and data center operations

ISO 27001

ISO/IEC 27001:2022 is a standard titled *Information security: Cybersecurity and privacy protection, Information security management systems, Requirements*, published by the ISO, which specifies requirements for establishing, implementing, maintaining, and continually improving an **information security management system (ISMS).** This standard provides requirements for organizations seeking ISO 27001 certification.

The key principles of this standard are:

- Risk assessment
- Risk treatment
- Statement of Applicability
- Continual improvement

ISO 27014

The standard ISO/IEC 27014:2020, titled *Information security: Cybersecurity and privacy protection, Governance of information security,* is published by the ISO and guides organizations seeking ISO 27001 certification or third-party assurance. The key principles of ISO 27014 cover understanding certification, selecting a certification body, and preparing for the certification audit.

ISO 27005

ISO/IEC 27005:2022 is a standard titled *Information security: Cybersecurity and privacy protection - Guidance on managing information security risks,* published by the ISO, which provides guidelines for information security risk management.

The key principles include:

- Establishing the context for the risk assessment
- Identifying and analyzing risks
- Evaluating and treating risks
- Communicating and consulting
- Monitoring and reviewing

ISO 31000

ISO 31000:2018, *Risk Management Guidelines,* is published by the ISO and provides principles and guidelines on risk management applicable to any organization, regardless of its size, type, or nature.

The key principles include:

- Creating value
- Integrate risk management
- Be systematic and structured
- Base decisions on the best available information
- Be human-centered and inclusive
- Be transparent and inclusive
- Be dynamic
- Be iterative and continually improve

ISO 27017

The standard ISO/IEC 27017:2015, titled as *Information technology: Security techniques, Code of practice for information security controls based on ISO/IEC 27002 for cloud service*s, is published by the ISO and provides guidelines for implementing and managing information security controls in cloud environments.

Some of the key principles of this standard are:

- Align with ISO 27001
- Address cloud-specific risks
- Guide different cloud service models

NIST CSF

NIST **Cybersecurity Framework (CSF)** is published by the **National Institute of Standards and Technology (NIST)** and provides a voluntary framework for managing cybersecurity risk to critical infrastructure and other sectors.

The CSF 2.0 is organized by six functions, namely:

- Govern
- Identify
- Protect
- Detect
- Respond
- Recover

Together, these functions, along with the underlying categories and sub-categories, provide a comprehensive view for managing cybersecurity risk. The resource and overview guide published by NIST provides brief details about each function, serving as potential starting points.

CSA CCM

The **Cloud Security Alliance (CSA) Cloud Controls Matrix (CCM)** is published by CSA and provides a comprehensive control framework for cloud computing, covering a wide range of security controls.

The key principles of CSA CCM include:

- Address the unique characteristics of cloud
- Computing
- Provide a comprehensive set of controls
- Enable continuous monitoring and improvement

GRC capability model

The GRC capability model (also referred to as the **Open Compliance and Ethics Group (OCEG)** Red Book) is a framework published by the OCEG. This is a unified framework for integrating GRC practices into an organization's culture and processes, fostering alignment and improved decision-making.

The key components of this framework cover the principles, practices, processes, performance, and people. Key points of the capability model include the following:

- **Purpose**: Help organizations reliably achieve objectives, address uncertainty, and act with integrity.
- **Structure**: Organized into four core components known as the *GRC capability model elements*, which form a continuous improvement cycle.
- **Principles-based**: It is flexible and scalable for organizations of all sizes and industries, emphasizing principles over rigid rules.

- **Focus areas**: Includes detailed practices for governance structures, risk assessments, compliance program management, performance monitoring, and continuous improvement.

- **Audit relevance**: Auditors can use the model as a benchmark to assess the maturity and effectiveness of an organization's GRC capabilities. It supports evaluating both internal controls and the broader integration of GRC processes.

The core components of the capability model, along with the underlying elements, are described in the following table:

Core component	Element	Description
LEARN	External context	Monitor regulatory, market, legal, and societal conditions.
	Internal context	Understand mission, strategy, structure, and internal dynamics.
	Culture	Analyze ethical values, behaviors, and organizational norms.
	Stakeholder expectations	Identify the needs and concerns of internal and external stakeholders.
ALIGN	Direction	Direct the organization with a clear mission, vision, and values that guide overall goals and strategies.
	Objectives	Define a set of measurable objectives.
	Identification	Identify the opportunities, obstacles, and obligations that might impact objectives.
	Analysis	Analyze current and planned approaches to quantify and address risk, reward, and compliance.
	Design	Develop a plan to achieve objectives within acceptable levels of risk.
PERFORM	Controls	Implement a mix of actions and control types, categories, and techniques.
	Policies	Implement policies to address opportunities, obstacles, and obligations.
	Communications	Implement communications to address opportunities, obstacles, and obligations.
	Education	Implement education and support for the workforce to develop job-specific awareness and skills.
	Incentives	Implement incentives to encourage the right conduct in the workforce.
	Notification	Implement multiple pathways for people and systems to report progress towards objectives.
	Inquiry	Implement multiple pathways to discover information from people and systems about progress towards objectives.
	Response	Implement responses that uncover and address root causes to correct and recover from unfavorable events.

Core component	Element	Description
REVIEW	Monitoring	Implement ongoing and periodic activities to gauge the effectiveness of actions and controls.
	Assurance	Objectively and competently evaluate priority areas to provide assurance to the stakeholders.
	Continuous improvement	Adapt and refine GRC capabilities based on learnings and changes.

Table 4.2: Core components of the capability model

The current version of the capability model enhances alignment with emerging standards like ISO 37301 and COSO frameworks, places greater emphasis on culture, ethical leadership, and organizational agility, and strengthens the integration of information and technology to optimize GRC processes.

Understanding and applying the OCEG GRC capability model allows auditors to evaluate not just compliance checkboxes, but the real effectiveness of how organizations manage risk, governance, and compliance holistically. It supports risk-based audit approaches and helps auditors identify systemic weaknesses that may not show up in isolated audits.

These GRC frameworks provide robust guidelines to ensure effective governance, risk management, and compliance. Auditors utilize these frameworks to benchmark practices, identify gaps, and provide actionable recommendations to strengthen an organization's GRC posture.

Common auditing aspects and key domains

GRC frameworks provide comprehensive guidance for managing organizational governance processes, addressing risks, and ensuring compliance. They also offer specific aspects to evaluate during audits and key domains to focus on for effective GRC practices.

Here is an overview of common auditing aspects:

- **Governance:**
  - Oversight and decision-making by leadership.
  - Alignment of IT and security strategies with organizational goals.
  - Transparency in resource allocation and policy enforcement.

- **Risk management:**
  - Identification, analysis, and mitigation of risks.
  - Continuous monitoring of emerging threats.
  - Implementation and effectiveness of risk treatment plans.

- **Compliance and control effectiveness:**
  - o Adherence to legal, regulatory, and industry-specific requirements.
  - o Assessment of implemented controls against established standards.
  - o Gap analysis and remediation planning.

- **Incident response and recovery:**
  - o Incident detection, reporting, and escalation procedures.
  - o Post-incident analysis and recovery timelines.
  - o Audits of business continuity and disaster recovery plans.

- **Cloud security and shared responsibility:**
  - o Data protection in cloud environments.
  - o Accountability between cloud service providers and customers.
  - o Alignment with cloud-specific standards and best practices.

The key domains for auditing vary depending on the framework, but often include the following:

- **IT and information security:**
  - o Assessment of IT governance and security measures.
  - o Evaluation of ISMS and cybersecurity practices.

- **Data protection and privacy:**
  - o Safeguarding sensitive information.
  - o Compliance with privacy regulations (e.g., GDPR).

- **Risk assessment and mitigation:** Processes for risk evaluation and control implementation.

- **Regulatory and legal compliance**: Ensuring adherence to laws and industry standards.

- **Cloud computing and virtual environments**: Assessment of cloud-specific security and compliance controls.

- **Process and performance monitoring**: Evaluating the efficiency of processes and achieving intended outcomes.

Grouping auditing aspects and key domains streamlines the approach for organizations to ensure alignment, accountability, and resilience in their GRC practices. The GRC framework empowers organizations to safeguard assets, ensure compliance, and build trust with stakeholders.

While traditional GRC frameworks serve as a foundation, their adaptation to cloud-specific characteristics, such as dynamic scalability and multi-tenancy, is crucial. Organizations should focus on flexibility, integrating these frameworks with the native controls of CSPs.

Risk management in cloud

Risk management is a systematic process used to identify, assess, and control potential threats or uncertainties that could negatively impact an organization's objectives. Organizations may leverage global risk management standards or frameworks such as ISO 31000, ISO 27005, or NIST SP 800-30 as a basis to formulate risk management methodology. Risk management helps organizations make informed decisions, improve their resilience, and protect their assets and reputation.

One should understand that fundamental risk management principles remain unchanged, whether your systems and data reside on-premises or in the cloud. You must still identify, evaluate, address, and track potential risks. However, cloud risk management necessitates a specific focus on the chosen service and deployment models, as these directly influence the security responsibilities shared between your organization and the cloud service provider.

Cloud risk management is a crucial process for organizations that leverage cloud computing services. It involves a series of steps to identify, assess, and mitigate potential risks associated with cloud environments.

Risk management process

Key steps in cloud risk management include risk identification, risk assessment, risk mitigation, and risk monitoring and review, which is depicted in the following figure:

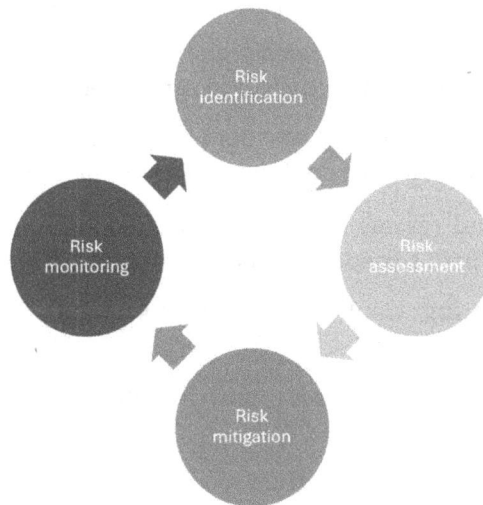

Figure 4.2: Risk management process

Let us understand this in detail:

- **Risk identification** is the process of recognizing and defining potential risks to the information assets in the cloud environment and involves the following steps:

- o **Inventory and mapping:** Identify and map all cloud resources, including virtual machines, databases, storage, and applications.

- o **Threat modeling:** Analyze potential threats, such as data breaches, outages, and compliance violations.

- o **Vulnerability scanning:** Regularly conduct vulnerability scans to proactively identify and address security weaknesses within the IT infrastructure.

- **Risk assessment** is the systematic process of identifying, analyzing, and evaluating the likelihood and potential impact of each risk, typically conducted in a sequential manner, as mentioned here:

  - o **Impact analysis:** Determine the potential impact of identified risks on business operations, data, and reputation.

  - o **Likelihood analysis:** Assess the likelihood of each risk occurring.

  - o **Risk prioritization:** Prioritize risk mitigation efforts based on a comprehensive assessment of each risk's potential impact and likelihood.

- **Risk mitigation** involves a proactive approach to managing risks, including the development and implementation of strategies to reduce their impact or likelihood, and involves the following steps:

  - o **Control implementation:** Implement appropriate security controls, such as access controls, encryption, and intrusion detection systems.

  - o **Cloud service provider security reviews:** Regularly review the security measures implemented by the cloud service provider.

  - o **Incident response plan:** Implement and maintain a robust incident response plan to effectively detect, contain, and remediate security breaches.

- **Risk monitoring and review** is the process of continuously tracking and adjusting risk management plans as needed and is performed in the following sequence of steps:

- **Continuous monitoring**: Continuously monitor cloud environments for threats and vulnerabilities.

- **Regular reviews**: Regularly review and update risk assessments and mitigation strategies.

- **Compliance audits**: Conduct regular compliance audits to ensure adherence to relevant regulations and standards.

Key considerations

The cloud introduces risks that differ from traditional on-premises setups, and the key considerations in cloud risk management include the following:

- **Responsibilities:** Understand the shared responsibility model between the organization and the cloud service provider, to ensure that there is no ambiguity in responsibility between the CSP and the client.

- **Data residency and sovereignty:** Challenges in ensuring data compliance across borders and regions.

- **Compliance requirements:** Ensure compliance with relevant industry regulations and standards.

- **Data security:** Implement robust data protection measures, including encryption, access controls, and data loss prevention.

- **Business continuity and disaster recovery:** Plan for business continuity and disaster recovery in the event of a cloud outage or security incident.

- **Vendor lock-in:** Dependence on a single CSP, which might lead to a single point of failure in disastrous situations affecting CSPs.

- **Cost optimization:** Optimize cloud spending while maintaining an appropriate level of security.

By following a comprehensive cloud risk management process, organizations can effectively mitigate risks, protect their data and systems, and ensure the successful adoption of cloud computing.

Auditors should also validate the alignment of the risk management methodology adopted for cloud risk assessments with the enterprise risk management methodologies.

Compliance requirements in cloud

The cloud has transformed the business landscape, offering businesses increased agility, reduced IT costs, and the ability to scale resources up or down based on their needs. However, migrating to the cloud also introduces new compliance challenges that organizations must address. To ensure data security, privacy, and regulatory adherence, a strong understanding of cloud compliance requirements is crucial. This is where the auditing community plays a vital role in assessing and verifying compliance within cloud environments. Compliance operates in conjunction with governance and risk management to form GRC.

Compliance ensures adherence to all relevant rules, from laws and regulations to internal policies and industry standards. It is a cornerstone of effective GRC, crucial for overseeing all computing activities, including cloud operations. A compliance framework provides the roadmap, including the policies, procedures, and technologies, that guide an organization in identifying and meeting its obligations.

Compliance assessments not only evaluate adherence but also consider the potential consequences of noncompliance. These costs, which can be significant, include financial penalties, reputational damage, and even legal repercussions for executives. While compliance necessitates investment, the potential costs of noncompliance far outweigh the proactive measures needed to ensure adherence.

In addition to organizational policies related to cloud computing, several frameworks and regulations drive and govern compliance requirements related to cloud computing, such as GDPR, HIPAA, SOX, ISO standards, and international and national regulations.

While the fundamental principles of compliance and auditing remain unchanged when using cloud services, as CSPs are essentially third-party providers, and organizations likely already have procedures for managing such relationships, specific compliance considerations arise when implementing cloud solutions. These will be discussed in detail in the *Challenges and considerations* section.

Role of auditors

Auditors play a crucial role in assessing and verifying cloud compliance. They provide independent assurance, allowing organizations to:

- **Adhere to relevant compliance standards:** Auditors evaluate an organization's cloud security posture against applicable regulations and frameworks, identifying any gaps or areas of non-compliance.

- **Implement effective controls:** They assess the effectiveness of security controls, such as access controls, data encryption, and incident response plans, within the cloud environment.

- **Maintain accurate records:** Auditors review documentation related to cloud service agreements, security assessments, and compliance certifications.

- **Conduct regular risk assessments:** They help organizations identify and mitigate potential risks associated with cloud adoption, such as data breaches, unauthorized access, and service disruptions.

- **Provide recommendations for improvement:** Auditors provide valuable insights and recommendations to enhance cloud security posture and improve overall compliance.

Challenges and considerations

Cloud computing offers numerous advantages, but it also introduces unique compliance challenges and considerations. Here are some key areas to focus on:

- **Dynamic nature of cloud computing:** The ever-evolving nature of cloud services can pose challenges for auditors in keeping up with the latest technologies and security threats.

- **Complexity of cloud environments:** Cloud environments can be complex and multi-layered, requiring specialized knowledge and expertise from auditors to navigate and assess effectively.

- **Emerging threats and vulnerabilities:** New threats and vulnerabilities constantly emerge in the cloud landscape, necessitating continuous adaptation of auditing methodologies and techniques.

Best practices for compliance

Organizations can effectively manage cloud compliance risks, maintain data security, and ensure adherence to relevant regulations by implementing these best practices, and some of the best practices are mentioned here:

- Conduct regular audits of cloud environments.

- Establish clear documentation for compliance processes.

- Use CSP tools like AWS Artifact or Azure Compliance Manager to track and maintain compliance.

- Enforce cloud security posture management using tools such as Prisma Cloud, Wiz, AWS Security Hub, etc.

- Implement fine-grained network controls by utilizing VPCs, subnets, and applying **Zero Trust networking (ZTN)** principles across all communication layers.

- Implement least privilege access, enforce **multi-factor authentication (MFA)** for all critical accounts, regularly audit permissions, rotate credentials, and prefer federated identities to reduce risks.

- Centralize cloud logs and security events into a SIEM to enable real-time monitoring, threat detection, incident response, and compliance reporting.

Cloud compliance is crucial for maintaining data security, ensuring regulatory adherence, and mitigating legal and financial risks associated with cloud computing. By working closely with the auditors, organizations can be assured that they meet regulatory requirements, protect sensitive data, and maintain a secure cloud environment. Auditors provide valuable expertise and assurance in navigating the complexities of cloud compliance and mitigating associated risks. As the cloud landscape continues to evolve, the role of the auditors will remain essential in helping organizations achieve and maintain a robust and compliant cloud posture.

Integrating cloud with enterprise GRC

The adoption of cloud technologies has become a cornerstone for organizations aiming to achieve agility, scalability, and cost-efficiency. However, integrating cloud services with enterprise GRC is a critical task that requires careful planning and execution. Here is an exploration of this topic, highlighting its significance, challenges, and best practices.

Significance of integrating cloud with GRC

Integrating cloud with GRC offers significant advantages for modern organizations. This is elaborated upon here:

- **Regulatory compliance:** Cloud adoption often involves handling sensitive data, which is subject to various regulations like GDPR, HIPAA, or CCPA. Integrating cloud operations into the GRC framework ensures that regulatory requirements are met consistently.

- **Risk management:** Cloud environments introduce new risks, such as data breaches, unauthorized access, or service outages. A GRC-aligned cloud strategy helps organizations identify, assess, and mitigate these risks.

- **Operational efficiency:** By embedding cloud processes within the GRC framework, organizations can streamline governance processes, reduce duplication of efforts, and enhance overall efficiency.

- **Enhanced security:** Integrating cloud systems with GRC ensures that robust controls are in place to safeguard data, providing visibility and accountability.

Challenges in integration

Integrating GRC with cloud environments presents several challenges, and some of these key challenges are as follows:

- **Complex cloud environments:** Hybrid and multi-cloud setups complicate the implementation of uniform GRC processes due to varied vendor policies and configurations.

- **Lack of visibility:** Cloud environments can lack transparency, making it difficult to monitor and manage compliance and risks effectively.

- **Dynamic nature of cloud:** The elastic and scalable nature of cloud computing leads to rapid changes in resource configurations, posing a challenge for maintaining real-time compliance.

- **Vendor dependency:** Cloud providers have their own compliance standards, which may not align perfectly with the organization's GRC requirements.

- **Skill gaps:** Many organizations face a lack of expertise in cloud-specific GRC integration, making it hard to design and implement effective strategies.

Key components for integration

Key components for a successful GRC integration with cloud environments include:

- **Unified GRC framework:** Establish a GRC framework that incorporates cloud-specific guidelines, controls, and compliance requirements.

- **Cloud risk assessment:** Identify and assess risks specific to the cloud environment, such as data residency, shared responsibility models, and vendor lock-in.

- **Policy alignment:** Ensure that the organization's internal policies align with cloud service providers' terms and industry regulations.

- **Automation and tooling:** Use cloud-native tools and third-party solutions for automated compliance checks, risk assessments, and continuous monitoring.

- **Vendor management:** Evaluate cloud providers for their compliance certifications, security measures, and risk management capabilities.

Best practices for effective integration

By following these best practices, organizations can effectively integrate GRC with their cloud environments, enhance their security posture, and achieve their business objectives:

- **Define clear roles and responsibilities**: Establish accountability for cloud GRC management between internal teams and external providers.

- **Continuous monitoring**: Implement tools and processes for real-time monitoring of compliance and security in the cloud.

- **Leverage frameworks**: Utilize industry standards such as ISO 27001, NIST standards that were discussed earlier, to design cloud-specific GRC practices.

- **Data classification and protection**: Classify data based on sensitivity and implement appropriate access controls and encryption mechanisms.

- **Regular audits and reviews**: Conduct periodic audits of cloud environments to ensure compliance with organizational and regulatory requirements.

- **Employee training**: Equip staff with knowledge of cloud-specific GRC challenges and best practices through ongoing training programs.

Emerging trends

Several emerging trends are shaping the future of GRC integration with cloud environments, and some of them are discussed here:

- **AI and ML for GRC:** Artificial intelligence and machine learning are being used to analyze vast amounts of cloud data, detect anomalies, and predict compliance issues.

- **Zero Trust security model:** A Zero Trust approach enhances the integration of security within the GRC framework, especially in cloud environments.

- **Cloud-native GRC tools:** Tools like AWS Security Hub, Microsoft Azure Policy, and Google Cloud Security Command Center are becoming essential for seamless integration.

- **Focus on environmental, social, and governance (ESG):** Organizations are aligning cloud adoption strategies with ESG goals, integrating sustainability metrics into their GRC frameworks.

Integrating cloud with enterprise GRC is essential for modern organizations to ensure seamless operations, robust compliance, and proactive risk management. By understanding the challenges, leveraging the right tools, and adopting best practices, organizations can build a resilient GRC framework that supports their cloud transformation goals while maintaining security, compliance, and operational excellence.

Auditors should play a critical role in ensuring that cloud operations are effectively integrated into an organization's GRC framework. Their expertise in assessing processes, controls, and compliance helps organizations navigate the complexities of cloud adoption while maintaining accountability and minimizing risks. By identifying risks, testing controls, and offering actionable recommendations, auditors enable organizations to confidently integrate cloud services into their broader governance and compliance strategy.

Role of auditors in cloud GRC implementation

Auditors play a critical role in ensuring the effective implementation of GRC frameworks in cloud environments. Their responsibilities include:

- **Assessing cloud service provider (CSP) security:** Evaluating the security controls and compliance posture of the chosen CSP to ensure it aligns with organizational requirements and industry standards.

- **Validating GRC framework implementation:** Verifying that the organization has implemented appropriate GRC processes, controls, and technologies in the cloud environment. This includes assessing access controls, data security measures, incident response plans, and compliance with relevant regulations (e.g., GDPR, HIPAA, SOX).

- **Identifying and mitigating risks:** Conducting risk assessments to identify potential threats and vulnerabilities in the cloud environment and ensuring that appropriate mitigation strategies are in place.

- **Monitoring compliance:** Continuously monitoring the cloud environment to ensure ongoing compliance with GRC requirements and identifying any deviations or emerging risks.

- **Providing assurance:** Providing assurance to management and stakeholders that the organization's cloud operations are secure, compliant, and aligned with business objectives.

By actively participating in the GRC implementation process, auditors can help organizations:

- **Reduce risks:** Mitigate potential security threats and data breaches in the cloud.
- **Improve compliance:** Ensure adherence to relevant regulations and industry standards.
- **Enhance operational efficiency:** Streamline GRC processes and reduce the burden of compliance.
- **Build trust:** Gain the trust of customers, partners, and regulators.

Key considerations for cloud auditors include the following:

- **Cloud-specific knowledge:** Auditors need to have a strong understanding of cloud computing concepts, technologies, and security best practices.
- **Collaboration:** Effective collaboration with management, IT teams, and cloud service providers is crucial for successful GRC implementation.
- **Continuous learning:** The cloud environment is constantly evolving, so auditors need to stay updated on the latest threats, vulnerabilities, and compliance requirements.

By effectively fulfilling their role, auditors can help organizations leverage the benefits of cloud computing while mitigating the associated risks and ensuring a secure and compliant environment.

GRC automation and tools for cloud

GRC automation refers to the use of technology to streamline and automate various aspects of GRC processes. This includes tasks such as:

- **Risk assessment:** Automating the identification, analysis, and prioritization of risks.
- **Compliance monitoring:** Continuously monitoring compliance with regulations and standards.
- **Control testing:** Automating the execution of controls and assessments.
- **Reporting and analytics:** Extracting meaningful insights from GRC data through advanced reporting and analytics techniques.

Benefits of GRC automation

GRC automation offers significant benefits for organizations, and some of these key benefits are discussed here:

- **Increased efficiency:** Automating manual tasks frees up valuable time and resources.

- **Reduced errors:** Automation significantly reduces the risk of human error, resulting in more accurate and reliable data and outcomes.

- **Improved consistency:** Automated processes ensure consistent application of controls and standards.

- **Enhanced visibility:** Real-time data and advanced analytics provide deeper insights into GRC performance, enabling proactive identification and mitigation of risks.

- **Faster response times:** Automated alerts and notifications enable faster response to incidents and deviations.

GRC tools for cloud environments

Cloud computing has introduced new challenges and complexities to GRC. Cloud-specific GRC tools address these challenges by providing features such as:

- **Cloud-native integration:** Seamless integration with major cloud providers (AWS, Azure, GCP).

- **Automated security assessments:** Continuous monitoring of cloud resources for vulnerabilities and misconfigurations.

- **Compliance automation:** Automating compliance with cloud-specific regulations and standards.

- **Cloud-specific reporting:** Generating reports on cloud security posture and compliance status.

Popular GRC tools for cloud environments

GRC tools help organizations manage and mitigate risks associated with their cloud environments. Here are some popular options:

- **ServiceNow GRC:** A comprehensive platform that covers various aspects of GRC, including risk management, compliance, and internal audit.

- **Archer:** A flexible platform that can be customized to meet specific GRC needs, including cloud security.

- **MetricStream:** A platform that provides a unified view of GRC processes, including cloud security and compliance.

- **SAP GRC:** A suite of solutions that address various GRC challenges, including cloud security and compliance.

- **IBM OpenPages:** An AI-driven GRC platform that helps enterprises manage risk, compliance, policies, and audits across cloud and hybrid environments through a single integrated solution.

- **LogicGate Risk Cloud:** A flexible, cloud-based GRC platform that enables organizations to automate and streamline risk management, compliance, and audit processes with customizable workflows and real-time insights.

- **OpenGRC:** A flexible, open-source platform, but it is generally less tailored for cloud environments compared to more specialized, cloud-native GRC tools. It can be used in cloud environments, but needs some customization or integrations to fully leverage cloud-specific capabilities.

GRC automation and tools are essential for organizations that want to effectively manage risk and compliance in the cloud. By automating key tasks and leveraging cloud-specific features, organizations can improve efficiency, reduce errors, and gain better insights into their GRC performance.

Conclusion

The adoption of cloud computing has revolutionized IT landscapes, bringing unparalleled scalability, flexibility, and efficiency. However, it also introduces unique challenges in GRC that organizations must address proactively. By adapting robust GRC practices tailored to cloud environments, businesses can secure their assets, meet compliance obligations, and align IT initiatives with overarching business goals.

As organizations continue their cloud transformation journeys, embedding GRC into every layer of cloud strategy is vital. The ability to balance innovation with robust controls will differentiate organizations that thrive in the cloud era from those that falter. Organizations should begin by assessing their current GRC posture, leveraging modern tools, and fostering a culture of compliance and risk awareness to achieve sustainable growth.

In the next chapter, we will discuss regulations that may need to be considered while transitioning data to the cloud and working with CSPs. We will primarily address the legal considerations of public and third-party hosted private clouds.

Points to remember

- **The strategic role of GRC**: GRC in the cloud is essential for aligning IT operations with business objectives, building stakeholder trust, and ensuring long-term organizational resilience.

- **Cloud-specific risks and solutions**: Organizations must address risks such as shared responsibility ambiguities, data breaches, and vendor lock-in with proactive risk management strategies, including encryption, **identity access management (IAM)**, and continuous monitoring.

- **Compliance complexity in the cloud**: Navigating diverse regulatory requirements like GDPR, HIPAA, and PCI DSS demands leveraging CSP compliance certifications and tools while maintaining clear documentation and internal accountability.

- **Integration of GRC across the enterprise**: Unifying cloud-specific GRC processes with enterprise-wide strategies ensures consistency and enhances overall organizational governance. Centralized platforms and APIs are key enablers.

- **The role of automation:** Automating GRC processes with tools like ServiceNow GRC and RSA Archer boosts efficiency, reduces errors, and scales seamlessly with dynamic cloud environments.

- **Auditor's impact on cloud GRC:** Auditors are instrumental in evaluating the effectiveness of GRC measures, ensuring regulatory adherence, and identifying vulnerabilities within cloud ecosystems.

Multiple choice questions

1. **Which of the following is not a standard for risk management?**

    a. NIST SP 800-30

    b. ISO 27001

    c. ISO 27005

    d. ISO 31000

2. **Which of the following organizations published the GRC capability model framework?**

    a. OCEG

    b. NIST

    c. ISO

    d. CSA

3. **Which of the following is not a challenge or consideration for cloud auditors?**

    a. Dynamic nature of cloud computing

    b. Complexity of cloud environments

    c. Emerging threats and vulnerabilities

    d. Increased efficiency

4. **Which of the following cannot be used for automating GRC?**

    a. ServiceNow

    b. Archer

    c. SolarWinds NPM

    d. MetricStream

5. **The potential consequences of noncompliance for an organization include which of the following?**

    a. Financial penalties

    b. Reputational damage

    c. Legal issues

    d. All of the above

Answers

1	b
2	a
3	d
4	c
5	d

Join our Discord space

Join our Discord workspace for latest updates, offers, tech happenings around the world, new releases, and sessions with the authors:

https://discord.bpbonline.com

CHAPTER 5

Common Cloud Regulations

Introduction

In today's complex regulatory landscape, compliance has become a critical aspect of managing cloud environments. Cloud-based systems host vast amounts of sensitive and confidential data, necessitating adherence to stringent regulatory requirements to protect information and ensure privacy. For organizations leveraging cloud services, compliance is not just a legal obligation but also a cornerstone of maintaining trust and integrity. This chapter explores key regulations governing cloud environments and emphasizes the vital role auditors play in ensuring adherence to these mandates.

Structure

This chapter covers the following topics:

- Overview of cloud regulations
- Sarbanes-Oxley Act and cloud compliance
- Importance of national and international regulations
- Roles of auditors in cloud compliance

Objectives

By the end of this chapter, readers will be able to understand relevant regulations and the necessity of involving an organization's legal counsel when procuring cloud services, especially when dealing with providers operating across multiple jurisdictions. Readers will also become familiar with regulations that may need to be considered when transitioning data to the cloud and working with **cloud service providers (CSPs)**.

However, as laws and regulations are subject to frequent changes, it is essential to verify the accuracy and applicability of the information presented here before relying on it.

Overview of cloud regulations

Cloud regulations are frameworks established to govern how data is processed, stored, and transmitted in cloud environments. These regulations ensure that organizations and CSPs implement appropriate security measures, adhere to privacy standards, and mitigate data breaches or misuse risks.

Depending on their industry and geography, cloud consumers may be subject to various regulations like the **Sarbanes-Oxley Act (SOX)**, **Payment Card Industry Data Security Standards (PCI DSS)**, and the **Health Insurance Portability and Accountability Act (HIPAA)**. **Federal Information Security Modernization Act (FISMA)**, or **Gramm-Leach-Bliley Act (GLBA)**. Since cloud consumers are accountable for data processed on a provider's systems, they must ensure that the cloud service provider assists them in complying with the relevant regulations.

At the same time, cloud consumers must be confident that legal recourse is available if cloud providers fail to comply with regulations or obligations. This is challenging because providers often treat their service implementation and configuration as proprietary information, limiting consumer visibility. This lack of transparency makes it difficult to verify compliance independently unless the provider undergoes regular audits by trusted third parties.

However, even with audits, the risk of non-compliance remains, as systems can gradually drift out of compliance between audits. Therefore, continuous monitoring of cloud configurations and health may be necessary for ongoing assurance.

The application of regulatory frameworks in cloud environments presents unique challenges. The shared responsibility model, which divides compliance obligations between CSPs and customers, demands a clear understanding of accountability. Furthermore, the global nature of cloud computing often results in jurisdictional overlaps, requiring organizations to comply with multiple, sometimes conflicting, regulatory requirements.

Regulatory compliance in cloud computing mitigates legal and financial risks and enhances organizational reputation and stakeholder trust. Auditors play a crucial role in assessing compliance by evaluating security controls, reviewing data protection measures, and ensuring alignment with applicable regulations.

General Data Protection Regulation

General Data Protection Regulation (GDPR) is a comprehensive data protection law enacted by the European Union to safeguard personal data and uphold individuals' privacy rights. It applies to all organizations processing the data of EU residents, irrespective of their location, making it particularly relevant in the globalized cloud ecosystem.

Key requirements for cloud compliance are as follows:

- **Lawful basis for processing**: Organizations must have a valid legal basis for processing personal data, such as consent or contractual necessity. This applies not only to data processed directly by the organization but also to personal data handled by third parties, including system integrators, acting on their behalf.

- **Data minimization**: Only data that is necessary for the stated purpose should be collected and processed.

- **Data subject rights**: Individuals have the right to access, rectify, and erase their personal data and object to its processing.

- **Data protection impact assessments (DPIAs)** are mandatory for high-risk processing activities, including those involving cloud services.

- **Security measures**: Organizations must implement robust technical and organizational measures to protect personal data.

- **Role of auditors**: Auditors evaluate the effectiveness of an organization's GDPR compliance program, particularly in cloud environments. They assess data protection practices, validate contractual agreements with CSPs, and review DPIAs to manage risks appropriately. Additionally, auditors ensure organizations have mechanisms to respond promptly to data breaches and subject access requests.

Health Insurance Portability and Accountability Act

The HIPPA establishes regulations to protect the confidentiality, integrity, and availability of **protected health information (PHI)**. HIPAA applies to covered entities, such as healthcare providers and their business associates, including CSPs handling PHI.

Key compliance requirements according to HIPAA are listed here:

- **Administrative safeguards**: Policies and procedures to manage the security of PHI, including workforce training and risk assessments.

- **Physical safeguards**: Controls to prevent unauthorized physical access to PHI stored in cloud data centers.

- **Technical safeguards**: Implementation of access controls, encryption, and audit trails to secure electronic PHI.

- **Business Associate Agreements (BAAs)**: Contracts ensuring CSPs adhere to HIPAA requirements.

- **Role of auditors**: Auditors play a pivotal role in verifying HIPAA compliance within cloud environments. They review BAAs, evaluate the implementation of safeguards, and conduct regular risk assessments to identify and mitigate vulnerabilities. By ensuring compliance, auditors help protect sensitive health information and reduce the risk of costly penalties and reputational damage.

Payment Card Industry-Data Security Standard

The **Payment Card Industry-Data Security Standard** (**PCI-DDS**) is a set of security standards designed to protect cardholder data. Organizations that process, store, or transmit payment card information must adhere to these standards to ensure data security and prevent fraud.

Some of the key control objectives of PCI-DSS are mentioned here:

- **Build and maintain a secure network**: Implement firewalls and strong access controls.

- **Protect cardholder data**: Encrypt sensitive data and secure its storage.

- **Maintain a vulnerability management program**: Regularly update systems and deploy anti-malware solutions.

- **Monitor and test networks**: Perform regular audits and vulnerability scans.

- **Challenges in cloud compliance**: Multi-tenant cloud environments complicate PCI-DSS compliance due to shared infrastructure and varying security practices among CSPs. Organizations must ensure their CSPs offer PCI-compliant solutions and maintain oversight of all data processing activities.

- **Role of auditors**: Auditors assess an organization's compliance with PCI-DSS by evaluating security controls, reviewing encryption practices, and conducting penetration tests. They also verify that CSPs provide adequate segmentation and logging capabilities to protect cardholder data.

SOX and cloud compliance

The SOX mandates strict financial reporting controls to ensure transparency and accountability. While traditionally focused on on-premises systems, SOX compliance is increasingly relevant in cloud environments as organizations migrate financial data to the cloud.

Key requirements of the SOX Act for cloud compliance are mentioned here:

- **Internal controls over financial reporting (ICFR)**: Implement and document controls to ensure accurate financial reporting.

- **Audit trails**: Maintain detailed logs of financial transactions and system changes.

- **Data integrity**: Ensure the accuracy and completeness of financial data.

- **Role of auditors**: Auditors evaluate the design and effectiveness of ICFR within cloud environments. They review access controls, logging mechanisms, and CSP certifications to ensure that financial data integrity and auditability are maintained.

Importance of national and international regulations

Cloud environments operate across borders, making compliance with national and international regulations essential. Organizations must navigate the global landscape of cloud-specific regulations to ensure compliance and safeguard data.

Some of the key challenges faced by organizations while complying with cloud regulations are as follows:

- **Jurisdictional overlap**: Organizations may face conflicting requirements from different regulatory regimes.

- **Cultural and legal differences**: Different regions prioritize specific data protection and privacy aspects.

Here are some key regulations related to cloud computing from various regions:

- **United States: Clarifying Lawful Overseas Use of Data (CLOUD)** Act, enacted in 2018, allows U.S. law enforcement agencies to access data stored by U.S.-based technology companies, regardless of whether the data is stored domestically or internationally. It also facilitates agreements with other countries to streamline cross-border data access for law enforcement purposes.

- **Saudi Arabia: Cloud Computing Regulatory Framework (CCF)**, established by the **Communications and Information Technology Commission (CITC)**, outlines the rights and obligations of CSPs and customers in Saudi Arabia. It emphasizes data protection, security measures, and compliance with local laws.

- **National Cybersecurity Authority (NCA) Cloud Cybersecurity Controls (CCC)** provides guidelines to enhance the cybersecurity posture of cloud services within the kingdom. They focus on risk management, data protection, and incident response to ensure the security of cloud environments.

- **United Arab Emirates**: The *National Cloud Computing Policy* is aimed at promoting cloud adoption while ensuring data security and compliance with national regulations. These policies aim to balance innovation with the protection of sensitive information.

- **China**: China's cybersecurity law requires that personal information and important data collected within the country be stored domestically. It also subjects cloud service providers to stringent security assessments and data localization requirements.

- **Australia**: The Australian government's cloud computing policy aims to drive greater adoption of cloud services by federal government agencies by adopting a 'cloud first' approach. Under the government's cloud policy, agencies now must adopt the cloud where it is fit for purpose, provides adequate data protection, and delivers value for money.

- **Malaysia**: The *National Cloud Policy* emphasized public service innovation, economic growth, strengthening data security, and digital inclusivity.

- **India**: Guidelines under the *GI Cloud Initiative* policy mandate that service providers offering cloud services to government agencies must ensure that all services provided, including data, will be guaranteed to reside in India.

It is crucial for organizations to stay informed about these regulations and ensure their cloud services comply with the relevant legal frameworks in each region of operation.

Role of auditors in cloud compliance

Auditors help organizations navigate these complexities by mapping compliance obligations, assessing cross-border data flows, and ensuring CSPs adhere to relevant regulations. Their expertise enables organizations to maintain compliance while operating efficiently in global markets.

Note: **It is important to note that this is not an exhaustive list, and regulations are constantly evolving.**

Organizations operating in the cloud, as well as the auditors assessing cloud environments, should stay informed about the latest developments in relevant regulations.

Auditors are instrumental in achieving and maintaining compliance in cloud environments, and their responsibilities include the following:

- Evaluating CSP certifications, such as SOC 2, ISO 27001, and CSA STAR certification.
- Conducting risk assessments and validating internal controls.
- Validate alignment between organizational policies and applicable regulations.
- Testing security measures and verifying regulatory alignment.
- Collaborating with CSPs and stakeholders to address compliance gaps.
- Identifying areas for improvement.
- Recommendations for optimizing resource utilization and improving security controls.

By identifying risks and recommending improvements, auditors ensure that organizations not only meet regulatory requirements but also enhance overall security and operational efficiency. Additionally, Auditors should be well-versed in the concept of order of precedence, which is crucial in various situations where multiple rules, standards, or documents might conflict.

Here are some examples where considering the order of precedence is essential:

- **Conflicting laws**: When national laws contradict local industry regulations, understanding the order of precedence helps determine which one takes precedence.

- **Policy conflicts**: When organizational policies contradict industry standards or best practices, establishing an order of precedence ensures consistent decision-making and risk mitigation.

By establishing a clear order of precedence, organizations, individuals, and societies can navigate complex situations and ensure consistency. The following figure depicts the order of precedence:

Figure 5.1: Order of precedence for compliance

The order of precedence for compliance, from highest to lowest, is generally as follows:

- **National and international regulations**: These are legally binding rules and laws that must be adhered to. Non-compliance can result in severe penalties, including fines and legal action.

- **Industry-specific standards**: These are established norms and guidelines specific to a particular industry or sector. They often provide a framework for best practices and can enhance an organization's reputation and competitiveness.

- **Organizational policies and standards**: These are internal rules and guidelines an organization sets to ensure consistent operations and ethical conduct. They should align with industry standards and regulations.

- **Best practices**: These are widely accepted methods or techniques that have proven effective in a particular field. While not legally binding, they can significantly improve efficiency and quality.

It is important to note that this is a general guideline, and the specific order of precedence may vary depending on the context and jurisdiction. In some cases, industry standards or organizational policies may take precedence over national regulations if they offer more stringent requirements.

It is important that auditors identify regulations that are applicable to the organization being audited during the audit planning stage to ensure audits are performed effectively. When in doubt, it is advisable to consult the legal department within the organization.

Ultimately, the goal is to achieve the highest level of compliance and ethical conduct, which may involve a combination of all these factors.

Conclusion

This chapter highlighted the importance of regulatory compliance in cloud environments and the critical role auditors play in safeguarding data and ensuring adherence to standards.

Key regulations such as GDPR, HIPAA, PCI-DSS, and SOX establish frameworks for protecting sensitive information and maintaining trust.

As discussed, auditors must stay informed about evolving regulations and leverage their expertise to evaluate compliance effectively. By balancing legal obligations with security and operational goals, auditors enable organizations to harness the benefits of cloud computing while mitigating risks.

In the next chapter, we will examine the **National Institute of Standards and Technology** (**NIST**) standards and frameworks, exploring their applicability to cloud auditing.

This chapter will cover key controls, risk management strategies, and practical guidance on cloud audit processes.

Points to remember

Here are some of the key takeaways from this chapter:

- Understanding the nuances of regulations is vital for effective auditing.
- It is important for the auditors to understand that laws and regulations are subject to frequent changes, and verifying their accuracy and applicability is essential.
- Regulatory compliance is a shared responsibility between organizations and CSPs.
- Continuous monitoring and collaboration are essential for maintaining compliance in dynamic cloud environments.
- When faced with conflicting rules, standards, or documents, auditors must prioritize their application based on a defined order of precedence.

Multiple choice questions

1. **Which of the following means 'only data that is necessary for the stated purpose should be collected and processed'?**

    a. Data anonymization

    b. Data quarantine

    c. Data encryption

    d. Data minimization

2. **What are the contracts that ensure CSPs adhere to HIPAA requirements called?**

    a. HIPAA agreements

    b. Business agreements

    c. Business associate agreements

    d. Cloud computing agreements

3. **ICFR is required for compliance with which of the following?**

    a. SOX Act

    b. GDPR

    c. HIPAA

    d. PCI-DSS

4. **Which of the following does not fall under the responsibilities of a cloud auditor?**

    a. Conducting risk assessments and validating internal controls

    b. Validate alignment between organizational policies and applicable regulations

    c. Testing security measures and verifying regulatory alignment

    d. Fix the compliance gaps in collaboration with CSPs

5. **Which of the following concepts is useful in situations where multiple rules, standards, or documents may conflict?**

    a. Legal counsel opinion

    b. Order of precedence

    c. Auditor's judgement

    d. CSP's cloud policy

Answers

1	d
2	c
3	a
4	d
5	b

Join our Discord space

Join our Discord workspace for latest updates, offers, tech happenings around the world, new releases, and sessions with the authors:

https://discord.bpbonline.com

CHAPTER 6

NIST Cloud Computing Standards

Introduction

National Institute of Standards and Technology (NIST) has developed a comprehensive set of standards and guidelines for cloud computing, with a primary focus on security and interoperability. By leveraging NIST's extensive suite of standards and guidelines, organizations can confidently navigate the complexities of cloud computing while ensuring the security, interoperability, and compliance of their cloud deployments. By aligning cloud audits with NIST standards, organizations can gain valuable insights into their security posture, identify areas for improvement, and demonstrate their commitment to protecting data and systems in the cloud.

Structure

This chapter covers the following topics:

- NIST cloud computing standards road map
- NIST Cybersecurity Framework
- Other related standards from NIST
- Risk assessment based on NIST cloud guidelines
- NIST cloud standards for auditors
- Using NIST framework in cloud auditing

Objectives

This chapter offers readers a detailed examination of the NIST frameworks and their application to cloud auditing. This chapter covers controls, risk management, and using the NIST framework in audits.

NIST cloud computing standards road map

Cloud computing has revolutionized IT services, enabling organizations to scale resources efficiently. However, with its benefits come challenges related to security, interoperability, compliance, and governance. To address these, the NIST developed **Special Publication (SP) 500-291r2**: Cloud Computing Standards Roadmap, which outlines the standardization landscape for cloud computing. This document identifies current standards, highlights gaps, and prioritizes standardization efforts to ensure security, portability, and interoperability within cloud environments.

This roadmap provides a structured approach for **cloud service providers (CSPs)**, consumers, regulators, and auditors to ensure cloud services align with best practices, security frameworks, and compliance requirements.

Key elements of the standards roadmap

NIST SP 500-291r2 is structured around several key areas crucial for the adoption and governance of cloud services. Let us look at them in detail:

- **Cloud computing definition and reference architecture**: NIST offers a clear definition of cloud computing and introduces a reference architecture that delineates various roles, including cloud consumers, providers, brokers, auditors, and carriers. This structured framework enables stakeholders to understand and effectively implement cloud services, standardizing roles and responsibilities to ensure accountability across cloud ecosystems.

- **Standards for interoperability and portability**: The roadmap emphasizes the necessity for standardized **application programming interfaces (APIs)** to facilitate seamless interoperability and portability, thereby establishing guidelines for standard APIs to ensure that data and applications can move between providers without vendor lock-in. Such standards ensure that consumers can migrate data and applications across different cloud providers without significant challenges. Supports hybrid and multi-cloud strategies, making it easier for organizations to switch or integrate cloud services.

- **Security and privacy standards**: Recognizing the paramount importance of security in cloud computing, the document identifies standards that address identity and access management, encryption, data protection, and compliance. These standards are crucial for safeguarding sensitive information and maintaining trust in cloud services. Auditors can assess whether cloud providers meet security benchmarks set by frameworks like ISO 27001, NIST 800-53, and SOC 2.

- **Performance standards**: The roadmap underscores the need for performance-related standards, including metrics for service agreements, monitoring, and auditing. Such standards enable consumers to objectively assess cloud services, validate performance claims, including availability and uptime guarantees, latency and response time, **recovery point objective (RPO)**, and **Recovery Time Objectives (RTO)**, and compare offerings from different providers. Auditors can validate whether cloud providers meet contractual SLAs and identify potential risks associated with service reliability.

- **Compliance and regulatory considerations**: Maps cloud security standards to compliance requirements, such as:

  o **Federal Risk and Authorization Management Program (FedRAMP)**: For U.S. government agencies

  o **General Data Protection Regulation (GDPR)**: For data protection in the EU

  o **Health Insurance Portability and Accountability Act (HIPAA)**: or healthcare data security

Auditors can use NIST's roadmap to ensure regulatory alignment and mitigate compliance risks.

NIST's Cloud Computing Standards Roadmap serves as an invaluable resource for the auditors. It provides a structured approach to evaluating cloud services, ensuring that they meet established standards for security, performance, and interoperability. Auditors can utilize this roadmap to:

- **Assess compliance**: Verify that cloud providers adhere to recognized standards, ensuring that security and privacy measures are robust and effective.

- **Enhance cloud security audits**: Use NIST-defined security guidelines to assess data protection, identity management, encryption, and compliance. Evaluate whether CSPs follow security best practices and risk management frameworks.

- **Improve cloud governance and risk management**: Assist organizations in adopting a structured cloud governance framework. Ensure ongoing compliance through continuous monitoring and audits.

- **Evaluate performance**: Use defined performance metrics to assess whether cloud services meet contractual obligations and service level agreements.

- **Ensure interoperability and portability**: Confirm that standardized APIs and protocols are implemented, facilitating seamless data migration and integration across platforms.

NIST Cloud Computing Standards Roadmap provides a list of their published standards and SPs relevant to cloud computing as per the following table:

NIST Federal Information Processing Standards and SPs relevant to cloud computing	
Standard	**Description of the Standard**
Federal Information Process Standards Publication (FIPS) 199	Standards for Security Categorization of Federal Information and Information Systems
FIPS 200	Minimum Security Requirements for Federal Information and Information Systems
NIST Special Publication 500-292	NIST Cloud Computing Reference Architecture, September 2011
NIST Special Publication 500-293	U.S. Government Cloud Computing Technology Roadmap, Release 1.0, Volume I High-Priority Requirements to Further USG Agency Cloud Computing Adoption, October 2014
NIST Special Publication 500-293	U.S. Government Cloud Computing Technology Roadmap, Release 1.0, Volume II: Useful Information for Cloud Adopters, November 2011
NIST Special Publication 800-37 Rev.1	Guide for Applying the Risk Management Framework to Federal Information Systems: A Security Life Cycle Approach
NIST Special Publication 800-53 Rev.4	Security and Privacy Controls for Federal Information Systems and Organizations
NIST Special Publication 800-92	Guide to Computer Security Log Management
NIST Special Publication 800-125	Guide to Security for Full Virtualization Technologies
NIST Special Publication 800-137	Information Security Continuous Monitoring for Federal Information Systems and Organizations
NIST Special Publication 800-144	Guidelines on Security and Privacy Issues in Public Cloud Computing
NIST Special Publication 800-145	The NIST Definition of Cloud Computing
NIST Special Publication 800-146	Cloud Computing Synopsis and Recommendations

Table 6.1: NIST standards and SPs related to cloud computing

By aligning their audit frameworks with the guidelines and standards outlined in NIST SP 800-53, auditors can enhance their ability to evaluate cloud services comprehensively, thereby bolstering organizational trust and confidence in cloud computing solutions.

NIST Cybersecurity Framework

The NIST released Version 2.0 of its CSF on February 26, 2024. This update expands the framework's applicability beyond critical infrastructure to organizations of all sizes and sectors, including CSPs and auditors.

The NIST CSF consists of the following key components, as depicted in the following figure:

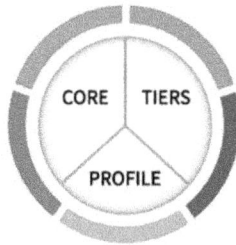

Figure 6.1: Depicting the NIST CSF components

The explanation is as follows:

- **CSF core**: The central element of the framework, providing a structured taxonomy of high-level cybersecurity outcomes that enables organizations to manage cybersecurity risks effectively. The CSF core is organized into a hierarchy of functions, categories, and subcategories, each detailing specific security outcomes. These outcomes are designed to be universally understandable by various stakeholders, including executives, managers, and cybersecurity practitioners, regardless of their technical expertise. Since the CSF core is neutral across industries, geographies, and technologies, it provides organizations with the flexibility to tailor it to their unique risks, technologies, and operational requirements.

- **CSF organizational profiles**: A tool for organizations to define their current and desired cybersecurity posture based on the outcomes outlined in the CSF core. These profiles enable organizations to assess their security maturity and develop targeted improvement plans.

- **CSF tiers**: A classification system used to evaluate the depth and effectiveness of an organization's cybersecurity risk governance and management within its organizational profile. Tiers help organizations understand their approach to cybersecurity risk and assess the robustness of their risk management processes.

CSF core

The CSF core is a structured collection of cybersecurity outcomes organized hierarchically into functions, categories, and subcategories. Rather than serving as a prescriptive checklist of tasks, it provides a flexible framework where the specific actions required to achieve each outcome will vary based on an organization's unique context and use case.

The responsibility for implementing these actions may also differ depending on the organization. Additionally, the arrangement and size of functions, categories, and subcategories do not imply a fixed order or level of priority. Instead, the CSF core is designed to be most relevant to those responsible for integrating cybersecurity risk management into an organization's operations.

Key components of NIST CSF 2.0 core include six functions, as depicted in the following figure:

Figure 6.2: Depicting the NIST CSF core

The explanation is as follows:

- **Govern**: Establishes organizational context, roles, and policies for cybersecurity governance.

- **Identify**: Focuses on understanding organizational assets, risks, and supply chain considerations.

- **Protect**: Involves implementing safeguards like access controls and data security measures.

- **Detect**: Entails developing capabilities to identify cybersecurity events.

- **Respond**: Covers actions taken during cybersecurity incidents.

- **Recover**: Focuses on restoring normal operations post-incident.

There are 22 categories and 106 sub-categories under these six functions under the CSF core. The categories represent a group of related cybersecurity outcomes that collectively comprise a CSF function, and the sub-categories are a group of more specific outcomes of technical and management cybersecurity activities that comprise a CSF category.

CSF profiles

A CSF organizational profile represents an organization's current and/or desired cybersecurity posture based on the outcomes outlined in the CSF core. It serves as a tool for understanding, customizing, evaluating, prioritizing, and communicating cybersecurity goals by considering factors such as mission objectives, stakeholder expectations, the evolving threat landscape, and regulatory requirements. This enables organizations to allocate resources strategically, focus on achieving specific security outcomes, and effectively communicate their cybersecurity priorities to stakeholders.

Each organizational profile consists of one or both of the following:

- **Current profile**: Identifies the core outcomes that the organization is currently meeting (or working toward) and provides insight into how well each outcome is being achieved.

- **Target profile**: Defines the cybersecurity outcomes the organization aims to achieve in alignment with its risk management strategy. It also considers future cybersecurity needs, including new regulatory requirements, technological advancements, and emerging threats.

CSF tiers

Organizations can incorporate tiers into their current and target profiles to assess and guide their cybersecurity risk management approach. Tiers represent the level of maturity and rigor in an organization's cybersecurity governance and risk management practices. They also provide context for how cybersecurity risks are perceived and managed within the organization.

The tiers categorize cybersecurity practices into four levels:

- **Partial (Tier 1)**: Cybersecurity risk management is informal, reactive, and lacks consistency.

- **Risk-informed (Tier 2)**: Some risk management practices are established, but they are not applied consistently across the organization.

- **Repeatable (Tier 3)**: Cybersecurity risk management processes are well-defined, consistently implemented, and regularly improved.

- **Adaptive (Tier 4)**: The organization demonstrates a proactive, agile, and continuously improving approach to managing cybersecurity risks.

These tiers illustrate a progression from unstructured, ad hoc security measures to a fully integrated, risk-informed, and continuously evolving cybersecurity strategy. By selecting an appropriate Tier, organizations can establish a strategic direction for managing cybersecurity risks effectively.

Cloud auditors should tailor the CSF 2.0 framework to specific cloud service models and provider environments to maximize effectiveness. Additionally, as cloud technology evolves, auditors must stay updated with NIST guidelines and emerging cybersecurity best practices to ensure comprehensive risk management in cloud environments.

Other related standards from NIST

Now let us discuss the related standards mentioned earlier in this chapter, including a brief about the standard, their relevance to the cloud, and their usefulness to the auditors:

- **FIPS 199**: This defines Standards for the Security Categorization of Federal Information and Information Systems. Defines how federal agencies categorize their information systems based on security impact levels (Low, Moderate, High) in terms of confidentiality, integrity, and availability. This standard is essential for determining the security requirements of cloud-based federal systems. Helps auditors verify whether organizations have correctly categorized their cloud-hosted information systems and applied appropriate security controls.

- **FIPS 200**: This defines minimum security requirements for federal information and information systems: Establishes minimum security controls for federal information systems in 17 security-related areas (e.g., access control, incident response). The standard provides the foundation for ensuring security compliance when migrating federal workloads to the cloud. Helps auditors assess if CSPs meet baseline security requirements for federal information systems.

- **NIST SP 500-292**: This defines the cloud computing reference architecture. Defines a standard cloud computing reference model, outlining key roles (cloud consumer, provider, auditor, etc.) and interactions. NIST SP 500-292 provides a structured approach for implementing and managing cloud services. Helps auditors understand the cloud ecosystem, its roles, and responsibilities, enabling them to assess security and compliance effectively.

- **NIST SP 500-293**: *US Government Cloud Computing Technology Roadmap Volume I* identifies high-priority security, interoperability, and portability requirements for federal cloud adoption. The standard guides agencies on transitioning to secure and efficient cloud solutions. Helps auditors assess whether cloud implementations align with federal cloud computing objectives and security requirements.

- **NIST SP 500-293**: *US Government Cloud Computing Technology Roadmap Volume II*: Provides detailed technical insights into cloud computing security, standards, and best practices. The standard serves as a guide for agencies implementing secure and compliant cloud solutions. Offers criteria for auditing technical security measures and compliance requirements in cloud environments.

- **NIST SP 800-37 Rev. 1**: This defines a risk management framework for information systems and organizations: Establishes a structured RMF for federal IT systems, emphasizing continuous monitoring and risk-based decision-making. The standard guides federal agencies in assessing and managing security risks in cloud environments. Helps auditors evaluate an organization's risk management approach, security authorization, and compliance with federal requirements.

- **NIST SP 800-53 Rev. 4**: This defines security and privacy controls for federal information systems and organizations. Provides a comprehensive set of security and privacy controls for federal information systems, including cloud services. Essential for implementing robust cloud security frameworks, especially for federal agencies. Serves as a key reference for auditing cloud security controls and ensuring compliance with federal regulations.

- **NIST SP 800-92**: It is a guide to computer security log management and outlines best practices for collecting, analyzing, and managing security logs. This standard is critical for detecting security incidents in cloud environments where logging is a key component of monitoring. Helps auditors assess whether cloud logging and monitoring practices comply with security policies and regulatory requirements.

- **NIST SP 800-125**: It serves as a guide to security for full virtualization technologies. Provides security guidelines for virtualized environments, which are foundational to cloud computing. It addresses security risks in virtualized infrastructures commonly used in cloud platforms. Helps auditors evaluate the security configurations and controls of virtualized cloud environments.

- **NIST SP 800-137**: **Information Security Continuous Monitoring (ISCM)** for federal information systems and organizations. Defines an approach for continuous security monitoring to support risk management. This standard ensures cloud environments maintain ongoing security compliance and risk mitigation. Provides criteria for auditing continuous security monitoring processes in cloud systems.

- **NIST SP 800-144**: **Guidelines on Security and Privacy in Public Cloud Computing**: Outlines key security and privacy considerations for using public cloud services. The standard provides best practices for federal agencies and organizations using public cloud solutions. Helps auditors assess cloud security and privacy protections, ensuring compliance with federal standards.

- **NIST SP 800-145**: Contains the NIST definition of cloud computing. Establishes the official NIST definition of cloud computing, including service models and deployment models. Standardizes cloud terminology, helping agencies and organizations adopt cloud technology effectively. Ensures auditors use a consistent framework when evaluating cloud service models and deployment types.

- **NIST SP 800-146**: **Contains cloud computing synopsis and recommendations**: Provides an overview of cloud computing, including risks, benefits, and security considerations. Helps organizations understand the implications of adopting cloud technology. Serves as a general reference for evaluating cloud implementations, security measures, and compliance.

These standards and publications provide essential guidelines for implementing, securing, and auditing cloud computing environments. Auditors can use them to perform the following:

- Assess security compliance of cloud-based systems.
- Verify risk management practices in cloud deployments.
- Ensure logging and monitoring are properly implemented.
- Evaluate security controls in virtualized and cloud environments.

Risk assessment based on NIST cloud guidelines

Risk assessment is a fundamental process in cloud security, ensuring that cloud services meet security, privacy, and compliance requirements. The NIST RMF and cloud-specific guidelines provide a structured approach to assessing risks in cloud environments.

Key NIST publications on cloud risk assessment

NIST has published several key documents that are relevant to cloud risk assessment.

The most notable ones include:

- **NIST SP 800-37: RMF**:
    - o Defines a six-step process for risk management as mentioned here:
        - ▪ Categorize the cloud system (based on FIPS 199).
        - ▪ Select security controls (using NIST SP 800-53).
        - ▪ Implement security measures in the cloud environment.
        - ▪ Assess the effectiveness of security controls.
        - ▪ Authorize the cloud system for operation based on risk acceptance.
        - ▪ Monitor continuously for security threats.

    Auditor's role: Verify that cloud-based systems follow the RMF steps and document risks effectively.

- **NIST SP 800-53: Security and privacy controls for cloud systems:**
    - o Provides a comprehensive set of security controls for risk mitigation in cloud environments. Key control areas as defined in the standard are:
        - ▪ Access control and identity management (e.g., multi-factor authentication).
        - ▪ Data protection and encryption for cloud storage and transmission.
        - ▪ Incident response and continuous monitoring to detect threats.
        - ▪ Configuration management to prevent misconfigurations.

    Auditor's role: Evaluate whether cloud providers and users have implemented the correct security controls based on the risk level.

- **NIST SP 800-144: Security and privacy in public cloud computing:**
    - o Highlights risk factors specific to public cloud environments, such as:
        - ▪ Data loss, leakage, and privacy concerns in multi-tenant environments.
        - ▪ Legal and compliance risks due to data location issues.

- Insider threats and external attacks in public cloud services.

Auditor's role: Assess cloud providers for data security, compliance, and contractual agreements to mitigate risks.

- **NIST SP 800-137: Continuous monitoring for risk management:**
  - Emphasizes real-time security monitoring for cloud systems.

Auditor's role: Ensure cloud environments have continuous security monitoring and automated alerts for risk detection.

- **NIST SP 800-92: Guide to security log management:**
  - Details best practices for log collection and analysis to detect security incidents.

Auditor's role: Verify logging policies, retention, and monitoring to support risk assessment and compliance.

Risk management approach

The stepwise risk management approach for cloud, as outlined by NIST, is presented in the following table:

Step	Description	Auditor's key checks
Identify risks	Understand cloud assets, data, and services.	Review CSP risk documentation and contracts.
Assess threats and vulnerabilities	Identify potential cyber threats, misconfigurations, and compliance gaps.	Evaluate security controls (e.g., access controls, data encryption).
Evaluate risk impact	Determine the effect of risks on confidentiality, integrity, and availability.	Check risk categorization (FIPS 199) and security control adequacy.
Mitigate and monitor risks	Implement security controls and establish continuous monitoring.	Assess real-time threat detection, logging, and incident response plans.

Table 6.2: Risk management approach in cloud based on NIST

Recommendations for auditors

Auditing risk management in cloud environments requires a structured approach to evaluate an organization's ability to identify, assess, and mitigate risks effectively.

Here are key recommendations for auditors:

- Verify cloud system risk categorization and compliance with FIPS 199 and FIPS 200.
- Ensure security controls (NIST SP 800-53) align with cloud risk levels.
- Assess logging, monitoring, and incident response practices (SP 800-92 and SP 800-137).

- Identify data privacy risks and compliance gaps (SP 800-144).
- Confirm cloud providers maintain continuous security monitoring.

By following NIST guidelines, auditors can effectively assess, manage, and mitigate risks in cloud environments while ensuring regulatory compliance.

NIST cloud standards for auditors

Here are the key takeaways from the NIST cloud standards for auditors that help auditors assess, verify, and report on cloud security compliance effectively. Let us look at them in detail.

Security categorization and risk management

NIST has several key standards and guidelines related to security categorization and risk management for cloud and traditional IT environments. Here are the most relevant publications:

- **FIPS 199 & FIPS 200**: Ensure cloud systems are properly categorized (Low, Moderate, High) and meet minimum security requirements.
- **NIST SP 800-37**: Auditors should verify that the RMF is followed, including risk assessments and continuous monitoring.

Cloud security and compliance controls

NIST provides standards and guidelines for securing cloud environments and ensuring compliance with regulatory frameworks. Here are the most relevant publications:

- **NIST SP 800-53 (Rev. 4)**: Provides the baseline security and privacy controls required for cloud environments. Auditors must ensure CSPs comply with these.
- **NIST SP 800-137**: Continuous monitoring is mandatory in federal cloud environments; auditors should check for real-time threat detection.
- **NIST SP 800-92**: Effective log management is critical for detecting security incidents in cloud environments.

Cloud architecture and governance

Here are some key publications that define cloud computing architecture while providing best practices in governance. They are developed by NIST to help organizations design, manage, and secure cloud environments while ensuring compliance and risk management:

- **NIST SP 500-292**: Defines the cloud computing reference model; auditors should verify the responsibilities of cloud providers, consumers, and auditors.
- **NIST SP 500-293 (Vol. I & II)**: Guides federal agencies in secure cloud adoption; auditors must ensure cloud implementations align with these best practices.

Virtualization and cloud-specific security concerns

The following key standards and guidelines, published by NIST, are used to address virtualization security. They also deal with cloud-specific security risks to help organizations secure virtualized environments, mitigate cloud-specific threats, and ensure compliance:

- **NIST SP 800-125**: Virtualization security is a major concern in cloud computing. Auditors should assess hypervisor security and VM isolation.

- **NIST SP 800-144**: Public cloud security and privacy risks must be addressed. Auditors should ensure that data protection, encryption, and access control are in place.

Cloud definitions and best practices

The following NIST publications define cloud computing and establish best practices for its secure and effective use. They also help organizations understand cloud models, architectures, security requirements, and risk management strategies:

- **NIST SP 800-145**: Defines cloud computing models, **Infrastructure as a Service (IaaS)**, **Platform as a Service (PaaS)**, and **Software as a Service (SaaS)**. Auditors must ensure that security measures align with the appropriate cloud model.

- **NIST SP 800-146**: Summarizes cloud computing risks and best practices; auditors should use this as a general framework for cloud assessments.

Key considerations for auditors

Auditing cloud environments requires a structured approach aligned with NIST best practices to ensure security, compliance, and risk management. Here are some key considerations auditors must keep in mind:

- Check security categorization and compliance with federal mandates.
- Verify cloud security controls and risk management practices.
- Assess logging, monitoring, and virtualization security.
- Ensure governance models are correctly implemented.
- Use NIST definitions & best practices for standardized cloud audits.

Using the NIST framework in cloud auditing

Cloud auditors can utilize CSF 2.0 to assess and enhance the security posture of cloud environments. Let us understand this in detail:

- **Govern**: Evaluate the cloud provider's governance policies and risk management strategies.

- **Identify**: Assess asset inventories, risk assessments, and supply chain risks.
- **Protect**: Verify implementation of security controls like encryption and identity management.
- **Detect**: Review logging, monitoring, and threat detection capabilities.
- **Respond**: Analyze incident response plans and communication strategies.
- **Recover**: Evaluate disaster recovery and business continuity plans.

Auditors can create a checklist based on the CSF 2.0, a sample of which is mentioned in the following table:

Sample audit checklist based on NIST CSF 2.0	
NIST CSF 2.0 function	**Audit question**
Govern	Are cybersecurity governance policies established and communicated?
Govern	Does the CSP have a formal risk management framework?
Identify	Is there an up-to-date inventory of cloud assets and data flows?
Identify	Are regular risk assessments performed?
Protect	Are data encryption and access controls effectively implemented?
Protect	Are identity and access management policies enforced with least privilege principles?
Detect	Are continuous monitoring and threat detection systems in place?
Detect	Is there SIEM integration for real-time threat intelligence?
Respond	Are incident response procedures documented and tested?
Respond	Is there a process for notifying affected parties in case of a security incident?
Recover	Are disaster recovery plans regularly updated and validated?
Recover	Does the cloud provider offer resilience mechanisms (e.g., multi-region redundancy)?

Table 6.3: Sample audit checklist based on NIST CSF 2.0

By integrating NIST CSF 2.0 into cloud auditing processes, organizations can enhance their cybersecurity strategies, ensuring they align with industry standards and effectively manage risks. The NIST Cybersecurity Framework 2.0 is a powerful tool for cloud auditors, offering a structured approach to evaluating security risks, governance, and compliance in cloud environments. By integrating CSF 2.0 into cloud auditing processes, organizations can enhance their security posture, improve regulatory compliance, and strengthen their incident response and recovery capabilities.

Conclusion

This chapter highlighted the application of NIST standards and frameworks in cloud computing, exploring their applicability to cloud auditing. It covered key controls, risk management strategies, and practical guidance on cloud audit processes.

The upcoming chapter aims to provide auditors with practical insights into the standards ISO 27017 and ISO 27018, addressing their unique challenges, audit techniques, and key focus areas. It is designed to serve as a comprehensive guide for auditors assessing cloud environments. It highlights the key controls and guidelines of ISO 27017 and ISO 27018, discusses audit challenges, and provides practical techniques to enhance the effectiveness of cloud security audits.

Points to remember

- **NIST developed SP 500-291r2**: Cloud Computing Standards Roadmap, which outlines the standardization landscape for cloud computing.

- The **National Institute of Standards and Technology (NIST)** released Version 2.0 of its CSF on February 26, 2024.

- The NIST CSF consists of three key components, namely the CSF:

  o Core

  o Profiles

  o Tiers

- The CSF core is organized into a hierarchy of six functions, 22 categories, and 106 subcategories, each detailing specific security outcomes.

- The NIST standards and publications related to cloud computing provide essential guidelines for implementing, securing, and auditing cloud computing environments.

- Cloud auditors can utilize CSF 2.0 to assess and enhance the security posture of cloud environments.

Multiple choice questions

1. **Which of the following is not a key component of the NIST Cybersecurity Framework?**

    a. Core

    b. Tiers

    c. Profile

    d. Function

2. Which of the following can be used as a tool for organizations to define their current and desired cybersecurity posture based on the outcomes outlined in the CSF core?

    a. CSF organizational profiles

    b. CSF Tiers

    c. Capability maturity model

    d. Audit report

3. Which of the following NIST standards is a risk management framework for information systems and organizations?

    a. NIST SP 800-53

    b. NIST SP 800-92

    c. NIST SP 800-37

    d. NIST SP 800-137

4. Which of the following steps in the risk management process identifies misconfigurations and compliance gaps?

    a. Identify risks

    b. Assess threats and vulnerabilities

    c. Evaluate risk impact

    d. Mitigate and monitor risks

5. Which of the following NIST CSF functions can cloud auditors utilize to analyze incident response plans?

    a. Protect

    b. Detect

    c. Respond

    d. Recover

Answers

1	d
2	a
3	c
4	b
5	c

CHAPTER 7
ISO/IEC 27017 and ISO/IEC 27018

Introduction

ISO 27017 and ISO 27018 are two important international standards that provide guidelines and controls for managing cloud security and protecting personal data in cloud environments. Both standards build upon ISO 27001, the leading standard for **information security management systems (ISMS)**, and address the specific needs of **cloud service providers (CSPs)** and their customers.

ISO 27017 provides additional controls beyond ISO 27001 to manage cloud-specific risks, while ISO 27018 focuses on protecting personal data in cloud environments and ensuring compliance with relevant privacy regulations.

Auditors play a critical role in ensuring compliance with these standards. Given the widespread adoption of cloud services and the increasing reliance on cloud infrastructures, the demand for audits focusing on cloud security and data privacy has grown significantly. The auditor community is now required to have a deep understanding of both ISO 27017 and ISO 27018, as well as their relationship with broader cybersecurity frameworks, such as ISO 27001 and national regulations like GDPR.

This chapter aims to provide auditors with practical insights into these standards, addressing their unique challenges, audit techniques, and key focus areas. It is designed to serve as a comprehensive guide for auditors assessing cloud environments. It highlights the key controls and guidelines of ISO 27017 and ISO 27018, discusses audit challenges, and provides practical techniques to enhance the effectiveness of cloud security audits.

Structure

This chapter covers the following topics:

- Overview of ISO/IEC 27017
- Overview of ISO/IEC 27018
- Certification process overview
- Auditor's role in ISO 27017/27018 certification
- Common audit findings
- Mapping to other standards and frameworks

Objectives

By the end of this chapter, readers will be equipped with practical insights into these standards, addressing their unique challenges, audit techniques, and key focus areas. This chapter is designed to serve as a comprehensive guide for auditors who are tasked with assessing cloud environments. It highlights the key controls and guidelines of ISO 27017 and ISO 27018, discusses audit challenges, and provides practical techniques to enhance the effectiveness of cloud security audits.

Overview of ISO/IEC 27017

The current version ISO/IEC 27017:2015, titled *Information technology—Security techniques—Code of practice for information security controls based on ISO/IEC 27002 for cloud services*, hereinafter referred to as ISO 27017, was developed in response to the growing use of cloud services and the need for specific controls to manage cloud security risks. Launched in 2015 by the **International Organization for Standardization (ISO)**, ISO 27017 offers guidelines that complement ISO 27001 and ISO 27002 by addressing risks associated with CSPs and customers.

ISO 27017 builds on the foundation of ISO 27001 and introduces several cloud-specific controls. These controls focus on areas such as shared responsibilities between CSPs and customers, secure development and management of cloud services, and risk management related to the virtual environment.

Some key principles of ISO 27017 include:

- **Segregation of environments**: Ensuring that cloud environments are appropriately isolated to prevent data leakage or compromise.
- **Virtual machine configuration**: Providing guidelines on securely configuring **virtual machines (VMs)** in cloud environments.

- **Customer responsibility agreements**: Establishing clear roles and responsibilities between CSPs and customers to avoid security gaps.

While ISO 27001 provides a broad framework for information security management, ISO 27017 goes deeper into cloud-specific issues, addressing the unique risks associated with virtualized environments, multi-tenancy, and the shared responsibility model.

Key cloud security challenges addressed by ISO 27017 include the following:

- **Shared responsibility ambiguities**: ISO 27017 clarifies the roles and responsibilities of CSPs and **cloud service customers** (**CSCs**). It ensures both parties understand their obligations regarding security controls, reducing confusion and gaps in accountability.

- **Data protection and privacy**: The standard emphasizes secure data handling in the cloud, including encryption for data at rest, in transit, and during backup storage. It also mandates secure deletion and retrieval of customer data upon contract termination to prevent unauthorized retention.

- **Multi-tenant environments**: ISO 27017 addresses risks associated with shared infrastructure by requiring segregation of customer data and virtual environments. This ensures that tenants in multi-tenant cloud setups are isolated from each other, preventing unauthorized access or data breaches.

- **Virtual machine security**: The framework includes controls for hardening virtual machines and minimizing vulnerabilities in line with business needs. This reduces risks associated with virtualization technologies commonly used in cloud environments.

- **Misconfiguration**: Cloud service misconfigurations, such as improper access controls or unsecured storage, can expose sensitive data and systems. ISO 27017 emphasizes secure configuration management practices and provider-user responsibility delineation to reduce these risks.

- **Logging and monitoring**: Enhanced logging and monitoring mechanisms are required to capture security-relevant events within the cloud environment. These logs must be protected from tampering to ensure effective detection and response to incidents.

- **Identity and access management (IAM)**: ISO 27017 highlights robust IAM practices, including multi-factor authentication, role-based access controls, and regular reviews of user permissions. These measures help prevent unauthorized access to cloud resources.

- **Incident response**: The standard stresses the importance of incident response plans specific to cloud environments. It includes mechanisms for reporting, investigating, and mitigating the impact of security incidents.

- **Asset management**: ISO 27017 mandates procedures for the secure removal or return of customer assets post-contract termination, ensuring no residual data remains vulnerable to exploitation.

- **Network security alignment**: The standard requires consistency between virtual network configurations and underlying physical networks to ensure seamless security across all layers of the cloud infrastructure.

- **Business continuity and disaster recovery (BCP/DR)**: Ensuring continuity of operations during service disruptions is critical in the cloud. ISO 27017 recommends that both cloud providers and customers establish and test robust BCP and DR plans, with clear roles and data recovery responsibilities outlined in SLAs.

- **Compliance with legal and regulatory requirements**: Organizations are guided on aligning their cloud security practices with applicable legal and regulatory frameworks, enhancing compliance while mitigating risks.

By addressing these challenges, ISO 27017 helps organizations establish a robust cloud security posture, reduce risks associated with cybersecurity incidents, and foster trust among stakeholders in the cloud ecosystem.

Overview of ISO/IEC 27018

The standard ISO/IEC 27018:2019 titled *Information technology — Security techniques — Code of practice for protection of personally identifiable information (PII) in public clouds acting as PII processors*, was introduced in 2014 and updated last in 2019. The standard is focused specifically on protecting PII in cloud environments. This standard aligns closely with global privacy regulations, including the **General Data Protection Regulation (GDPR)**, **Health Insurance Portability and Accountability Act (HIPAA)**, and other privacy laws.

ISO 27018 outlines best practices for handling personal data in the cloud.

The key principles revolve around ensuring that CSPs perform the following:

- **Process personal data transparently**: Cloud providers must disclose how and where personal data is processed.

- **Limit data access**: Providers must limit access to personal data only to authorized personnel.

- **Enable data subject rights**: Cloud services should facilitate the exercise of rights, such as the right to access or delete data, by the data subjects.

ISO 27018 is often regarded as a standard that complements various privacy regulations, including GDPR. For organizations using cloud services, compliance with ISO 27018 ensures that they meet international privacy requirements, mitigating non-compliance risks.

When auditing cloud environments for compliance with ISO 27018, auditors should focus on the following:

- Ensuring the CSP has clear policies for processing personal data.

- Verifying that data access control mechanisms are sturdy and that only authorized personnel can access sensitive data.

- Evaluating how well the CSP supports data subject rights (e.g., data access, deletion, and portability).

- Reviewing data breach notification processes and how the CSP informs its customers of incidents involving personal data.

- Ensuring the protection of **Personally Identifiable Information** (**PII**) in the cloud, which includes verifying that robust audit logging mechanisms are in place, profiling restrictions are enforced to prevent unauthorized or excessive behavioral analysis, and that clear procedures exist for breach notification and incident reporting.

- Assess whether effective consent management is demonstrated to ensure lawful processing of PII in alignment with user expectations and regulatory requirements.

The following table provides a summary of the standards ISO/IEC 27017 and ISO/IEC 27018 for easier understanding:

Feature	ISO/IEC 27017	ISO/IEC 27018
Focus	Cloud security in general	Protection of PII in public clouds
Relationship to ISO 27001	Provides cloud-specific controls that complement ISO 27001	Aligns with ISO 27001 and addresses privacy requirements, particularly for PII
Key principles	Segregation of environments Secure VM configuration Shared responsibility agreements	Transparency in data processing Limited data access Enabling data subject rights
Cloud challenges addressed	Data segmentation Data location control Cloud infrastructure security DR/Availability	Compliance with privacy regulations (GDPR, HIPAA, etc.) Protecting PII in the cloud
Auditing focus	Shared responsibility agreements Environment isolation VM security Access control	Data processing policies Data access controls Support for data subject rights Data breach notification

Table 7.1: Summary of ISO/IEC 27017 & ISO/IEC 27018

Certification process overview

One has to understand that while ISO 27001 is a standard that provides requirements for implementing ISMS and is certifiable, ISO 27017 and ISO 27018 provide *guidance* specific to cloud security and privacy, respectively. These two standards are not certifiable.

However, certain certification bodies *certify* against ISO 27017/27018 standards during an ISO 27001 certification process, because ISO 27001 is the only certifiable standard in the ISO 27000 series.

Based on the above, organizations seeking ISO 27017/27018 certifications must incorporate the relevant controls from these standards into their existing ISMS, which was initially established in accordance with ISO 27001 requirements. This process generally includes the following steps:

1. **Risk assessment and treatment**: Conduct a thorough risk assessment to identify and evaluate potential threats and vulnerabilities to cloud security and data privacy. Based on the assessment, appropriate controls from ISO 27017/27018 are selected and incorporated into the organization's risk treatment plan.

2. **Implementation and documentation**: Effectively implementing the chosen controls and documenting the implementation process. This includes updating relevant policies, procedures, and work instructions.

3. **Statement of Applicability (SoA)**: SoA to reflect the inclusion of ISO 27017/27018 controls. The SoA outlines the specific controls adopted by the organization and justifies any deviations from the standard.

4. **Certification body notification**: Informing the certification body about the changes to the ISMS, including the inclusion of ISO 27017/27018 controls. This allows the certification body to adjust the scope and focus of subsequent certification and surveillance audits accordingly.

A typical certification process is depicted in the following figure:

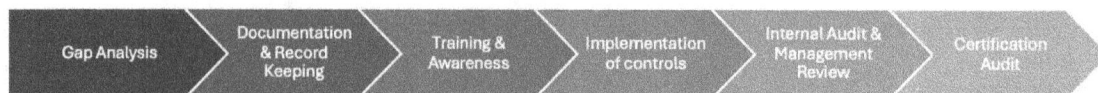

Figure 7.1: Typical certification process for ISO/IEC 27017 & ISO/IEC 27018

Achieving certification in ISO 27017 and ISO 27018 typically follows a structured process similar to ISO 27001.

The prerequisite is the implementation of requirements from the ISO 27001 standard, and the process involves the following stages:

- **Gap analysis**: A pre-audit stage where organizations identify the gaps between their current security posture and the requirements of the ISO standards.

- **Documentation**: Organizations must diligently document and maintain records to demonstrate their commitment to cloud security/data privacy, streamline audits, and continuously improve the posture of information security and data privacy in the cloud.

- **Training and awareness**: Organizations must implement training and awareness programs to enhance cloud security posture, reduce the risk of incidents, and demonstrate their commitment to compliance with ISO 27017 / 27018 standards.

- **Implementation**: Organizations must address the gaps identified and implement necessary controls to comply with ISO 27017 or ISO 27018.

- **Internal audit**: Prior to the formal certification audit, organizations must conduct an internal audit to ensure readiness.

- **Management review**: Management review must be conducted to evaluate the effectiveness of controls related to security & privacy in the cloud and ensure continuous improvements.

- **Certification audit**: A formal audit conducted in two stages by a certification body to evaluate compliance with the standards.

- **Certification**: If the organization meets the necessary requirements, it is awarded the certification, which is typically valid for three years.

Auditor's role in ISO 27017 / 27018 certification

Auditors play a pivotal role in both the pre-certification and certification stages of ISO audits. The specific roles and responsibilities of an auditor may vary slightly depending on whether they are internal to the organization or external. However, their core responsibilities generally encompass the following:

- Conducting gap analyses to help organizations identify areas where they fall short of ISO 27017 or ISO 27018 requirements.

- Evaluating the effectiveness of security and privacy controls during the certification audit.

- Providing recommendations on how to implement and improve controls.

For auditors to prepare for an ISO 27017 or ISO 27018 audit, they must include:

- Familiarize themselves with the organization's cloud infrastructure and the specific cloud service models in use, such as **Infrastructure as a Service (IaaS)**, **Platform as a Service (PaaS)**, or **Software as a Service (SaaS)**.

- Understand the organization's business context and its regulatory environment, as this impacts how controls should be applied.

- Review prior audit reports, if available, to understand the organization's audit history and identify any recurring issues.

CSPs often face challenges during the certification process, particularly in these two scenarios:

- **Managing compliance across multiple jurisdictions**: CSPs that operate globally must meet various regulatory requirements that differ between countries.

- **Ensuring transparency with customers**: CSPs must maintain clear communication with their customers about how security and privacy controls are implemented.

Auditors should know these challenges and work closely with the CSP to ensure compliance while promoting transparency and accountability.

Key audit considerations for ISO 27017

As ISO 27017 builds upon the foundation of ISO 27001 by adding specific controls and implementation guidance related to cloud-specific, auditors should focus on the following in addition to the ISO 27001 controls:

- **Shared roles and responsibilities**: Cloud environments involve shared responsibilities between the CSPs and their customers. Auditors should ensure that roles are clearly defined, documented, and agreed upon. This includes operational, technical, and legal responsibilities.

- **Data ownership and asset management**: Customers must retain ownership of their data and have clear procedures for retrieving or deleting their data upon contract termination. Auditors should confirm that data return, removal, and destruction processes are in place and aligned with contractual obligations.

- **Customer data isolation**: In multi-tenant environments, strong isolation mechanisms are essential. Auditors should examine how virtual computing resources are segregated to prevent unauthorized access to customer data across shared infrastructure.

- **Contractual security requirements**: Security requirements must be embedded in service agreements between CSPs and cloud customers. This includes data protection obligations, compliance expectations, and service level agreements. Auditors should review contract language to ensure it covers these elements.

- **IAM**: Effective IAM is a critical control area in ISO/IEC 27017. Auditors should give special attention to the implementation of federated identity for integrating with enterprise directories and minimizing identity sprawl. Additionally, the use of **multi-factor authentication (MFA)** should be verified, especially for privileged accounts and access to cloud management interfaces, to mitigate the risk of credential compromise.

- **Logging and monitoring**: Visibility into cloud operations is essential for security assurance. Auditors should evaluate whether adequate logging and monitoring are in place, and whether customers receive regular reports or audit summaries from the provider.

- **Incident response in the cloud**: Both providers and customers should have defined incident response procedures, with clear communication protocols. Auditors should ensure incidents are detected, managed, and reported effectively in a shared environment.

- **Business continuity and exit planning**: Cloud providers should support customers' business continuity plans and provide clear exit strategies for service migration or termination. Auditors should assess availability measures and data portability mechanisms.

Key audit considerations for ISO 27018

Data Privacy and Protection Controls ISO 27018 is centered around safeguarding personal data in cloud environments. Auditors must carefully assess the privacy-related controls set out in the standard. Key areas to focus on include the following:

- **Data minimization**: Auditors should verify that the CSP collects, processes, and stores only the minimal personal data necessary for the cloud service.

- **Consent management**: The audit should ensure that proper consent mechanisms are in place for collecting and processing personal data, especially in jurisdictions with stringent data privacy laws.

- **Data retention and deletion**: CSPs must have clear policies for data retention and secure data deletion. Auditors should confirm that personal data is deleted once it is no longer needed or upon request by the customer.

General considerations for ISO 27017 & ISO 27018

For auditors, it is crucial to evaluate not only whether the controls listed in these standards are in place but also their level of maturity. However, it should be remembered that the auditors performing the certification audits are not concerned with the maturity levels. Maturity models can help determine the strength of controls across the following stages:

- **Initial**: Controls are ad hoc and reactive, with little formalization.

- **Managed**: Controls are documented and somewhat consistent but may still be applied on a case-by-case basis.

- **Defined**: Controls are standardized and integrated into the organization's overall security management practices.

- **Quantitatively managed**: Performance data is regularly gathered to improve control efficiency.

- **Optimized**: Continuous improvement of controls, with proactive adaptation to new threats.

For each cloud-specific control, auditors should assess the organization's maturity level and whether it meets its risk profile.

Future trends and understanding the auditor's role

As cloud technologies evolve, so too do the threats facing cloud environments. Auditors must stay ahead of these trends by continuously updating their knowledge of cloud security risks. Emerging threats may include:

- **Cloud misconfiguration**: Poorly configured cloud services remain one of the most significant security risks, exposing organizations to data breaches.

- **Insider threats**: The risk of insiders intentionally or unintentionally compromising cloud environments is rising, necessitating stronger internal controls.

- **Sophisticated cyberattacks**: Threat actors are becoming more adept at targeting cloud infrastructures, often using advanced techniques like AI-driven attacks and ransomware.

- **Artificial intelligence (AI)**: Attackers can utilize AI for phishing, automation of attacks, and evading detection.

- **Multi-cloud environment complexities**: Threats mainly stem from the increased attack surface, lack of visibility, and inconsistent security controls across different cloud platforms.

- **Quantum computing**: In the future, quantum computers could break today's encryption, rendering cloud data protection methods obsolete.

- **Automation**: While automation enhances efficiency, it also introduces potential risks as automated tasks can sometimes lead to unintended consequences, such as scripts inadvertently exposing sensitive data.

Auditors must be well-versed in these evolving threats and tailor their audit procedures accordingly.

Regarding the future of cloud audits, one should consider AI, automation, and continuous auditing. The future of cloud audits will likely involve greater use of AI and automation tools. Continuous auditing, where audits are conducted in real time using automated systems, can help identify and address security gaps before they become serious issues. AI-driven audits can automatically scan cloud environments for vulnerabilities and non-conformities. Continuous monitoring ensures that security controls remain effective, providing auditors with real-time data on the organization's security posture.

Auditors should develop competencies using these advanced tools to remain effective.

The evolving regulatory landscape, driven by new regulations such as the CCPA and GDPR updates, is significantly impacting the auditing field. To maintain effectiveness, auditors must proactively adapt their audit procedures to align with these dynamic regulatory requirements.

Common audit findings

During ISO 27017 audits, specific issues commonly arise. These may include:

- **Inadequate data segmentation**: In multi-tenant cloud environments, improper data segregation can expose sensitive data to unauthorized parties.

- **Weak IAM**: Mismanagement of user credentials, roles, and permissions can result in unauthorized access to cloud resources.

- **Lack of clarity in shared responsibility agreements**: A failure to clearly define responsibilities between the CSP and the customer often leads to security gaps.

- **Insufficient monitoring and logging**: Cloud environments must have comprehensive logging and monitoring to detect and respond to threats promptly.

When conducting ISO 27018 audits, auditors frequently encounter the following issues:

- **Insufficient consent management**: Many cloud providers struggle to implement comprehensive consent management mechanisms that comply with local and international privacy regulations.

- **Non-transparent data processing**: Auditors may find that the cloud provider lacks sufficient documentation or transparency regarding how, where, and by whom personal data is processed.

- **Weak incident notification procedures**: A failure to promptly notify customers in the event of a personal data breach can lead to significant regulatory non-compliance, particularly under GDPR.

Auditors should also look for evidence of privacy by design, which is the proactive embedding of privacy features into cloud systems. CSPs are increasingly expected to design their services with privacy as a default setting, not an afterthought. This requires close collaboration between the CSP and customers to ensure that privacy features are built into all aspects of the cloud solution, from data storage to user management.

Auditors should ensure these areas are thoroughly reviewed and tested during the audit process.

In pursuit of high-quality cloud security audits conforming to ISO 27017/27018, auditors must consider best practices tailored to auditing cloud-specific controls, as mentioned in the following points:

- **Review CSP documentation**: Ensure that the CSP's documentation clearly defines security roles, data ownership, and shared responsibilities.

- **Test access controls**: Validate that access controls are implemented as specified and that they align with the organization's risk appetite.

- **Check for encryption**: Auditors should verify that data in transit and at rest is encrypted using industry-standard methods.

- **Assess incident management**: Review the cloud provider's incident response procedures to ensure they can effectively detect, respond to, and recover from security incidents.

Case studies: Two case studies on auditing a cloud-based environment using ISO 27017 and ISO 27018 standards are discussed here:

- To illustrate how ISO 27017 audits are conducted, consider the following hypothetical case:

  A global e-commerce company is migrating to a public cloud platform to host its online services. The organization has obtained ISO 27017 certification as part of its risk management strategy. During the audit, while assessing various controls such as geo compliance, logging & monitoring, data security, and encryption, the auditors discovered that the company's customer data is not properly segmented from other tenants on the shared cloud infrastructure, creating a potential data leakage risk. The auditors recommend the implementation of better data segmentation controls and improvements to the company's cloud monitoring and logging capabilities. The preceding case highlights the importance of thorough assessments, especially when handling sensitive customer data in cloud environments.

- The second case study relates to auditing personal data in the cloud using ISO 27018, and considers the following example:

  A healthcare organization stores patient records in a cloud-based system. During an ISO 27018 audit, it was found that the CSP does not have adequate access controls in place for sensitive medical data. Additionally, the organization is unable to demonstrate how it would notify patients in the event of a data breach. The auditors recommend implementing stricter access control policies and developing a clear incident notification plan that aligns with GDPR requirements. This case underscores the importance of ensuring access control and compliance with regulatory standards for protecting personal data in the cloud.

Cloud audit challenges

Evaluating the compliance of CSPs is one of the main challenges auditors face. Since CSPs may host multiple clients on the same infrastructure, auditors must scrutinize how well the provider protects each tenant's data.

Risk assessments in cloud environments are inherently complex due to the shared responsibility model. Auditors must assess how risks are jointly managed between the CSP and the customer. Identifying the boundaries of control and responsibility is essential to conducting a practical risk assessment.

Now, let us understand some common pitfalls in cloud audits:

- **Shared responsibility**: Auditors may encounter difficulty in precisely determining the allocation of security control responsibilities between the CSP and the customer.

- **Lack of transparency from CSPs**: Some CSPs may not fully disclose their security measures, making it difficult for auditors to evaluate compliance.

- **Dynamic environments**: The constantly evolving nature of cloud infrastructure means that audit findings may quickly become outdated.

To mitigate these challenges during cloud audits, auditors should adapt certain techniques for effectiveness. Let us look at some of them:

- Use automated tools for continuous monitoring of cloud environments.

- Engage with CSPs to establish transparency regarding their security controls and incident management processes.

- Focus on reviewing CSP contracts to clarify security roles and responsibilities.

Mapping to other standards and frameworks

As discussed earlier, ISO 27017 and ISO 27018 are specialized extensions of the ISO/IEC 27001 standard, designed to address cloud-specific security and privacy requirements. Mapping these standards to other frameworks enables organizations to streamline compliance efforts, identify gaps, and achieve a more integrated approach to risk management.

Let us look at how these two standards can be mapped to other standards and frameworks and simplify the compliance process:

- **ISO/IEC 27001**:
  - **Relation**: Both ISO 27017 and ISO 27018 are extensions of ISO 27001, sharing its core structure of Annex A controls.
  - **Focus**: ISO 27001 provides the foundational ISMS framework, while ISO 27017 and ISO 27018 add specific guidance for cloud services and privacy.

- **General Data Protection Regulation (GDPR)**:
  - **Key connections**: Data protection impact assessments in ISO 27018 align with GDPR's Article 35. ISO 27018 ensures transparency, consent, and data subject rights, echoing the GDPR's principles.
  - **Benefit**: ISO 27018 acts as a practical guideline for operationalizing GDPR compliance in cloud environments.

- **Service Organization Control 2 (SOC 2)**:
  - **Overlap**: ISO 27017 aligns with SOC 2's Trust Services Criteria, such as Security, Confidentiality, and Availability, and ISO 27018 supports SOC 2 Privacy criteria with PII-specific guidance.
  - **Streamlining**: Organizations can leverage ISO compliance evidence for SOC 2 audits and vice versa.

- **CIS Controls**:
  - **Mapping**: CIS Control 13 (Data Protection) aligns with ISO 27018's PII safeguarding measures. CIS Control 16 (Application Software Security) resonates with ISO 27017's cloud application-specific guidelines.
  - **Focus**: ISO standards provide detailed process-based approaches, complementing CIS's prescriptive technical controls.

- **Cloud Security Alliance (CSA) Cloud Controls Matrix (CCM)**:
  - **Synergy**: ISO 27017 directly supports CSA CCM domains like IAM, encryption, and compliance. ISO 27018 aligns with CCM privacy controls, ensuring adherence to cloud privacy frameworks.
  - **Benefits**: Joint use provides cloud providers and customers with a comprehensive security and privacy baseline.

Mapping ISO 27017 and ISO 27018 to other frameworks bridges gaps between security, privacy, and compliance requirements. By leveraging these mappings, organizations can create a unified compliance strategy, reduce audit fatigue, and enhance trust in cloud services.

Building a **Unified Compliance Framework** (UCF) is one commonly used approach to integrating multiple standards and regulatory requirements into a single, cohesive framework. This enables organizations to address overlapping requirements efficiently.

Now, let us look at a sample UCF mapping ISO 27017, ISO 27018 and other standards/ frameworks in the following table:

Unified control ID	Control description	Source frameworks	Responsible party	Compliance status
UC-001	Define roles and responsibilities for cloud security	ISO 27017 (5.1.1), CSA CCM (GOV)	Cloud Provider/ Customer	Compliant
UC-002	Implement encryption for PII in cloud storage	ISO 27018 (8.1.3), GDPR (Art. 32), SOC 2 (Security)	Cloud provider	Partially compliant
UC-003	Monitor cloud service usage and security events	ISO 27017 (9.1.1), CIS Control 6	IT security team	Non-compliant
UC-004	Conduct regular risk assessments for cloud services	ISO 27001 (A.12.6.1), ISO 27017 (12.1.1)	Risk management team	Compliant

Table 7.2: Sample UCF

UCF avoids duplication of effort by mapping controls from various standards, regulations, and best practices into a single control set.

Conclusion

This chapter highlighted the importance of ISO 27017 and ISO 27018 standards for auditing cloud environments for addressing the growing concerns around cloud security and data privacy.

To remain effective, auditors must continually update their knowledge of cloud technologies, emerging threats, and evolving regulations. By embracing new tools and techniques such as AI and continuous auditing, auditors can ensure that they provide valuable insights that enhance cloud security and privacy practices.

The upcoming chapter introduces the CSA's CCM, **Consensus Assessments Initiative Questionnaire (CAIQ)**, and how auditors can leverage it for cloud security assessments. It discusses controls related to compliance, risk, and governance, and the STAR program of CSA.

This chapter will cover an overview of CCM, an overview of CAIQ, key CSA resources and tools for auditors, the STAR program, and the benefits.

Points to remember

- Auditors ISO 27017 and ISO 27018 are essential standards for auditing cloud environments, providing a framework for securing cloud services and protecting personal data.

- Auditors must focus on the unique risks and controls related to cloud security and data privacy, leveraging best practices to ensure compliance with these standards.

- Auditors need to be well-versed in evolving cloud-specific threats and tailor their audit procedures accordingly.

- Risk assessments in cloud environments are inherently complex due to the shared responsibility model, and auditors should focus on identifying the boundaries of control and responsibility.

- Building a UCF helps integrate multiple standards and regulatory requirements into a single, cohesive framework, enabling organizations to address overlapping requirements efficiently.

Multiple choice questions

1. **Which of the following ISO standards offers guidelines to address cloud security risks?**

    a. ISO/IEC 27017

    b. ISO/IEC 27018

    c. ISO/IEC 27001

    d. ISO/IEC 27002

2. Which of the following standards details the controls and guidance relevant to the protection of personal data in cloud environments?

    a. ISO/IEC 27017

    b. ISO/IEC 27018

    c. ISO/IEC 27001

    d. ISO/IEC 27002

3. Which of the following documents outlines the specific controls adopted by the organization and justifies any deviations from the ISO 27001 standard?

    a. Statement of intent

    b. Statement of purpose

    c. Statement of applicability

    d. Statement of information

4. Which one of the following is not one of the common pitfalls in cloud audits?

    a. Ambiguity in the shared responsibility model

    b. Dynamic cloud environments

    c. Lack of transparency from CSPs

    d. Scalability and flexibility

5. Which of the following is not an advantage of having a UCF?

    a. Reduced complexity

    b. Improved efficiency

    c. Reduced audit fatigue

    d. Initial setup complexity

Answers

1	a
2	b
3	c
4	d
5	d

CHAPTER 8

CSA – CCM and STAR Program

Introduction

The **Cloud Security Alliance (CSA)** is a leading organization dedicated to promoting best practices for securing cloud computing environments. This comprehensive overview will explore the CSA's key initiatives, including the **Cloud Controls Matrix (CCM),** the **Consensus Assessments Initiative Questionnaire (CAIQ),** and the **Security, Trust, Assurance,** and **Risk (STAR)** program. We will examine how auditors can leverage these tools for cloud security assessments, with a focus on controls related to compliance, risk, and governance.

Structure

This chapter covers the following topics:

- Introduction to Cloud Security Alliance
- Cloud Controls Matrix overview
- Overview of CAIQ
- Mapping CCM to other standards
- Key CSA resources and tools for auditors
- STAR program and its benefits

Objectives

By the end of this chapter, readers will understand the CSA's Cloud CCM and CAIQ and how auditors can leverage them for cloud security assessments. It also discusses controls related to compliance, risk, and governance, and the CSA STAR program.

Introduction to Cloud Security Alliance

The CSA was conceived in November 2008 at the forum of the **Information Systems Security Association (ISSA)** and **Chief Information Security Officers (CISOs)** in *Las Vegas.*

Founded by industry leaders *Jim Reavis and Nils Puhlmann,* the CSA was formally established in December 2008 with the mission to promote the use of best practices for providing security assurance within cloud computing environments.

The CSA has achieved numerous milestones since its inception. Some key milestones are mentioned here:

- **2008:** The CSA was founded at the ISSA CISO Forum in *Las Vegas. Jim Reavis and Nils Puhlmann* outlined the initial mission and strategy.

- **2009:** Released the first comprehensive best practices guide for secure cloud computing, *Security Guidance for Critical Areas of Focus for Cloud Computing.*

- **2010:** Created the CCM and introduced the **Certificate of Cloud Security Knowledge (CCSK).**

- **2010:** CSA launched the CAIQ. This provides a standardized set of questions that cloud customers or auditors can use to assess the security posture of cloud providers. It's closely tied to the CCM and helps organizations gain transparency into the security controls implemented by cloud providers.

- **2011:** Hosted the White House to announce the US Federal Cloud Strategy.

- **2012:** Established CSA Europe and launched the **Security, Trust, and Assurance Registry (STAR).**

- **2013:** Expanded to Asia Pacific and launched CSA STAR Certification.

- **2015**: Introduced the **Certified Cloud Security Professional (CCSP)** certification with ISC2.

- **2017:** Released major updates to Guidance v4.0 and issued the code of conduct for GDPR compliance.

- **2022:** CSA launched the **Certificate of Competence in Zero Trust (CCZT).** This certification validates an individual's knowledge and skills in implementing and managing zero-trust security frameworks, a crucial approach in today's cloud-centric world.

Cloud Controls Matrix overview

The CCM is a cybersecurity control framework specifically designed for cloud computing. It consists of 197 control objectives structured across 17 domains, covering all key aspects of cloud technology that address critical aspects of cloud security, including application security, compliance, data governance, and risk management. The CCM serves as a comprehensive tool for the systematic assessment of cloud implementations and provides guidance on security controls that should be implemented by various actors within the cloud supply chain.

The 17 domains of the CCM are represented in the following figure:

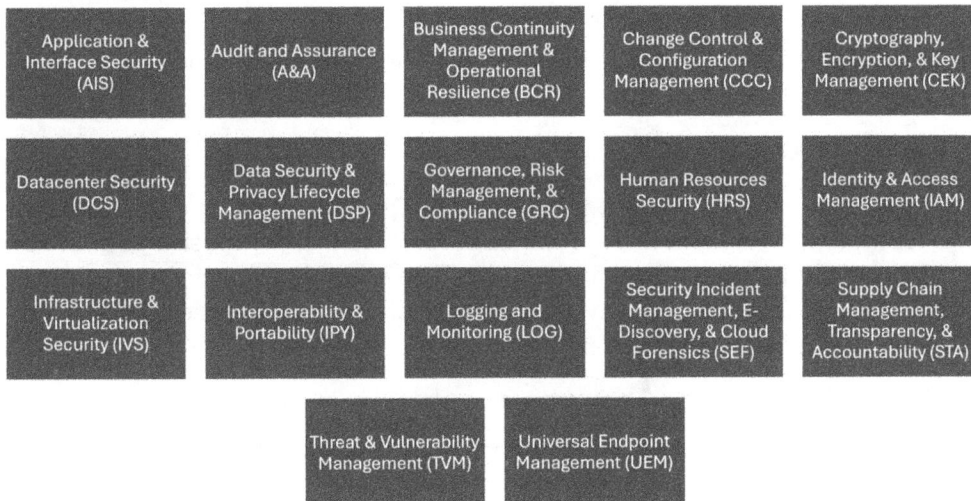

Application & Interface Security (AIS)	Audit and Assurance (A&A)	Business Continuity Management & Operational Resilience (BCR)	Change Control & Configuration Management (CCC)	Cryptography, Encryption, & Key Management (CEK)
Datacenter Security (DCS)	Data Security & Privacy Lifecycle Management (DSP)	Governance, Risk Management, & Compliance (GRC)	Human Resources Security (HRS)	Identity & Access Management (IAM)
Infrastructure & Virtualization Security (IVS)	Interoperability & Portability (IPY)	Logging and Monitoring (LOG)	Security Incident Management, E-Discovery, & Cloud Forensics (SEF)	Supply Chain Management, Transparency, & Accountability (STA)
	Threat & Vulnerability Management (TVM)	Universal Endpoint Management (UEM)		

Figure 8.1: The 17 domains of CSA CCM

Key features of CCM include the following:

- **Vendor-neutral:** The CSA CCM does not favour or align with any specific cloud service provider or technology vendor. It is designed to be broadly applicable across different environments.

- **Provider-agnostic:** It is intended to be used with any cloud provider or deployment model, meaning the controls are general enough to apply across the board, not tied to any one provider's way of doing things.

- **Comprehensive coverage:** The CCM addresses a wide range of cloud security concerns, ensuring a holistic approach to security assessment.

- **Alignment with industry standards**: The framework is aligned with the CSA security guidance for Cloud computing, making it a de facto standard for cloud security assurance and compliance.

- **Role-based structure:** The CCM provides clarity on responsibilities among **cloud service providers (CSPs)** and cloud customers, fostering shared accountability.

- **Flexibility**: The CCM can be customized to fit the specific needs of different organizations and cloud service models.

- **Regular updates**: The CSA continuously updates the CCM to keep pace with evolving cloud technologies and security threats.

The matrix is designed for all cloud deployment models (public, private, hybrid) and service models (Infrastructure as a Service, Platform as a Service, and Software as a Service). Here are some of the key benefits of CCM:

- Simplifies compliance by mapping to multiple regulations and frameworks.

- Enhances risk management by offering actionable controls.

- Provides a benchmark for CSPs to demonstrate security assurance.

Overview of CAIQ

The CAIQ is a complementary tool to the CCM, designed to provide a standardized set of questions for assessing the security capabilities of CSPs. The CAIQ consists of a series of yes/ no control-assertion questions that can be tailored to meet the specific needs of individual cloud customers. It enables CSPs to document their security practices and demonstrate compliance with CCM controls.

CAIQ is closely tied to the CCM. The purpose and benefits of CAIQ include:

- **Standardization:** CAIQ offers a uniform approach to documenting security controls across various cloud service models (IaaS, PaaS, SaaS).

- **Efficiency:** It reduces the complexity of due diligence and eliminates the need for multiple questionnaires from individual cloud consumers, streamlining the assessment process.

- **Transparency:** By completing the CAIQ, cloud providers can offer increased visibility into their security practices, fostering trust with potential customers.

- **Risk assessment:** Organizations can use CAIQ responses to evaluate potential risks associated with different CSPs.

- **Certification:** Aligns with CSA STAR, supporting certification efforts.

Here are some example questions from the CAIQ (refer to *Table 8.1*), covering a few different domains:

- **Access control:**
  - o Does the CSP have a documented process for granting, modifying, and revoking user access to cloud services?
  - o Does the CSP enforce multi-factor authentication for all privileged users?

- o Does the CSP have controls in place to prevent unauthorized access to sensitive data?

- **Data security and information lifecycle management:**
  - o Does the CSP encrypt sensitive data at rest and in transit?
  - o Does the CSP have a data retention policy that complies with applicable regulations?
  - o Does the CSP provide data backup and recovery services?

- **Governance, risk management, and compliance:**
  - o Does the CSP have a documented security incident response plan?
  - o Does the CSP conduct regular security assessments and penetration testing?
  - o Does the CSP comply with relevant industry standards and regulations?

Mapping CCM to other standards

One of the key strengths of the CCM is its extensive mapping to other industry-accepted security standards, regulations, and control frameworks. This mapping allows organizations to efficiently address multiple compliance requirements simultaneously.

The CCM is mapped against numerous standards and frameworks, including but not limited to the following points:

- **ISO 27001/27002/27017/27018:** These are international standards for information security management systems, with 27017 specifically addressing cloud security and 27018 focusing on data privacy in the cloud.

- **NIST SP 800-53:** This is a U.S. government standard for security and privacy controls for federal information systems and organizations.

- **AICPA Trust Services Criteria (SOC 2):** These criteria are used for reporting on controls at a service organization relevant to security, availability, processing integrity, confidentiality, and privacy.

- **PCI DSS:** This is the **Payment Card Industry Data Security Standard (PCI DSS),** a set of security requirements for organizations that handle credit card information.

- **HIPAA:** The Health Insurance Portability and Accountability Act, a *U.S.* law that protects the privacy and security of health information.

- **GDPR:** The GDPR, an EU regulation on data protection and privacy.

- **Center for Internet Security (CIS) controls:** The CIS controls provide a set of prioritized, specific, and actionable security actions that organizations can take to defend against cyber-attacks.

- **Federal Risk and Authorization Management Program (FedRAMP):** The **FedRAMP**, a U.S. government program that provides a standardized approach to security assessment, authorization, and continuous monitoring for cloud products and services.

- **BSI C5:** A German standard for cloud security.

Now, let us look at an example of CCM mapping to other standards and frameworks in the following table:

Control information	Control description	Mappings
CCM V4 Control Domain: Audit and Assurance Control Title: Audit and Assurance Policy and Procedures Control ID: A&A-01	Establish, document, approve, communicate, apply, evaluate, and maintain audit and assurance policies and procedures and standards. Review and update the policies and procedures at least annually.	AICPA TSC 2017 – CC2.2, CC2.3, CC3.2, CC5.3
		CIS V8.0 – 8.1
		ISF SOGP 2022 – AS1.1, AS2.1
		NIST 800-53 Rev 5 – CA-1
		NIST CSF 2.0– GV.PO-01, GV.PO-02
		PCI-DSS v4.0 – 12.1.1, 12.1.2
		ISO 27001:2022 – 5.1, 5.2, 7.3, 7.4, 7.5, 9.1, 9.2, 9.2, A.5.1, A.5.4, A.5.37
		ENX ISA v6.0 – 1.1.1, 1.5.1

Table 8.1: Example of CCM control mapping

CCM mapping, compared to other standards and frameworks, offers many benefits that include the following:

- **Efficiency**: Organizations can fulfill multiple compliance requirements by addressing CCM controls.

- **Comprehensive coverage**: The mapping ensures that no critical security aspects are overlooked when complying with various standards.

- **Simplified audits**: Auditors can use CCM as a central reference point when assessing compliance with multiple standards.

- **Cost-effective compliance**: By addressing CCM controls, organizations can reduce the time and resources required to achieve compliance with multiple frameworks.

Key CSA resources and tools for auditors

CSA provides a range of resources and tools that auditors can leverage to enhance their cloud security assessments, which are discussed here:

- **CCM and CAIQ:** Auditors can use the CCM as a comprehensive checklist for evaluating cloud security controls. The CAIQ serves as a standardized questionnaire for gathering information from CSPs.

- **CSA STAR registry:** The STAR registry is a publicly accessible database of cloud provider security practices.

  Auditors can use this resource to perform the following:

  - Compare security practices across different providers
  - Verify self-reported security measures
  - Identify industry benchmarks and best practices

- **CSA guidance:** The CSA regularly publishes guidance documents that provide in-depth information on various aspects of cloud security. These resources can help auditors stay informed about emerging threats and best practices.

- **CSA Cloud Academy:** *Provides programs designed to equip cloud computing professionals, including auditors,* with the skills needed for cloud security evaluations. The programs offered include certifications such as **CCSK, Certificate of Cloud Auditing Knowledge (CCAK), CCZT**, and several trainings, including the STAR lead auditor training.

- **CSA research**: The CSA conducts ongoing research into various aspects of cloud security. Auditors can leverage these research findings to inform their assessment methodologies and stay current with emerging trends and threats in cloud security.

- **Cloud computing threat report:** Provides insights into emerging threats and mitigative strategies.

- **CSA code of conduct:** A framework that supports GDPR compliance for CSPs.

STAR program and its benefits

The STAR program is a comprehensive initiative by the CSA to provide assurance within the cloud computing ecosystem. The program offers various levels of assessment and certification, catering to different organizational needs and risk profiles.

The STAR Program has two levels of assurance, each designed to provide increasing levels of transparency and rigor in assessing CSPs. Here is an overview of the levels:

- **STAR Level 1 (Self-assessment):** Organizations can complete a self-assessment using the CAIQ or the CCM. The self-assessment is published in the CSA STAR registry and provides a basic level of transparency for customers about the provider's security practices.

  This level is suitable for the following:

  - Organizations operating in low-risk environments
  - Those seeking to increase transparency around their security controls
  - Companies looking for a cost-effective way to improve trust and transparency

- **STAR Level 2 (Third-party certification):** This level involves independent assessment by third-party auditors. It offers a higher degree of assurance and is suitable for organizations operating in more sensitive or regulated environments. The certification details are published in the CSA STAR Registry and offer a higher level of assurance by validating the provider's security practices through a formal certification process.

- **Variations of Level 2:** There are different variations in collaboration with other entities, such as STAR Attestation for SOC 2, STAR certification for ISO/IEC 27001, and C-STAR for the Greater *China* market. The attestation reports are published in the CSA STAR registry and provide the highest level of assurance, as they involve a detailed examination of the provider's controls and practices by an independent auditor.

Level 2 is considered the highest level of assurance and provides the most comprehensive view of an organization's security posture.

Benefits of STAR program

The CSA STAR program is CSA's flagship certification and assessment program, designed to provide assurance of CSPs' security practices. It integrates CCM and CAIQ, enabling CSPs to achieve varying levels of assurance based on their maturity and compliance.

This program offers many benefits, and some of the key benefits are mentioned here:

- **Market advantage:** STAR certification serves as a competitive advantage for CSPs.

- **Enhanced transparency:** STAR program promotes openness about security practices, fostering trust between cloud providers and customers.

- **Enhanced trust:** STAR-certified CSPs signal robust security practices, fostering customer confidence.

- **Standardized assessment:** By using common frameworks like CCM and CAIQ, the STAR program ensures a consistent approach to security assessment across the industry.

- **Competitive advantage:** Cloud providers can differentiate themselves by demonstrating their commitment to security through STAR certification.

- **Streamlined compliance:** The program reduces the complexity of meeting multiple standards by consolidating requirements.

- **Risk reduction:** Organizations can make more informed decisions about cloud providers by leveraging the information available through the STAR program.

- **Auditor efficiency:** It provides auditors with standardized tools and documentation for assessments.

- **Continuous improvement:** The program encourages ongoing assessment and improvement of security practices.

CCM and STAR in cloud auditing

Auditors can effectively use the CCM and STAR program to enhance their cloud security assessments in the following ways:

- **Comprehensive control coverage**: The CCM provides a thorough list of controls that auditors can use as a baseline for their assessments. This ensures that all critical aspects of cloud security are evaluated.

- **Standardized approach:** By using the CAIQ, auditors can ensure consistency in their information-gathering process across different CSPs.

- **Benchmarking:** The STAR registry allows auditors to compare a provider's security practices against industry standards and peer organizations.

- **Risk assessment:** Auditors can use the CCM and STAR certifications to evaluate the risk posture of cloud providers and identify potential areas of concern.

- **Compliance mapping:** The CCM's mapping to various standards helps auditors efficiently assess compliance with multiple regulatory requirements.

- **Continuous monitoring:** The STAR program's emphasis on ongoing assessment aligns with the need for continuous monitoring in cloud environments.

CCM GRC controls

The CCM comprises several domains, organized into 16 key aspects of cloud security that specifically address governance, risk, and compliance. Within these domains, there are 133 control objectives that organizations should implement to mitigate risks and ensure the confidentiality, integrity, and availability of their data in the cloud. Let us discuss the key aspects of GRC controls in the CSA CCM.

Governance controls focus on the organizational and strategic aspects of cloud security, ensuring that cloud deployments are aligned with business objectives and comply with relevant regulations and standards.

Some key aspects of governance controls are discussed here:

- **Baseline requirements**: Establishes minimum security requirements for the development or acquisition of information systems.

- **Policy reviews**: Mandates regular reviews and updates of security policies and procedures.

- **Policy enforcement**: Ensures that violation of security policies results in appropriate disciplinary action.

The CCM emphasizes the importance of establishing a formal **risk management** program to identify, assess, and treat cloud security risks. This includes conducting regular risk assessments, developing risk treatment plans, and monitoring the effectiveness of controls. Some key controls related to risk management are mentioned here:

- **Risk assessments**: Mandates regular risk assessments to identify and address potential threats to the cloud environment.

- **Mitigation/risk treatment**: Requires the development and implementation of risk treatment plans.

- **Business/policy change impacts**: Ensures that changes to business objectives or risk tolerance are reflected in the security program.

By implementing CSA CCM *compliance controls*, organizations can significantly improve their cloud security posture and reduce their risk of security breaches. Let us look at them in detail:

- **Audit planning:** Ensures audit activities are planned and agreed upon in advance to minimize disruption to business processes.

- **Independent audits:** Regular independent reviews of the organization's security program are required.

- **Information system regulatory mapping:** Ensures information systems are regularly reviewed for compliance with applicable laws and regulations.

Conclusion

This chapter discussed how the CSA, through its CCM, CAIQ, and STAR program, provides a comprehensive framework for assessing and improving cloud security and how these tools offer significant benefits to both CSPs and consumers, promoting transparency, standardization, and continuous improvement in cloud security practices.

For auditors, the CSA's resources offer a robust foundation for conducting thorough and consistent cloud security assessments. By leveraging these tools, auditors can ensure comprehensive coverage of security controls, streamline the assessment process, and provide valuable insights to their clients or organizations.

The CSA's CCM and CAIQ are foundational tools that enable organizations to secure their cloud environments effectively. By leveraging these resources, auditors can perform thorough assessments, ensuring compliance, mitigating risks, and establishing robust governance.

CSA's STAR program also offers a comprehensive certification path that enhances trust and transparency in cloud security practices. As cloud adoption continues to grow, CSA's frameworks and resources remain indispensable for organizations seeking to navigate the complexities of cloud security and compliance.

The upcoming chapter will cover auditing the underlying cloud infrastructure, including virtualization, containerization, and multi-tenancy. It discusses tools for auditing resource allocation and usage.

Points to remember

- The CCM is a comprehensive set of security controls organized into 17 domains specifically designed for cloud computing and covers all key aspects of cloud technology. CCM provides guidance on which security controls should be implemented by different actors in the cloud supply chain.

- The CCM's controls are mapped to other industry-accepted security standards and regulations, including ISO 27001, NIST SP 800-53, and others.

- The CCM serves as the foundation for the STAR program, providing the set of controls against which cloud providers are assessed.

- The STAR program is built on the principles of transparency, rigorous auditing, and harmonization of standards and is designed to provide transparency and assurance around the security of cloud services.

- The STAR program offers different levels of assurance, from self-assessment to third-party certification.

- The CSA and the STAR program are committed to continuous improvement, regularly updating the CCM and the program to address the latest threats and best practices.

Multiple Choice Questions

1. **CCM can be best described as:**
   a. A cloud service provider's security certification.
   b. A set of security controls for cloud computing.
   c. A legal framework for cloud data protection.
   d. A risk assessment methodology for cloud migrations.

2. **The CCM is organized into how many domains?**
   a. 12
   b. 14
   c. 17
   d. 20

3. **What is the primary purpose of the STAR registry?**
   a. To list certified cloud security professionals.
   b. To provide a public database of cloud provider security assessments.
   c. To track cloud security incidents.
   d. To host cloud security training materials.

4. **The CAIQ stands for:**

    a. Cloud Application Infrastructure Qualification

    b. Consensus Assessments Initiative Questionnaire

    c. Certified Cloud Infrastructure Quality

    d. Critical Asset Identification Questionnaire

5. **STAR level 1 attestation involves which of the following:**

    a. Audit & attestation by CSA

    b. Any third-party audit

    c. Audit & attestation by a CPA Self-attestation

    d. Self-attestation

Answers

1	b
2	c
3	b
4	b
5	d

Join our Discord space

Join our Discord workspace for latest updates, offers, tech happenings around the world, new releases, and sessions with the authors:

https://discord.bpbonline.com

CHAPTER 9

Auditing Cloud Infrastructure

Introduction

Cloud computing has become a cornerstone of modern information technology infrastructure, offering scalability, flexibility, and cost efficiency. However, the shift from traditional on-premises environments to the cloud introduces new risks and complexities that necessitate thorough auditing processes. Auditing cloud infrastructure involves evaluating its security, compliance, and operational integrity, ensuring that the cloud environment remains resilient and secure. This chapter explores the auditing of underlying cloud infrastructure, covering key areas such as virtualization, containerization, multi-tenancy, resource allocation, and usage monitoring.

Structure

This chapter covers the following topics:

- Cloud infrastructure overview
- Key risks in cloud infrastructure
- Auditing cloud infrastructure
- Evaluating resilience and availability of cloud infrastructure
- Tools for auditing cloud infrastructure
- Common cloud infrastructure vulnerabilities and findings

Objectives

By the end of this chapter, readers will be able to understand the specifics of auditing the underlying cloud infrastructure, including virtualization, containerization, and multi-tenancy. It discusses tools for auditing resource allocation and usage.

Cloud infrastructure overview

Cloud infrastructure consists of several key components, or foundational resources, that enable the delivery of computing resources over the Internet. The conceptual layout of cloud infrastructure is depicted in the following figure:

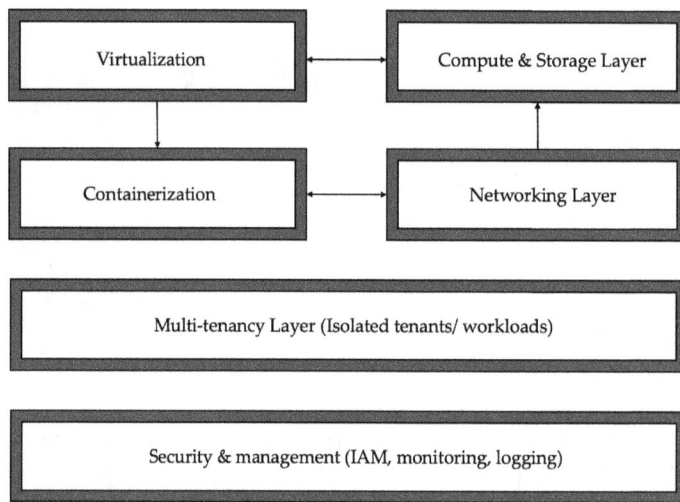

Figure 9.1: Conceptual layout of cloud infrastructure components

The key components of the cloud infrastructure are explained here:

- **Virtualization:** Allows several operating systems to operate on one physical machine, maximizing the efficiency of resource utilization.

- **Containerization:** Uses lightweight, portable containers to run applications consistently across environments.

- **Multi-tenancy:** Allows multiple users or organizations to share the same cloud resources while maintaining data segregation.

- **Networking:** Includes virtual networks, subnets, firewalls, and load balancers to ensure secure connectivity.

- **Storage and compute:** Comprises cloud-based storage solutions (block, object, file storage) and compute instances such as **virtual machines (VMs)** and Kubernetes clusters.

- **Security and management:** Achieved through **identity and access management (IAM),** encryption, and monitoring tools to help secure and optimize cloud resources.

Cloud infrastructure is typically delivered through public, private, or hybrid cloud models by providers like **Amazon Web Services (AWS**), Microsoft Azure, and Google Cloud. Organizations leverage cloud infrastructure for scalability, cost efficiency, and flexibility in their information technology operations.

Key risks in cloud infrastructure

Cloud infrastructure presents unique risks that auditors must evaluate to ensure security, compliance, and operational resilience. These risks are represented in the following figure:

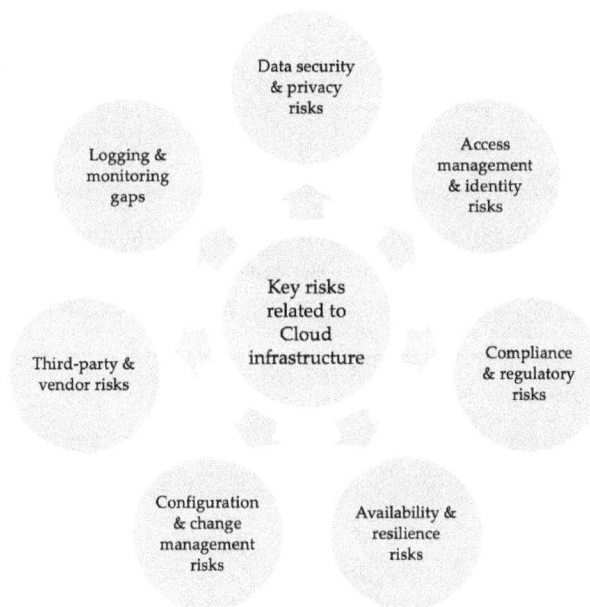

Figure 9.2: Key risks related to cloud infrastructure

Key risks related to cloud infrastructure include the following:

- **Data security & privacy risks**: Sensitive information can be exposed due to unauthorized access, data breaches, or weak encryption. Auditors should assess data protection measures, including encryption, access controls, and compliance with regulations, e.g., **General Data Protection Regulation (GDPR), Health Insurance Portability and Accountability Act (HIPAA).**

- **Access management & identity risks**: Weak authentication mechanisms and excessive user permissions increase the risk of insider threats and unauthorized access. Auditors should review IAM policies, **multi-factor authentication (MFA),** and **role-based access controls (RBAC)**.

- **Compliance & regulatory risks**: Cloud providers operate in different jurisdictions, leading to potential non-compliance with legal and industry regulations. Auditors should verify whether cloud services align with required compliance frameworks, e.g., **Service Organization Controls 2 (SOC 2), ISO 27001, Payment Card Industry Data Security Standard (PCI-DSS).**

- **Availability & resilience risks**: Service outages, misconfigurations, or lack of redundancy can impact business continuity. Auditors should evaluate **disaster recovery (DR)** plans, backup strategies, and **service level agreements (SLAs).**

- **Configuration & change management risks**: Misconfigurations, unpatched vulnerabilities, or unauthorized changes can introduce security gaps. Auditors should assess configuration management processes, automated compliance checks, and security monitoring tools.

- **Third-party & vendor risks**: Cloud infrastructure relies on third-party providers, which can introduce risks related to service reliability, security practices, and contractual obligations. Auditors should review vendor risk assessments, contracts, and security certifications.

- **Logging & monitoring gaps**: Insufficient monitoring can make it difficult to detect security incidents or policy violations. Auditors should ensure centralized logging, real-time monitoring, and incident response procedures are in place.

When assessing and analyzing the risks associated with cloud infrastructure, auditors should focus on and prioritize the following:

- **Risk assessments and governance**: Evaluate cloud risk management frameworks and security policies.

- **Access and identity controls**: Review IAM policies, user privileges, and authentication mechanisms.

- **Compliance and security posture**: Validate adherence to regulatory and industry standards.

- **Incident response and monitoring**: Assess logging, monitoring, and forensic capabilities.

By addressing these risks, auditors help organizations strengthen cloud security, maintain regulatory compliance, and ensure the integrity of cloud-based operations.

Auditing cloud infrastructure

Now that we have an understanding and overview of cloud infrastructure and the key risks associated with cloud infrastructure, we will move on to explore the auditing aspects of various components of cloud infrastructure in detail. This will help us understand how to assess controls, ensure compliance, and manage potential vulnerabilities across the cloud environment.

Network management

Auditing network management in cloud infrastructure is crucial for ensuring security, compliance, and operational resilience. Cloud networks control how data flows between systems, applications, and external entities, making them a critical area for auditors to evaluate.

Regular audits enable early detection of security incidents, minimizing potential damages and ensuring that workloads remain secure, and some of the key areas to audit in cloud network management are as follows:

- **Network architecture and design review:** During the review of network architecture and design, auditors should assess how secure, efficient, and resilient the network is. Here are the key aspects to look for:

  o Assess whether the cloud network follows industry best practices and security frameworks.

  o Verify the segmentation of environments, e.g., production vs. development, to minimize risk.

  o Review the use of **virtual private cloud (VPC),** subnets, and network isolation techniques.

- **Access controls and identity management:** Auditors should assess access and identity management, with a goal to ensure only authorized users have the minimum necessary access, and that identities are securely managed across the cloud environment. Key areas to assess are mentioned here:

  o Ensure that network access is restricted using least privilege and RBAC.

  o Check the configuration of firewalls, security groups, and **network access control lists (NACLs).**

  o Review VPNs, Direct Connect, or other secure tunnels for remote access.

- **Security controls and threat protection:** Auditors should evaluate whether preventive, detective, and responsive security measures are properly implemented and whether they align with the organization's risk posture and compliance requirements. Some of the key areas to assess are:

  o Validate the use of **intrusion detection and prevention systems (IDPS)** for threat monitoring.

  o Assess encryption protocols **Transport Layer Security (TLS)** and **Internet Protocol Security (IPSec)** used for data in transit.

  o Review the implementation of **distributed denial-of-service (DDoS)** protection and **web application firewalls (WAFs)** to prevent attacks.

- **Network logging and monitoring:** Auditors evaluate whether the organization has effective logging and monitoring controls in place to detect, investigate, and respond to network-related activities and security events. The key aspects to look for are:

  o Ensure that network traffic logs, e.g., VPC flow logs, CloudTrail, Azure Network Watcher, are enabled and stored securely.

  o Assess real-time monitoring tools for detecting suspicious activity, e.g., AWS GuardDuty, Azure Sentinel.

  o Verify whether automated alerts are in place for abnormal network behaviors.

- **Configuration and change management:** Auditors should evaluate how well an organization manages and controls changes to its cloud infrastructure and how securely configurations are maintained. Key aspects to assess are:

  o Review how network changes, e.g., firewall rule updates, routing modifications, are controlled and documented.

  o Ensure configuration management tools, e.g., Terraform, CloudFormation, are used for consistency.

  o Check for regular vulnerability assessments and penetration testing on network components.

- **Compliance and regulatory alignment:** Auditors should aim to ensure that cloud usage aligns with industry standards, legal requirements, and internal policies, and the key aspects to look for during audits are:

  o Ensure that the network adheres to security and compliance standards, e.g., **National Institute of Standards and Technology (NIST),** ISO 27001, PCI-DSS, and any applicable national and international regulations.

  o Verify that third-party integrations and cloud service providers comply with relevant regulations.

Auditors may adapt to the following approaches and best practices for performing an effective audit of network management in the cloud:

- **Review policies and procedures:** Ensure documented policies exist for network security and management.

- **Perform configuration audits**: Validate cloud network settings against best practices and compliance requirements.

- **Test network controls**: Conduct simulated security testing to assess firewall and access control effectiveness.

- **Analyze logs and incident reports:** Review past incidents to identify gaps in monitoring or response processes.

By systematically auditing network management, organizations can strengthen their cloud security posture, mitigate risks, and ensure compliance with industry standards.

Configuration management

Configuration management is a critical component of cloud infrastructure, ensuring consistency, security, and compliance across cloud resources. Auditors must assess whether configurations are properly managed to prevent misconfigurations, security vulnerabilities, and operational risks.

Periodic configuration audits of cloud infrastructure ensure several critical aspects of cloud security, compliance, and operational efficiency. Some of the key areas to focus on while auditing configuration management in the cloud are mentioned here:

- **Configuration policies and standards:** Assessing configuration policies and standards is a key part of cloud auditing, especially as misconfigurations are one of the most common causes of cloud security incidents.

  Typically, auditors should look for the following:

  o Verify that the organization has well-documented configuration management policies aligned with industry best practices, e.g., NIST, **Center for Internet Security (CIS)** Benchmarks.

  o Assess whether cloud configurations follow vendor-recommended security guidelines (AWS Well-Architected Framework, Azure Security Best Practices, Google Cloud Security Foundations).

- Ensure that configuration standards are consistent across multi-cloud and hybrid environments.

- **Infrastructure as Code (IaC) and automation:** Auditors should look at how these tools are used to enforce consistency, reduce risk, and improve governance, and the key aspects to look for during the audit are:

  o Review the use of IaC tools like Terraform, AWS CloudFormation, or Azure Resource Manager.

  o Ensure version control mechanisms, e.g., Git repositories, are in place to track configuration changes.

  o Assess whether automated **continuous integration and continuous delivery (CI/CD)** pipelines enforce security policies before deployment.

- **Configuration change management and version control:** Auditors should begin by verifying that the organization has a documented and enforced process for managing configuration changes in cloud environments.

Key aspects of the audit should include the following:

- o Evaluate the change management process to ensure all configuration changes are approved, tested, and documented.

- o Verify the existence of change logs tracking who made changes, when, and why.

- o Assess rollback mechanisms to restore previous configurations in case of failure.

- **Misconfiguration and compliance audits:** Misconfigurations are among the most common causes of cloud security incidents, and compliance audits help ensure cloud environments meet regulatory and policy requirements.

Here is what auditors should assess:

- o Check for common misconfigurations, such as open storage buckets, unrestricted firewall rules, or excessive IAM permissions.

- o Ensure the organization conducts regular configuration audits using cloud-native tools such as:

    - ▪ AWS Config

    - ▪ Azure Policy and Security Center

    - ▪ Google Cloud Security Command Center

- o Validate compliance with security frameworks like CIS Benchmarks, PCI-DSS, ISO 27001, and NIST 800-53.

- **Monitoring and logging of configuration changes:** Auditors should pay close attention to how well these processes are implemented and monitored.

Key aspects auditors typically assess in this area are:

- o Ensure configuration changes are logged and monitored using **CloudTrail (AWS), Activity Logs (Azure),** or **Audit Logs (Google Cloud).**

- o Assess real-time alerts and automated remediation for unauthorized changes.

- o Verify whether **security information and event management (SIEM)** solutions integrate with cloud logs for centralized monitoring.

- **Backup and disaster recovery of configurations:** Auditors should evaluate whether the organization can restore critical settings, infrastructure, and data quickly and accurately in the event of failure, misconfiguration, or a security incident.

Key aspects of an audit are:

- o Confirm that configuration backups are taken regularly and stored securely.

- o Assess the organization's DR strategy for restoring cloud configurations after a security event.

- o Validate that automated backup policies are in place to prevent accidental data loss.

The following audit approach and best practices may be adapted by the auditors while evaluating configuration management in the cloud:

- **Review configuration policies**: Ensure documentation exists for configuration management standards.

- **Perform automated scans**: Use cloud security tools to detect misconfigurations and non-compliance.

- **Test change management controls**: Verify whether configuration changes are reviewed and approved before deployment.

- **Analyze logs and incidents**: Assess past configuration-related incidents to identify gaps in controls.

By systematically auditing configuration management, organizations can reduce security risks, improve compliance, and enhance the reliability of cloud infrastructure.

User device management

User device management is a crucial aspect of cloud infrastructure security, as improperly managed devices can become entry points for unauthorized access, data breaches, and malware infections. Auditors should assess how organizations control, secure, and monitor endpoints (laptops, mobile devices, and other user endpoints) that access cloud services. Some of the key areas to focus on while auditing user device management in the cloud are mentioned here:

- **Device security policies and compliance:** Auditors should validate that user devices accessing cloud services are secure, managed, and aligned with organizational and regulatory security requirements.

  Some of the key aspects to be assessed are:

  o Review the organization's user device management policy, ensuring it aligns with security best practices, e.g., NIST, CIS, ISO 27001.

  o Verify that corporate and personal devices accessing cloud resources comply with security standards, e.g., device encryption, strong passwords.

  o Assess compliance with regulatory requirements like GDPR, HIPAA, and PCI-DSS, if applicable.

- **Endpoint security and access controls:** This is to ensure that endpoints accessing cloud resources are secure and that access controls effectively protect sensitive data and services from unauthorized access or misuse.

  Some key aspects to look for during the audit are:

  o Evaluate the use of **endpoint detection and response (EDR)** or **mobile device management (MDM)** solutions, e.g., Microsoft Intune, Jamf, VMware Workspace ONE.

- o Ensure MFA is enforced for all devices accessing cloud applications.
- o Verify whether **Zero Trust Network Access (ZTNA)** principles are applied to restrict device access based on security posture.

- **Device inventory and asset management:** Auditors should assess if all the devices and cloud assets are accurately tracked, managed, and secured throughout their lifecycle to reduce risks and maintain control over the IT environment.

  Key aspects of the assessment are:
  - o Check whether the organization maintains an inventory of all authorized devices accessing cloud infrastructure.
  - o Assess how device enrolment and deprovisioning are managed when users leave or change roles.
  - o Ensure unauthorized or unmanaged devices are detected and blocked.

- **Patch management and software updates:** This is to ensure that all systems, applications, and devices in the cloud environment are regularly updated to fix security vulnerabilities, improve performance, and maintain compliance by assessing the following aspects:
  - o Verify that automated patch management is in place for operating systems, applications, and security software.
  - o Review policies for regular security updates and vulnerability scanning to detect outdated software.
  - o Assess whether non-compliant or vulnerable devices are restricted from accessing cloud services.

- **Data protection and encryption:** The auditors should assess if the sensitive data stored, processed, or transmitted in the cloud is properly secured through encryption and other protection measures to prevent unauthorized access, loss, or breaches by assessing the following:
  - o Confirm that devices accessing cloud services use full-disk encryption, e.g., BitLocker, FileVault, to protect data.
  - o Evaluate **data loss prevention (DLP)** controls to prevent unauthorized data transfer.
  - o Ensure that cloud-based applications enforce encryption for data in transit and at rest.

- **Remote access and endpoint monitoring:** Auditors should evaluate if remote connections to cloud resources are secure and that all endpoints are continuously monitored to detect and respond to threats effectively by assessing the key aspects listed here:

o   Assess the use of VPNs, secure tunnelling, or cloud-based security gateways for remote access.

o   Verify whether real-time monitoring is in place to detect compromised devices.

o   Review logs from SIEM tools, e.g., Splunk, Azure Sentinel, AWS Security Hub, to track device-related security incidents.

- **Incident response and device decommissioning:** This is to ensure that security incidents are promptly and effectively managed, and that devices are properly decommissioned to prevent data leaks or unauthorized access.

Auditors should review the following key aspects:

o   Ensure there are defined procedures for handling lost, stolen, or compromised devices.

o   Verify that remote wipe capabilities are enabled for corporate-managed devices.

o   Review how devices are removed from the system when employees leave the organization.

Auditors may adapt to the following approaches and best practices for conducting an effective audit of user device management in the cloud:

- **Review device management policies**: Ensure documentation exists for securing user devices.

- **Perform compliance checks:** Use MDM tools to verify whether devices meet security policies.

- **Test access controls**: Simulate access from unmanaged devices to confirm restrictions are enforced.

- **Analyze logs and incidents:** Assess past security incidents related to user devices.

By auditing user device management, organizations can strengthen endpoint security, reduce cloud security risks, and ensure compliance with security frameworks.

Logging and monitoring

Logging and monitoring are critical components of cloud security and compliance, enabling organizations to detect, investigate, and respond to security incidents. Auditors should assess whether logging and monitoring mechanisms are effectively implemented, ensuring visibility into cloud activities and adherence to regulatory requirements. The key areas to focus on while auditing logging and monitoring on the cloud are mentioned here:

- **Logging policies and compliance requirements:** Auditors should assess if logging is properly implemented, managed, and retained to support security monitoring, incident response, and compliance with regulatory standards.

This can be assessed by looking at the following:

- o Review the organization's logging and monitoring policy to ensure it aligns with industry standards, e.g., NIST, ISO 27001, CIS, PCI-DSS.

- o Verify compliance with regulatory frameworks requiring log retention and audit trails, e.g., GDPR, HIPAA, **Sarbanes–Oxley Act (SOX).**

- o Ensure logs capture relevant events, including authentication attempts, administrative actions, access requests, and data modifications.

- **Centralized logging and log management:** This is to ensure that logs from various cloud services and systems are collected, stored, and managed in a centralized, secure, and efficient manner to support security operations and compliance. This can be done by assessing the following key aspects:

  - o Assess whether the organization uses a centralized logging solution, e.g., AWS CloudTrail, Azure Monitor, Google Cloud Logging, SIEM tools like Splunk, ELK Stack, or IBM QRadar.

  - o Verify that logs from multiple sources, e.g., servers, applications, databases, and network devices, are aggregated and correlated.

  - o Ensure log data is tamper-proof, securely stored, and protected from unauthorized modifications.

- **Log retention and storage:** Auditors should ensure that logs are securely stored and retained for appropriate durations to support security investigations, operational needs, and regulatory compliance.

  This can be done by evaluating the following key aspects:

  - o Check log retention policies to ensure they meet compliance requirements e.g., PCI-DSS requires at least one year of log storage.

  - o Review log encryption and access controls to prevent unauthorized access.

  - o Verify that logs are archived in a secure and scalable storage solution with defined retention periods.

- **Real-time monitoring and alerting mechanisms:** Auditors should assess if security events and anomalies are continuously monitored, and timely alerts are generated to enable rapid detection and response to threats.

  This can be done by reviewing the following key aspects:

  - o Evaluate the use of real-time monitoring tools, e.g., AWS GuardDuty, Azure Sentinel, Google Security Command Center.

  - o Ensure automated alerts are configured for critical security events, e.g., failed login attempts, privilege escalation, unauthorized access.

- o   Assess whether **Security Operations Center (SOC)** teams or IT administrators actively monitor alerts.

- **Incident detection and response:** The following key aspects must be assessed by auditors to ensure that the organization can quickly detect, analyze, and respond to security incidents in the cloud to minimize impact and maintain security and compliance:

  - o   Verify whether the organization has a **Security Incident and Event Management (SIEM)** solution to analyze logs for security threats.

  - o   Review incident response procedures and determine how security teams investigate and remediate issues.

  - o   Check if past security incidents were properly logged, reviewed, and mitigated in a timely manner.

- **Monitoring coverage and scope:** Auditors should evaluate if all critical cloud resources, services, and activities are appropriately monitored to detect security events, performance issues, and policy violations by reviewing the following aspects:

  - o   Confirm that all cloud services and resources, e.g., VMs, databases, API endpoints, are covered under the logging and monitoring strategy.

  - o   Ensure third-party integrations, e.g., SaaS applications, external APIs, are monitored for security events.

  - o   Assess whether **user behavior analytics (UBA)** is used to detect anomalies, e.g., unusual access patterns, data exfiltration attempts.

Auditors may adapt to the following approaches and best practices for achieving an effective audit of user logging and monitoring in the cloud:

- **Review policies and compliance standards**: Ensure the organization has documented policies for logging and monitoring.

- **Test log collection and retention**: Verify that logs are collected, stored, and retained according to regulatory requirements.

- **Assess alerting and response mechanisms**: Check if security teams act on alerts and investigate incidents in real time.

- **Perform log integrity checks**: Ensure logs are protected from unauthorized modification or deletion.

- **Analyze past security incidents**: Review previous log data for unresolved threats or weaknesses in monitoring controls.

By effectively auditing logging and monitoring, organizations can enhance their threat detection capabilities, improve compliance, and strengthen their cloud security posture.

Change management

Change management is a critical control area in cloud infrastructure auditing, ensuring that changes to cloud resources (such as configurations, applications, and security settings) are authorized, documented, tested, and monitored. Poor change management can lead to security vulnerabilities, service disruptions, or compliance failures.

Auditors should pay attention to the following key focus areas while auditing change management in the cloud:

- **Change management policies and procedures:** Auditors should evaluate the effectiveness of change management governance aspects by reviewing the following:
  - Review whether the organization has a formalized change management policy aligned with industry best practices, e.g., **Information Technology Infrastructure Library (ITIL),** NIST, ISO 27001.
  - Assess if the policy defines roles and responsibilities for approving and implementing changes.
  - Verify that emergency change procedures exist for urgent fixes and security patches.
- **Change request and approval process:** This is to ensure that all changes to systems, applications, or infrastructure are formally requested, reviewed, and approved before implementation to maintain control, accountability, and minimize risk.

  This can be achieved by reviewing the following:
  - Evaluate the change request workflow, ensuring changes require formal approval before implementation.
  - Verify that all changes go through a **Change Advisory Board (CAB)** or an equivalent review process.
  - Check if significant changes undergo risk assessment and business impact analysis.
- **Version control and audit trail:** Auditors should perform an assessment to make sure every change is tracked and traceable. Hence, organizations can understand what changed, when, and by whom, and undo it if needed, by reviewing the following:
  - Ensure that changes are tracked using version control systems, e.g., Git, AWS CodeCommit, Azure Repos.
  - Review audit logs to confirm that changes are properly documented, e.g., AWS CloudTrail, Azure Monitor, Google Cloud Logging.
  - Check whether logs include who made the change, what was changed, when it was changed, and why.

- **Testing and validation of changes:** Auditors should assess if all changes to systems, applications, and infrastructure are thoroughly tested and validated before deployment to prevent disruptions, vulnerabilities, or performance issues.

  They can do so by reviewing the following key aspects:

  o Verify that all major changes undergo testing in a staging environment before deployment.

  o Assess whether automated testing and configuration validation tools are used, e.g., Terraform, AWS Config, Azure Policy.

  o Ensure that rollback procedures exist to restore previous configurations if a change causes issues.

- **Deployment and release management:** This is to ensure that changes are deployed into production in a controlled, secure, and consistent manner, minimizing disruptions and aligning with organizational policies.

  Such compliance requirements can be assessed by reviewing the following:

  o Review whether the organization follows controlled deployment processes, such as CI/CD pipelines.

  o Check if infrastructure changes are automated using IaC tools like Terraform or CloudFormation.

  o Assess how hotfixes, patches, and new releases are rolled out to avoid disruptions.

- **Security and compliance considerations:** The auditors should make sure every change supports security and compliance, not undermines them.

  Keep systems safe and aligned with legal and policy requirements by assessing the following:

  o Verify that security-related changes, e.g., firewall rules, IAM policies, undergo additional scrutiny.

  o Ensure changes comply with regulatory standards, e.g., PCI-DSS, HIPAA, GDPR, SOC 2.

  o Assess if unauthorized or unexpected changes trigger real-time alerts for investigation.

- **Post-change monitoring and review:** Auditors should assess if the changes are evaluated after implementation to confirm they function as intended, do not introduce new issues, and align with operational, security, and compliance expectations.

  This can be achieved by evaluating the following:

  o Confirm whether organizations conduct post-implementation reviews to assess the impact of changes.

   o   Evaluate if there are automated monitoring tools, e.g., AWS Config, Azure Security Center, that detect unauthorized or misconfigured changes.

   o   Check whether security teams analyze change-related incidents for lessons learned.

The following approaches and best practices may be adapted by the auditors for conducting an effective audit of change management in the cloud:

- **Review change management policies:** Ensure proper governance exists.

- **Test the change approval process:** Verify if changes require authorization.

- **Analyze change logs:** Check audit trails for compliance and security risks.

- **Assess testing and validation controls:** Ensure changes are properly tested before deployment.

- **Verify security monitoring:** Confirm if unauthorized changes trigger alerts.

- **Evaluate incident response:** Review past incidents caused by poor change management.

By auditing change management, organizations can enhance cloud security, operational stability, and regulatory compliance while reducing risks from unauthorized or faulty changes.

Evaluating resilience and availability

Resilience and availability are critical factors in cloud computing, ensuring that services remain operational despite failures or disruptions. Here are some key concepts that the auditors should be well aware of prior to evaluating the resilience and availability of cloud infrastructure:

- **Resilience**: The ability of cloud systems to recover from failures and continue operations with minimal disruption.

- **Availability**: The percentage of time a cloud service remains accessible and operational as per SLAs.

- **Fault tolerance**: The capability of cloud environments to continue functioning even when components fail.

- **DR**: Strategies and mechanisms implemented to restore services after major incidents.

Auditor's role

Auditors play a key role in evaluating whether cloud infrastructure meets these requirements by assessing design, controls, and response mechanisms. Here are some of the key aspects:

- **Review of cloud service architecture:** Assess the design of the cloud infrastructure, including multi-region deployments and redundant components. Evaluate the use of load balancing, auto-scaling, and failover mechanisms.

- **Verification of service level agreements (SLAs):** Examine SLAs between cloud providers and customers for uptime guarantees. Validate historical availability metrics and compare them against SLA commitments. Review penalties and compensations for non-compliance with SLAs.

- **Assessment of high availability (HA) mechanisms:** Verify the presence of redundancy in key infrastructure components, e.g., storage, databases, and networks. Test failover capabilities through simulated disruptions. Check the implementation of real-time monitoring and alerting mechanisms.

- **Evaluation of backup and DR plans:** Confirm that backup procedures are regularly performed and tested. Assess RTO and **recovery point objectives** (RPO) compliance. Review DR testing frequency and effectiveness.

- **Examination of monitoring and incident response:** Evaluate the use of monitoring tools for proactive issue detection. Verify automated incident response mechanisms and escalation procedures. Assess documentation and reporting of past incidents and resolutions.

- **Compliance with industry standards:** Check adherence to frameworks like NIST SP 800-53, ISO 27001, and CSA CCM. Ensure compliance with regulatory requirements such as GDPR, HIPAA, or SOC 2.

Evaluating the resilience and availability of cloud infrastructure is a fundamental aspect of cloud auditing. Auditors must review architectures, SLAs, HA mechanisms, DR plans, monitoring tools, and compliance requirements to ensure that organizations can maintain continuous operations in the cloud. Effective audits not only validate current resilience but also highlight areas for improvement in cloud strategies.

Tools for auditing cloud infrastructure

With the increasing adoption of cloud computing, organizations must ensure their cloud environments are secure, compliant, and optimized. Auditing cloud infrastructure is essential for identifying security vulnerabilities, performance issues, and compliance risks. There are various tools available that help in auditing cloud infrastructure across different **cloud service providers (CSPs)** like AWS, Azure, and Google Cloud.

Some of the common tools for auditing cloud infrastructure are detailed in the following table:

Tool name	Provider/type	Purpose	Key features
AWS audit manager	AWS	Automates evidence collection for compliance (e.g., GDPR, HIPAA, ISO 27001)	Continuous compliance monitoring; Integration with AWS services; Automated assessment reports
Azure Security Center	Microsoft	Security posture management and compliance auditing	Security score, Compliance tracking, AI-driven threat protection
Google Cloud Security Command Center	Google	Centralized security & risk management	Identifies misconfigurations, threat detection, and compliance monitoring
Prisma Cloud	Palo Alto Networks (CSPM)	Multi-cloud security monitoring & compliance	Automated remediation; Compliance audits (PCI-DSS, GDPR, etc.)
Dome9	Check Point (CSPM)	Cloud security & access auditing	Identity & access auditing; Misconfiguration detection; Threat intelligence
Lacework	Lacework (CSPM)	Cloud workload protection & anomaly detection	Behavioral anomaly detection; Real-time insights, Automated compliance
Cloud custodian	Open-source	Policy-driven cloud governance & automation	Multi-cloud support, Automated security audits, Custom policies
Scout suite	Open-source	Multi-cloud auditing tool	Detects security misconfigurations; Generates audit reports
Prowler	Open-source	AWS security and compliance auditing	CIS benchmark checks; CLI-based integration, Lightweight and fast
Microsoft Defender for Cloud Apps	Microsoft (CASB)	Cloud access security & policy enforcement	Monitors cloud service usage; Risk analytics
McAfee MVISION Cloud	McAfee (CASB)	Cloud threat protection	DLP; Compliance enforcement
Netskope	Netskope (CASB)	Cloud visibility and control	Real-time monitoring; Risk scoring; Policy enforcement
AWS trusted advisor / Azure advisor	AWS / Microsoft	Cloud resilience, availability, and best practices	Configuration evaluation; Fault tolerance checks
Cloud monitoring tools - *Prometheus/ Datadog/ AWS CloudWatch*	Open-source/ Datadog/ AWS	Real-time monitoring and metrics	Alerting, performance tracking, Log visibility
Gremlin	Chaos engineering tool	Tests fault tolerance and resilience	Controlled failure injection; Outage simulation; Recovery testing

Table 9.1: Common tools for auditing cloud infrastructure

Auditing cloud infrastructure is a critical practice for security and compliance. Organizations can choose from cloud-native tools, third-party CSPM solutions, or open-source alternatives based on their needs. Regular audits help detect misconfigurations, enforce security policies, and ensure regulatory compliance, ultimately strengthening the overall cloud security posture.

Common audit observations

Here are some of the common cloud infrastructure vulnerabilities and findings that are frequently observed during audits:

- **Misconfigured access controls:** This can allow unauthorized access to sensitive data or systems, e.g., overly permissive IAM roles, lack of MFA.

- **Inadequate identity and authentication mechanisms**: This increases the risk of account compromise, e.g., shared user accounts, Weak password policies, and no MFA for admin accounts.

- **Lack of proper encryption:** This might result in sensitive data being exposed to unauthorized parties, e.g., data at rest not encrypted and data in transit not protected.

- **Poor configuration management:** Resulting in an increase in the risk of exploitation due to known flaws, e.g., default settings left unchanged, outdated software, or unpatched vulnerabilities.

- **Lack of network segmentation:** Making lateral movement easier for attackers e.g. all resources in a single flat network, no firewall rules or access control lists.

- **Poor backup and disaster recovery planning:** Increasing the impact of system failure or data loss, e.g., backups not performed regularly, no tested recovery procedures.

During a cloud infrastructure audit, auditors should ensure that these areas are thoroughly reviewed and tested, and a comprehensive review across security, compliance, and operational resilience is conducted during the audit process.

Conclusion

This chapter discussed how auditing cloud infrastructure is essential for maintaining security, compliance, and operational efficiency. By leveraging best practices, implementing strong security controls, and using auditing tools, organizations can mitigate risks and ensure their cloud environments remain resilient and secure. Regular audits, continuous monitoring, and proactive threat assessments are key to maintaining a robust cloud security posture.

The upcoming chapter will discuss auditing cloud security controls, focusing on IAM, encryption, and network security. It covers the tools and methodologies used to evaluate security in cloud environments.

Points to remember

- Understanding common risks to cloud infrastructure is essential for auditors to deliver effective, relevant, and value-driven audits.

- IAM practices must be assessed to confirm that access is restricted based on the principle of least privilege, with RBAC and MFA in place.

- Security configurations of cloud resources should be evaluated to ensure that public access is restricted, unnecessary ports are closed, and encryption is applied to data in transit and at rest.

- Change and configuration management processes must be verified to ensure changes are tracked, approved, and implemented through structured workflows, preferably using IAC and version control.

- Auditors should confirm that logging, monitoring, and alerting are in place, with centralized log collection, active monitoring, and alerts for unauthorized or suspicious activities.

- Data protection and privacy controls must be reviewed to ensure sensitive data is encrypted, classified appropriately, and handled in compliance with legal and regulatory requirements, including data residency obligations.

- The security posture of third-party integrations should be reviewed to ensure vendors are properly vetted, and secure communication channels and access restrictions are enforced.

- Disaster recovery and business continuity capabilities should be assessed to ensure that backup and recovery strategies are tested, effective, and aligned with defined RTOs and RPOs.

- Compliance with regulatory frameworks and industry standards must be verified, with controls mapped to standards such as ISO 27001, NIST 800-53, SOC 2, PCI-DSS, HIPAA, or GDPR, as applicable.

- The use of native cloud security tools should be confirmed, ensuring that platforms like AWS Security Hub, Azure Defender, and GCP Security Command Center are utilized to enhance visibility and compliance.

- A complete and up-to-date cloud asset inventory should be maintained to ensure that all deployed resources are accounted for and that unauthorized or shadow IT resources are detected and addressed.

- Auditors should engage with cloud stakeholders, including but not limited to security, compliance, and infrastructure teams, to validate implementation of controls and awareness of policies.

- Finally, auditors should be aware of common audit observations to ensure prioritizing high-risk areas and ensure that critical vulnerabilities are not overlooked.

Multiple Choice Questions

1. **What is the core purpose of using virtualization in cloud computing?**
   a. To use portable containers to run applications consistently across environments
   b. To allow multiple operating systems to share a single physical machine, improving resource utilization
   c. To allow multiple users or organizations to share the same cloud resources
   d. To achieve security through various tools to help secure and optimize cloud resources

2. **Auditors can review network architecture and design to verify all the following, except which one?**
   a. To assess whether the cloud network follows industry best practices
   b. To verify the segmentation of environments
   c. To review the use of VPC, subnets, and network isolation techniques
   d. To ensure that network access is restricted using RBAC

3. **Why is it important for auditors to assess whether system configurations are properly managed?**
   a. To ensure software updates are released on time
   b. To reduce system performance for better control
   c. To identify potential security vulnerabilities and misconfigurations
   d. To improve system speed by reducing unnecessary services

4. **When auditing user device management in a cloud environment, which of the following should auditors primarily assess?**
   a. The brand and model of user devices
   b. Verify if the devices accessing cloud resources comply with security standards
   c. The operating system version installed on all user devices
   d. Assess how frequently users charge their devices

5. **Which of the following best describes the ability of cloud systems to recover from failures and continue operations with minimal disruption?**
   a. Fault-tolerance
   b. Resilience
   c. Auto-scaling
   d. Load balancing

Answers

1	b
2	d
3	c
4	b
5	b

Join our Discord space

Join our Discord workspace for latest updates, offers, tech happenings around the world, new releases, and sessions with the authors:

https://discord.bpbonline.com

CHAPTER 10
Auditing Cloud Security

Introduction

In today's digital landscape, cloud computing has firmly established itself as a core component of information technology infrastructure for organizations around the globe. No longer a cutting-edge innovation, it is now a strategic necessity. The benefits of scalability, flexibility, cost-effectiveness, and accelerated innovation have fuelled widespread migration to cloud platforms such as AWS, Azure, and Google Cloud. However, this transition introduces a distinct set of security challenges and complexities.

Simply adopting cloud services does not inherently ensure security. While **cloud service providers** (**CSPs**) are responsible for securing the underlying infrastructure (i.e., security *of* the cloud), customers remain accountable for security *in* the cloud, such as securing the data, access controls, etc.

Cloud security audits differ significantly from traditional on-premises audits due to the dynamic, automated, and abstract nature of cloud environments. Auditors must possess specialized expertise in cloud platforms and the shared responsibility model. Rather than relying on physical inspections, they often depend on configuration analysis, **application programming interface** (**API**) integrations, and automated assessment tools.

Auditing cloud security is a vital function for any organization leveraging cloud services. It offers crucial visibility into an organization's security posture, ensures compliance, builds stakeholder confidence, and helps protect sensitive data in an increasingly complex cloud ecosystem. Ensuring the confidentiality, integrity, and availability of cloud-based data and services depends on effective and continuous security auditing.

This chapter provides a hands-on guide to auditing cloud security controls, with a focus on data protection, **identity and access management (IAM)**, vulnerability management, **incident response (IR)**, and evaluating the security posture of CSPs. It outlines the tools, techniques, and best practices necessary for thorough and effective audits in cloud environments.

Structure

This chapter covers the following topics:

- Cloud security basics and key risks
- Auditing cloud security
- Assessing CSP's security posture
- Tools and techniques
- Common audit observations

Objectives

By the end of this chapter, readers will have a comprehensive grasp of auditing cloud security controls, with an emphasis on securing data, managing identities and access, vulnerability management, responding to incidents, and evaluating the security posture of CSPs, as well as tools, techniques, and industry best practices essential for conducting rigorous and effective audits within dynamic cloud infrastructures.

Cloud security basics and key risks

Before exploring the specific methods used in auditing cloud security, it is crucial to first understand the broader context, namely, the common risks associated with cloud environments and the foundational controls designed to mitigate them. An auditor's core responsibility is to assess how effectively these controls address relevant threats. A solid grasp of this foundation is essential for any meaningful audit.

This foundation must be viewed through the lens of the shared responsibility model (explained in *Chapter 3, Challenges in Cloud Auditing*). In this model, the CSP is responsible for securing the underlying infrastructure, while the customer is accountable for securing their own data, configurations, applications, and access controls within that infrastructure. Most cloud security failures, and therefore the primary focus of audits, occur on the customer's side of this model.

Conducting a thorough cloud security audit requires deep knowledge of key domains where risks frequently arise and where controls must be carefully assessed. While the cloud introduces a wide array of challenges, auditing cloud security typically focuses on five core areas as depicted in the following table:

Domain	Core concept	Key risks
Data security	Protecting the confidentiality, integrity, and availability of data throughout its lifecycle.	Data leaks from misconfigured storage Unauthorized access or tampering Inadequate backups Non-compliance with data laws Insecure data transfers
Application security	Securing cloud-based applications from design through deployment to prevent exploitation of software vulnerabilities.	Insecure coding practices Lack of input validation Exposure of sensitive data via APIs Inadequate security testing Hardcoded secrets in codebases
IAM	Ensuring only authorized entities have appropriate access, following the principle of least privilege.	Compromised credentials Privilege escalation Weak authentication Orphaned accounts Poor API key management
Vulnerability management	Identifying and addressing weaknesses in cloud assets like VMs, containers, and code.	Unpatched CVEs Misconfigurations Delayed vulnerability remediation
IR	Detecting, containing, and recovering from cloud security incidents effectively.	Missed detections Inadequate response plans Poor logging Downtime Legal non-compliance
CSP's security posture	Evaluating the CSP's built-in security capabilities and understanding the shared responsibility boundary.	Misunderstood responsibility splits Over-reliance on CSP Lack of transparency CSP outages or vulnerabilities

Table 10.1: Core areas of cloud security audit

Cloud security audit covering the key security domains is depicted in *Table 10.1*.

Refer to the following figure:

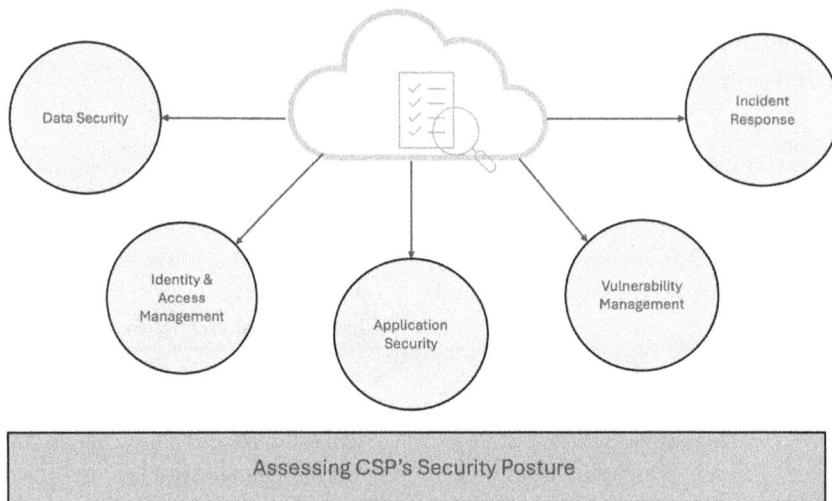

Figure 10.1: Cloud security audit

A comprehensive cloud security audit depends on systematically reviewing these five pillars. Auditors must collect evidence to confirm that the customer has implemented robust security controls within their areas of responsibility and that they are effectively utilizing and evaluating the security capabilities of their chosen CSP. This structured approach provides crucial insights into the organization's overall ability to manage cloud risk.

Auditing cloud security

Let us now examine the auditing considerations for each of the five pillars discussed in the previous section, organized by domain for greater clarity and depth.

Data security

Auditing data security in the cloud is a critical component of modern risk management. As organizations increasingly rely on cloud services to store, process, and share sensitive data, the need for a comprehensive, well-structured data security audit has become paramount. These audits assess the policies, controls, technologies, and operational practices that ensure the **confidentiality, integrity, and availability (CIA)** of cloud-hosted data, while also verifying compliance with internal standards and external regulations.

Cloud environments introduce dynamic, distributed, and often complex infrastructures. As a result, auditing must go beyond traditional perimeter-based reviews and adopt a holistic, risk-based approach that addresses cloud-specific challenges and technologies, including **information rights management (IRM)**, which plays a key role in protecting data *after* it leaves the immediate cloud environment.

Defining scope of data security audit

Establishing a clear audit scope ensures focus and alignment with business objectives, legal obligations, and technological realities, and the scope should cover the following aspects:

- **Service and deployment models**:
  - o Define organizational responsibilities under the shared responsibility model.
  - o Understand architectural differences and audit implications across environments.
- **Key scope considerations**:
  - o **Data sensitivity and classification: Personally Identifiable Information (PII)**, financial, proprietary, and regulated data.
  - o **Geographic data location**: Data residency, cross-border flows, and jurisdictional constraints.
  - o **Compliance requirements**: National and International regulatory requirements and industry-specific mandates.

Core audit areas and key checkpoints

A thorough data security audit should examine key areas as detailed in the following table:

Audit area	Audit objective	Auditor checkpoints
Data classification and discovery	Ensure sensitive data is identified, categorized, and appropriately handled.	Is there a formal, enforced data classification policy? Are automated tools used for data discovery and classification? Is data tagged/labelled based on sensitivity? Are classifications reviewed and updated regularly?
Data encryption	Protect data confidentiality and integrity in transit, at rest, and potentially in use.	Is data encrypted at rest across all cloud storage and databases? Are strong protocols (e.g., TLS/SSL) used for data in transit? Are encryption keys securely generated, stored, rotated, and revoked? Is key access monitored and restricted? Is the choice between client-side/server-side encryption documented and appropriate?
Data loss prevention (DLP)	Prevent unauthorized data leakage or exfiltration.	Are DLP solutions implemented across cloud environments? Are policies configured to detect/prevent unauthorized data transfers? Is user activity monitored for data misuse? Are DLP measures extended to endpoints accessing cloud data?

Audit area	Audit objective	Auditor checkpoints
IRM	Control how data is used, shared, and accessed especially post-distribution.	Is IRM applied to sensitive data within collaboration tools? Do IRM policies reflect data sensitivity and usage constraints? Can access to documents be revoked after sharing? Are audit logs available to track document usage and violations? Are users trained on how to use IRM-protected content?
Data backup and recovery	Ensure business continuity and resilience through reliable backup and recovery.	Are backup schedules defined and executed for all cloud assets? Are backups encrypted and geo-redundant? Are data recovery procedures documented and tested? Are **recovery time objective (RTO)** and **recovery point objective (RPO)** targets clearly defined and consistently met?
Data retention and disposal	Ensure compliance with legal / regulatory requirements and minimize data exposure.	Are retention schedules automated and enforced? Are deletion processes secure (e.g., cryptographic wiping)? Are regulatory deletion requests fulfilled reliably? Is there an audit trail for deleted data and decommissioned assets?
Data residency and sovereignty	Comply with geographic-specific data handling laws and contractual obligations.	Are data residency laws identified and documented? Are data storage regions configured to comply with these laws? Are CSP commitments to data residency defined in the contractual agreement? Are tools in place to verify actual data locations?
Logging, monitoring, and alerting	Enable timely detection and response to unauthorized access or anomalies.	Are logs collected for data access, system changes, and user activity? Are logs centralized in a SIEM or cloud-native logging tool? Are alerts configured for unauthorized or unusual behavior? Are logs retained securely and reviewed regularly?
Configuration management	Prevent misconfigurations, which are leading causes of cloud data breaches.	Are secure templates or baselines used for deploying cloud resources? Are misconfigurations and vulnerabilities scanned periodically? Is there a change control process for configuration updates? Are **cloud security posture management (CSPM)** tools deployed and monitored for ongoing posture management?
Third-party and vendor management	Validate the security posture and accountability of CSPs.	Are CSP certifications (e.g., SOC 2, ISO 27001) reviewed regularly? Is the shared responsibility model clearly understood and mapped? Do contracts contain SLAs, data protection clauses, and right-to-audit provisions? Are third-party risk assessments conducted periodically?

Table 10.2: Data security audit checklist

Cloud-specific challenges and considerations

Auditing data security in the cloud presents unique challenges as follows:

- **Shared responsibility model:** Clearly understanding and auditing controls within the organization's responsibility vs. the CSP's is crucial. Auditors need to verify that the organization is fulfilling its part and that the CSP meets its obligations (often verified via CSP attestations).

- **Lack of physical access:** Auditors typically cannot physically inspect the CSP's data centers. Reliance is placed on CSP reports, certifications, and virtual audit capabilities.

- **Dynamic and ephemeral resources:** Cloud resources can be spun up and down quickly. Audits need to adapt to this dynamic nature, possibly using continuous auditing techniques.

- **Multi-tenancy:** In public clouds, resources are shared. The audit must ensure that logical isolation controls are effective in protecting data from other tenants.

- **Complexity of cloud services:** CSPs offer a vast array of services, each with its own security configurations and considerations. Auditors need specialized knowledge.

- **API security:** APIs are fundamental to cloud services. Auditing API security (authentication, authorization, rate limiting, input validation) is critical.

- **Vendor lock-in and integration:** Dependence on specific CSP tools and services can create lock-in. Audits should consider the security implications of these dependencies and integrations.

Auditing data security in the cloud is an ongoing and evolving discipline. It requires a deep understanding of cloud technologies, security best practices, and the specific risks associated with an organization's cloud deployments. By adopting a structured audit approach, focusing on key control areas, and leveraging appropriate tools, organizations can gain valuable insights into their cloud data security posture, identify areas for improvement, and ultimately enhance the protection of their critical data assets in the cloud. Regular audits, combined with continuous monitoring and a proactive security culture, are vital for navigating the complexities of cloud security and maintaining trust in the digital age.

Application security

In cloud environments, **application security** (**AppSec**) is a critical component of an organization's security posture. With the increasing use of cloud-native applications, containers, microservices, and APIs, the attack surface has significantly expanded. Cloud application security must go beyond traditional perimeter defenses to address dynamic deployments, shared responsibility models, DevOps practices, and third-party integrations.

A cloud security audit must thoroughly evaluate the security controls and practices implemented at each stage of the **software development lifecycle** (**SDLC**), starting from design, code development, and testing to deployment and ongoing monitoring. The goal is to ensure applications are secure by design, resilient to threats, and compliant with regulatory requirements.

The following table provides a detailed checklist for auditing application security in cloud environments as part of the cloud security audit process:

Audit area	Key focus areas	Auditor verification objectives
Secure SDLC integration	Secure coding practices Threat modelling Security checkpoints in CI/CD Developer training and awareness	Confirm security is integrated into all SDLC phases Review developer training and secure code practices Assess threat modeling and code review coverage Verify use of CI/CD security gates
Code and dependency security	Static and dynamic analysis (SAST/DAST) **Software composition analysis (SCA)** Use of trusted libraries and registries	Verify regular use of SAST, DAST, and SCA tools Ensure third-party components are scanned and managed Check for known vulnerabilities (CVEs) in libraries
API security	API authentication and authorization Input validation and rate limiting API gateways and monitoring OWASP API Top 10 awareness	Evaluate access control on APIs (OAuth, JWT, etc.) Confirm input validation and protection against injection Check use of API gateways and throttling Review documentation and security testing of APIs
Cloud-native and serverless security	Securing serverless functions (e.g., AWS Lambda) Container hardening and image scanning Service mesh policies Ephemeral resource protection	Review serverless function configurations (least privilege, timeout, logging) Validate container image provenance and scanning Check service mesh or sidecar proxy security enforcement Assess controls for auto-scaling and short-lived resources
Identity and access controls	IAM roles used by applications Role-based and attribute-based access control (RBAC/ABAC) Secrets and key management practices	Verify IAM roles follow the principle of least privilege Audit RBAC/ABAC implementations at the app level Ensure secrets are stored securely (e.g., AWS Secrets Manager)

Audit area	Key focus areas	Auditor verification objectives
Vulnerability and patch management	Timely patching of app components Auto-updates in containers Vulnerability disclosure process	Check vulnerability tracking and remediation SLAs Verify automated patching or rebuilds in containers Review bug bounty or coordinated disclosure mechanisms
Application configuration and secrets management	Secure configuration practices Use of environment variables and config files Key rotation and encryption in transit/at rest	Validate configurations for misconfigurations or defaults Detect hardcoded credentials or secrets in code repos Ensure encryption and key lifecycle management is enforced
Web and mobile application security	OWASP Top 10 testing (XSS, SQLi, CSRF, etc.) Session management Secure cookies, headers, CORS policies	Review pen testing results and security scans Check cookie flags (Secure, HttpOnly, SameSite) Validate session handling and logout mechanisms
Logging, monitoring, and incident detection	App-level logging (e.g., user actions, errors) Integration with SIEM tools- Alerts for abnormal behavior Forensic readiness	Confirm centralized logging of security-relevant events Evaluate log integrity and retention policies Ensure alerts trigger appropriate IR workflows
Third-party and open-source risk management	Use of SaaS/PaaS components Dependency tracking Licensing and code provenance	Identify all third-party components in the software stack Ensure legal and security reviews are performed Review risk assessments for third-party integrations
Compliance and regulatory alignment	PCI DSS, HIPAA, GDPR, SOC 2, etc. Data residency and handling App-level audit trails	Confirm compliance-related controls in applications Verify audit trails for data access and transactions Ensure applications meet industry-specific regulatory needs
Testing, reviews, and continuous improvement	Regular code audits and pen testing Red team/blue team exercises DevSecOps maturity assessments	Validate frequency and scope of testing efforts Review findings from red/blue team simulations Assess maturity of DevSecOps and continuous feedback loops

Table 10.3: Application security audit checklist

Auditing application security in the cloud is a critical and dynamic process that must adapt to the evolving nature of modern development practices and cloud-native architectures. It requires a comprehensive understanding of cloud platforms, secure SDLC, and the unique threats posed by APIs, serverless functions, containers, and continuous deployment pipelines. A structured audit approach, grounded in industry standards and tailored to cloud environments, enables organizations to systematically evaluate application-layer controls, identify security weaknesses, and ensure adherence to secure coding, access control, and vulnerability management best practices. By integrating regular audits with automated testing, developer training, and real-time monitoring, organizations can not only reduce application-level risk but also foster a culture of security within their DevOps processes. In today's cloud-driven world, maintaining resilient and trustworthy applications depends on this continuous, proactive auditing of application security.

Identity and access management

IAM is a framework of policies, processes, and technologies that enables the right users to access the right resources at the right times for the right reasons. In cloud environments, IAM is the cornerstone of security, controlling who (identities) can do what (permissions) on which resources. A misconfigured IAM can lead to unauthorized access, data breaches, compliance violations, and significant financial and reputational damage. Therefore, regularly auditing IAM is not just a best practice but a critical necessity for maintaining a robust cloud security posture.

The key areas of auditing IAM along with the objectives and auditor checkpoints are illustrated in the following table:

Audit area	Audit objective	Auditor checkpoints
User accounts and identities	Ensure user identities are well-managed, secure, and aligned with access policies.	Evaluate onboarding/ offboarding procedures. Identify stale, orphaned, dormant or inactive accounts. Review usage of shared accounts; ensure accountability. Validate time-bound access for external/guest users. Check adherence to naming conventions.
Roles and permissions	Verify that access rights are strictly based on job functions and follow the principle of least privilege.	Audit roles for excessive or broad permissions. Assess use and justification of custom vs. predefined roles. Match role assignments to job responsibilities. Detect privilege creep across users. Validate use of permission boundaries (AWS-specific). Evaluate implementation of RBAC and its alignment with job functions.
IAM policies	Ensure policies are secure, specific, and minimize the risk of over-permissions.	Review for wildcard permissions (*:*). Check use of conditions (IP, MFA, time). Audit resource-based policies for unintended access. Review policy lifecycle management and version control. Assess the use of ABAC and verify correct attribute conditions and mappings.

Audit area	Audit objective	Auditor checkpoints
Groups	Simplify access control and minimize errors by using group-based access assignments.	Confirm access is managed primarily through groups. Audit group memberships for sensitive roles. Ensure group names are clear and purposes documented.
Multi-factor authentication (MFA)	Strengthen user authentication to reduce the risk of account compromise.	Check if MFA is enforced for all users, especially admins. Review the strength and type of MFA methods in use. Assess recovery procedures for lost MFA access.
Access keys and credentials	Ensure secure handling of programmatic credentials and access secrets.	Verify regular access key rotation. Identify and remove unused keys. Detect hardcoded credentials in code/configs. Evaluate password policy strength and enforcement.
Service accounts and roles	Restrict non-human identities to the minimal required permissions and secure their credentials.	Enforce least privilege on service accounts/principals. Review management of service credentials (IAM roles, managed identities). Periodically validate the necessity and permissions of each service account.
Federated access and 3rd-party integrations	Safeguard integrations with external identity providers and vendors.	Review configuration and trust relationships with identity providers. Validate attribute mappings and session controls. Audit permissions granted to third-party applications.
Logging and monitoring	Maintain visibility into IAM activity and detect unauthorized actions.	Ensure IAM actions are logged via CloudTrail, Activity Log, etc. Confirm log integrity and retention policy. Review alerting for suspicious behavior (root login, failed logins, etc.). Check that IAM logs are actively reviewed.
Separation of duties (SoD)	Prevent concentration of power that could lead to fraud or abuse.	Detect users with conflicting roles or excessive permissions. Verify role design supports SoD principles. Review SoD controls across critical workflows.
Privileged access management (PAM)	Secure and monitor use of highly privileged accounts.	Audit PAM solutions for configuration and enforcement. Verify limited and controlled use of root/admin accounts. Assess break-glass emergency access procedures.

Table 10.4: IAM audit checklist

When a **Cloud Access Security Broker** (**CASB**) is implemented, IAM audits extend beyond just reviewing native cloud controls. CASBs act as intermediaries between users and cloud services, providing visibility, governance, and data security. An IAM audit in this context must evaluate how identity and access controls are extended, enforced, or overridden through the CASB.

Key aspects of IAM audit with CASB in place are illustrated in the following table:

Key aspects	Audit focus
Identity federation and SSO integration	Ensure CASB integrates correctly with enterprise identity providers (e.g., SAML, OAuth). Verify user identities and session attributes are properly passed through to cloud services.
Access policy enforcement	Review policies defined in the CASB for user access based on context (e.g., device posture, geolocation, role). Validate the enforcement of least privilege and time-limited access.
Shadow IT detection	Examine how CASB identifies unauthorized or unsanctioned cloud applications. Confirm actions are taken to block or limit risky access.
Privileged access control	Validate how CASB monitors and restricts privileged access to SaaS and IaaS resources, including admin actions.
Activity monitoring and anomaly detection	Ensure CASB logs user activities across sanctioned and unsanctioned apps. Audit alerts triggered for anomalous IAM behaviour (e.g., impossible travel, mass downloads).
Data access control	Confirm that the CASB applies data-centric IAM controls, such as restricting downloads or sharing based on user role or content sensitivity.
API and admin console security	Audit how the CASB governs access to APIs and management consoles for third-party services.
Multi-cloud IAM harmonization	Verify consistent identity and access policies across multiple cloud platforms (e.g., AWS, Azure, GCP) as enforced by CASB.
Integration with native IAM tools	Check whether the CASB complements or conflicts with existing IAM solutions (e.g., IAM policies, RBAC). Ensure there is no policy overlap or contradiction.

Table 10.5: Key audit aspects of CASB in IAM

In short, IAM audits in CASB-enabled environments must ensure that CASB policies enhance and do not bypass cloud-native IAM controls, and that they offer visibility and enforcement over both sanctioned and unsanctioned cloud activity.

Auditing IAM is a fundamental and ongoing activity in securing cloud environments. It requires a meticulous approach, a deep understanding of the cloud provider's IAM services, and a commitment to the principle of least privilege. By regularly performing comprehensive IAM audits, organizations can significantly reduce their risk of security breaches, ensure compliance, and maintain a strong defense against evolving cyber threats.

Vulnerability management

Effective vulnerability management is an indispensable pillar of robust cloud security. As organizations accelerate their migration of workloads and data to the cloud, a meticulous audit of vulnerability management processes is paramount for proactive risk mitigation, maintaining a strong security posture, and ensuring compliance. An audit in this domain scrutinizes the entire lifecycle of identifying, assessing, remediating, and reporting on security weaknesses within the cloud environment. This is not merely a static check but a continuous, dynamic process vital for protecting sensitive assets.

Here is a breakdown of key aspects to consider when auditing vulnerability management in the cloud:

- Scope definition, asset inventory, and responsibility model: The audit's scope must be meticulously defined, encompassing all cloud assets across **Infrastructure as a Service (IaaS)**, **Platform as a Service (PaaS)**, and **Software as a Service (SaaS)** models. This includes **virtual machines (VMs)**, storage instances, databases, network components, applications, APIs, containerized environments, serverless functions, and associated code repositories and CI/CD pipelines.

A foundational step is verifying the completeness and accuracy of the cloud asset inventory. Auditors must ensure all resources, including dynamic and ephemeral ones, are identified and tracked. Without this, vulnerability management efforts will inherently possess blind spots.

Crucially, the audit must establish a clear understanding of the shared responsibility model with the CSP(s). This delineates where the CSP's responsibility for vulnerability management ends and the customers' begin. This understanding will heavily influence the audit approach, especially for PaaS and SaaS.

- **Vulnerability identification processes**: The auditors should evaluate the following aspects of the vulnerability identification processes:

  - **Scanning tools and techniques:** Evaluate the array of tools and techniques for vulnerability scanning:

  - **Network-based scanners:** For open ports, network service misconfigurations, and known vulnerabilities.

  - **Host-based agents:** For in-depth inspection of VMs and container images.

  - **Application security testing (AST) tools: Static AST (SAST), Dynamic AST (DAST), Interactive AST (IAST)**, and SCA for custom code and third-party libraries.

  - **CSPM tools:** For detecting cloud service misconfigurations and ensuring compliance.

  - **Container image scanning:** Integrated into CI/CD pipelines and registries.

o **Infrastructure as Code (IaC) scanning:** To identify vulnerabilities in code that defines infrastructure.

o **Scan frequency and coverage:** Assess the regularity (e.g., continuous, daily, weekly, upon deployment) and comprehensiveness of scans across all scoped assets.

o **Authenticated vs. unauthenticated scans:** Verify appropriate use. Authenticated scans offer deeper insights, while unauthenticated scans simulate an external attacker.

o **Threat intelligence integration:** Determine if vulnerability identification is enriched with up-to-date threat intelligence to prioritize actively exploited vulnerabilities.

- **Penetration testing**: While vulnerability scanning is crucial for breadth, penetration testing provides depth by simulating real-world attack scenarios. Auditors should examine:

   o **Scope and objectives:** Are penetration tests regularly conducted? Is the scope clearly defined (e.g., specific applications, cloud environments, network segments) and aligned with business risks? Are tests objective-based (e.g., attempt to access specific data, compromise a system)?

   o **Methodology and rules of engagement**: Is a recognized methodology followed (e.g., PTES, OWASP)? Are the rules of engagement clearly established with the CSP (if required) and internal teams?

   o **Tester qualifications**: Are tests performed by qualified and certified professionals (internal or third-party) with experience in cloud environments?

   o **Frequency:** Is the frequency of penetration tests adequate, considering the organization's risk profile, compliance requirements, and major changes to the environment?

   o **Findings management and remediation**: How are penetration testing findings integrated into the overall vulnerability management lifecycle? Is there a process for prioritizing and remediating findings, followed by re-testing to validate fixes?

- **Vulnerability assessment and prioritization**: Auditors are expected to perform a comprehensive examination of the processes and activities associated with vulnerability prioritization, as detailed as follows:

   o **Risk-based prioritization:** Audit the methodology for prioritizing vulnerabilities. This should be risk-based, considering:

      ▪ CVSS scores (as one factor among many).

      ▪ Exploitability (known exploits, ease of exploitation).

- Potential business impact (data breach, service disruption, financial loss, reputational damage).

- Asset criticality and data sensitivity.

- Effectiveness of compensating controls.

  o **Contextualization:** Ensure findings are contextualized within the specific cloud environment, business processes, and the shared responsibility model.

  o **False positive management:** Review the process for identifying, validating, and managing false positives to prevent wasted remediation efforts.

- **Remediation and patch management**: While remediation focuses on identifying and addressing security vulnerabilities, effective patch management is essential to ensure that known software flaws are systematically corrected in a timely manner. Inadequate patch management can leave systems exposed to exploits, even after vulnerabilities have been identified, thereby undermining the overall effectiveness of the remediation process. Auditors are expected to conduct a comprehensive assessment of the processes and activities related to remediation and patch management, as detailed here:

  o **Defined service level agreements (SLAs):** Verify clearly defined and consistently met SLAs for remediating vulnerabilities based on severity.

  o **Patch management process:** Evaluate the effectiveness of patch management for OS, applications, and applicable cloud services (where customer-managed). This includes patch testing and rollback plans.

  o **Configuration management:** Assess how misconfigurations (a primary source of cloud breaches) are identified, remediated, and prevented, leveraging IaC best practices and CSPM tools.

  o **Remediation tracking and verification:** Audit the system for tracking remediation and verifying the effectiveness of fixes.

  o **Automated remediation:** Inquire about the use of automation for routine remediation tasks to improve response times.

- **Auditing CSP-managed vulnerability management**: In many PaaS and SaaS models, the CSP is responsible for vulnerability management of the underlying platform. If an organization is *not allowed* to perform its own vulnerability scanning or patching on these CSP-managed layers, the auditor's focus shifts to due diligence and oversight:

  o **Verification of CSP responsibilities:** Scrutinize contracts, SLAs, and official documentation from the CSP that detail their vulnerability management program. This includes their scanning frequency, patching policies, tools used, and commitments to security standards.

  o **Right to audit and third-party reports:** Determine if the customer has the right to audit the CSP's controls or, more commonly, can obtain and review the CSP's third-party audit reports (e.g., SOC 2 Type 2, ISO 27001, CSA STAR Attestation). The auditor should assess the scope and relevance of these reports to the services consumed.

o **Vulnerability disclosure:** How does the CSP inform customers about vulnerabilities affecting the services they use, especially those requiring customer action (e.g., configuration changes, updates to client-side software)?

o **Remediation transparency:** Does the CSP provide adequate transparency into their remediation timelines and status for platform-level vulnerabilities?

o **Configuration audits:** Even with CSP-managed platforms, customers are typically responsible for securely configuring the services, managing identity and access, and securing data. The audit must cover these customer-controlled aspects. For example, auditing user access controls, network configurations (security groups, firewalls if applicable at PaaS level), and application-level settings in SaaS.

o **Data security practices:** Assess the organization's practices for securing their data within the CSP-managed environment (e.g., encryption, access controls).

o **API security:** Scrutinize the security of APIs used to interact with or build upon PaaS/SaaS offerings.

o **IR coordination:** Evaluate the processes for coordinating IR with the CSP in the event of a security breach originating from a vulnerability in the CSP-managed layer. Are communication channels and responsibilities clear?

o **Monitoring and logging:** Assess what logs and monitoring capabilities the CSP provides to the customer and how the customer utilizes these for their own security monitoring and detection of anomalous activities that might indicate exploited vulnerabilities.

- **Reporting and documentation**: Accurate and comprehensive reporting, along with well-maintained documentation, is essential for ensuring transparency, accountability, and traceability of security-related activities. Auditors are expected to conduct a thorough evaluation of the reporting and documentation practices associated with the organization's security processes, as outlined:

o **Clear and actionable reporting:** Review internal vulnerability reports for clarity, conciseness, and actionable remediation guidance.

o **Metrics and key performance indicators (KPIs):** Assess metrics like time-to-detect, time-to-remediate, scan coverage, open critical vulnerabilities, and repeat findings.

o **Documentation:** Ensure comprehensive and updated documentation of policies, procedures, tool configurations, and shared responsibility agreements.

- **Roles and responsibilities**: Auditors are expected to perform a detailed assessment of the defined roles and responsibilities within the organization's security framework, as described:

  o **Clearly defined internal roles:** Verify clear roles and responsibilities for any customer-managed vulnerability management tasks, as well as for overseeing CSP-provided services.

  o **Training and awareness:** Assess security training for personnel regarding their roles, especially in understanding the shared responsibility model.

- **Continuous improvement and monitoring**: Continuous improvement and monitoring together help maintain a proactive security posture, reduce risk, and support compliance with evolving industry standards and threat landscapes, as described:

  o **Program review:** The vulnerability management program (including oversight of CSPs) should be regularly reviewed and updated.

  o **Integration with IR:** Ensure tight integration with the IR plan.

  o **Continuous monitoring (Customer-Side):** Evaluate the use of continuous monitoring for customer-controlled configurations and applications.

Challenges in auditing vulnerability management

Auditing VMs in the cloud presents several unique challenges due to the dynamic, abstracted, and shared-responsibility nature of cloud environments.

Here are the key challenges:

- **Shared responsibility nuances:** Precisely delineating and auditing responsibilities is paramount.
- **Dynamic cloud environments:** Auditing must account for ephemeral resources and continuous deployment models.
- **Multi-cloud and hybrid complexity:** Increases the scope and intricacy of the audit.
- **API security:** Often overlooked but critical, as APIs are key integration points.
- **DevSecOps integration:** Assessing the embedding of vulnerability management within CI/CD pipelines.

Auditing vulnerability management in cloud environments demands a nuanced approach that considers the specific cloud service models in use, the shared responsibility model, and the organization's reliance on CSPs. By systematically evaluating the organization's direct vulnerability management processes, its framework for penetration testing, and its due diligence in overseeing CSP-managed security, auditors can provide vital assurance. This includes verifying that even when direct action is restricted, the organization diligently ensures its cloud services are operated securely by the CSP, and that all customer-side responsibilities are robustly addressed. Such an audit delivers actionable recommendations to fortify the cloud security posture against an ever-evolving threat landscape.

Incident response

A robust IR capability is essential to any modern cloud security strategy. As organizations increasingly depend on cloud services for critical operations, the ability to quickly detect, contain, eradicate, and recover from security incidents is crucial for reducing risk, ensuring continuity, and maintaining trust with stakeholders.

A cloud security audit must therefore include a comprehensive evaluation of the organization's **incident response plan (IRP)**, its structure, real-world effectiveness, and how well it addresses the unique aspects of cloud environments.

The following table outlines a comprehensive checklist for evaluating IR mechanisms in cloud environments as part of the cloud security audit process:

Audit area	Key focus areas	Auditor verification objectives
IRP review and governance	Documented IRP for cloud Accessibility during incidents Scope, roles, objectives Integration with BC/DR Governance and updates	Confirm the existence of a cloud-specific IRP Ensure roles and escalation paths are defined Check the regular review and formal approval process Validate alignment with broader security strategy
Preparation and prevention	IAM, WAFs, encryption, awareness Logging/monitoring tools (SIEM, cloud-native) Baselines for normal behavior CSP collaboration procedures	Assess the adequacy of proactive security controls Verify tooling and resource readiness Confirm incident collaboration frameworks with CSPs
Identification and detection	Use of cloud-native detection (e.g., GuardDuty) SIEM/XDR/IDS integration Multi-source detection Incident classification criteria	Evaluate the effectiveness of monitoring and alerts Check diverse detection inputs and alert triage Confirm clear criteria for incident declaration
Containment, eradication, recovery	Tailored containment strategies Root cause eradication methods Recovery procedures and RTO/RPOs Evidence preservation practices	Validate IRP coverage for different cloud incidents Ensure recovery from backups or golden images Review forensic readiness in cloud contexts

Audit area	Key focus areas	Auditor verification objectives
Post-incident activities	Lessons learned/post-mortems IRP improvement processes Control refinements Incident documentation and reporting	Confirm the presence of structured reviews Ensure feedback loops update the IRP Check formal reporting to stakeholders/regulators
Cloud-specific considerations	Shared responsibility model awareness Use of CSP tools and support IR automation (e.g., SOAR) Ephemeral resources & serverless API incident handling Data sovereignty issues	Assess how cloud nuances are addressed Verify automation practices for rapid response Evaluate treatment of serverless & API-based incidents
Testing, training, drills	Regular IRP testing (tabletop, simulated) Realistic cloud attack scenarios CSP involvement Personnel training and awareness	Confirm periodic, realistic scenario-based testing Validate staff competence and training sufficiency Ensure drills involve relevant CSPs
Communication plan	Internal/external protocols CSP escalation contacts Pre-approved media templates	Evaluate communication planning for incidents Ensure CSP contacts/escalation paths are documented Review media/regulatory communications procedures
Legal and regulatory compliance	Alignment with GDPR, HIPAA, PCI DSS, etc. Legal counsel involvement during incidents	Verify compliance with regulatory mandates Confirm timely legal consultation procedures

Table 10.6: Checklist for auditing IR

Auditing the organization's cloud IR capability is vital to ensure it can respond effectively to security events. A strong IRP, well-documented, frequently tested, cloud-aware, and backed by trained personnel and adequate technology, is central to reducing operational, reputational, and regulatory risks. The auditor's role is to ensure these components are not only present but operationally effective and to provide actionable recommendations for continuous improvement.

Assessing CSP's security posture

Migrating to the cloud brings major advantages in scalability, flexibility, and cost savings. However, it also introduces new security complexities and redefines the boundaries of responsibility between the customer and the CSP. A thorough cloud security audit must therefore include an assessment of the CSP's own security posture, viewed through the lens of the shared responsibility model.

The shared responsibility model outlines how security duties are split between CSPs and their customers, as described:

- **CSP responsibilities: Security of the cloud**: Securing physical infrastructure, hardware, software, networking, and the foundational services powering the cloud.

- **Customer responsibilities: Security in the cloud**: Securing data, applications, identity, and access, and configuration within the cloud environment.

The scope of responsibility shifts depending on the cloud service model, as depicted in the following table:

Model	CSP responsibility	Customer responsibility
IaaS	Infrastructure only	Everything above (OS, applications, data, IAM, network configurations)
PaaS	Infrastructure + **operating system (OS)**, middleware	Applications, data, user access, application-level security
SaaS	Nearly everything (infrastructure, software)	Data, user access, application settings

Table 10.7: Shared responsibilities in the cloud

Even though customers bear significant responsibility, their security depends on the strength of the CSP's foundation. A weak or non-compliant CSP undermines customer efforts, and that is the reason why the security posture of CSPs should be evaluated.

Key goals of evaluating a CSP include the following aspects:

- Verifying core infrastructure security
- Understanding inherited controls
- Confirming compliance with regulations and applicable industry standards
- Assessing business continuity and disaster recovery capabilities
- Ensuring transparency and effective support

The key areas for assessing the security posture of CSPs are best described in the following table:

Area	What to look for	Audit actions
Compliance and certifications	Relevant certifications (SOC 2, ISO 27001, PCI DSS, etc.)	Review third-party audit reports Confirm scope and recency
Physical and environmental security	Data center controls for physical access, fire, flood, and power	Rely on compliance reports (e.g., SOC 2) Review CSP documentation
Infrastructure security	Host OS, hypervisor, patching, vulnerability management	Review SOC 2/certification details Check CSP security whitepapers
Network security	Core network protections, DDoS mitigation, segmentation	Examine CSP architecture documents and compliance evidence
IAM platform security	Resilience and protection of IAM services	Evaluate CSP IAM documentation and best practice guidance
IR	Detection, response, and notification processes for CSP incidents	Review policies, SLAs, and transparency reports
Business continuity and disaster recovery (BCDR)	Redundancy, backups, and failover across regions	Assess CSP BCDR plans, SLAs, and regional infrastructure capabilities

Table 10.8: Key areas for assessing CSP's security posture

Since direct access to audit public CSP infrastructure (e.g., AWS, Azure, GCP) is limited, the following methods of assessment should be relied upon:

- **CSP documentation:** Whitepapers, security practices, architecture details
- **Compliance reports:** SOC 2, ISO, PCI DSS, etc., via CSP portals
- **Contracts and SLAs:** Evaluate security, availability, and notification commitments
- **Security dashboards/tools:** AWS Security Hub, Azure Security Center, etc.
- **CSA CAIQ:** Standardized CSP responses to security questions

It should be ensured that CSP assessment is integrated into the cloud security audit, and a comprehensive audit must evaluate both of the following:

- **CSP's compliance**: Ensuring the provider meets its security obligations for infrastructure and services.
- **Customer's controls**: Verifying proper configuration, data protection, IAM, and application security practices.

Evaluating a CSP's security posture is essential for ensuring a secure cloud environment. By aligning the audit with the shared responsibility model and leveraging documentation, certifications, and platform tools, organizations can gain confidence in their cloud foundation. A balanced audit of both CSP and customer responsibilities leads to a more resilient, compliant, and secure cloud deployment.

Tools and techniques

Auditing cloud environments demands a customized strategy that combines native cloud capabilities, third-party tools, and structured assessment methodologies.

The following table provides a detailed breakdown of tools and techniques applied across the key core cloud security domains, organized for clarity and focus:

Data security		
Category	**Tools**	**Key audit techniques**
CSPM	AWS Security Hub, Azure Defender, GCP Security Command Center, Wiz, Prisma Cloud, SentinelOne Horizon, CrowdStrike	Configuration audits (e.g., public access, encryption, versioning) Compliance checks (e.g., CIS, NIST, ISO 27001) Automated misconfiguration scans
DLP	Amazon Macie, Microsoft Purview, Google DLP API, third-party DLP platforms	Policy verification and classification accuracy Reviewing DLP incident logs Data discovery effectiveness validation
Encryption and key management	AWS KMS, Azure Key Vault, Google Cloud KMS, HSMs	Encryption policy and certificate audits Key lifecycle reviews (generation, rotation, destruction) Access control analysis for key material
Logging and monitoring (data access)	AWS CloudTrail, Azure Monitor, GCP Audit Logs, SIEMs (Splunk, QRadar, Sentinel)	Review of access logs for anomalies Alert configuration and investigation effectiveness
Backup and disaster recovery	AWS Backup, Azure Backup, GCP Backup & DR, third-party tools	Backup policy scope, frequency, and encryption reviews Disaster recovery testing and RTO/RPO validation
Manual techniques	Interviews, policy reviews, evidence collection	Documenting and validating data security controls Interviewing stakeholders and collecting control evidence

Table 10.9: Tools and technologies for auditing data security

In continuation, the following table provides a detailed breakdown of tools and techniques applied across the key core cloud security domains, organized for clarity and focus:

Identity and access management		
Category	**Tools**	**Key audit techniques**
Native IAM tools	AWS IAM, Azure AD, Google Cloud IAM	Permission and entitlement reviews Role and policy analysis Audit of service accounts and trust relationships
MFA	IAM console reports, custom scripts	MFA enforcement audits for critical roles Evaluation of MFA types used (e.g., TOTP, push, hardware tokens)
PAM	Azure PIM, CyberArk, BeyondTrust, Delinea	Inventory of privileged accounts JIT access review Session recording checks Password rotation and vaulting assessments
IAM logging & analysis	AWS CloudTrail, Azure AD Logs, GCP IAM Logs, SIEMs	Log analysis for anomalies (e.g., failed logins, policy changes) Alerting on critical IAM activities
CIEM (Entitlement management)	Wiz, Ermetic, Zscaler, SentinelOne	Least privilege and effective access reviews Visualization of identity-to-resource paths Automated remediation suggestions
Manual techniques	Policy and Process Reviews, SoD Checks	Policy completeness and enforcement validation Review of onboarding/ offboarding workflows Segregation of duties analysis

Table 10.10: Tools and technologies for auditing IAM

In continuation, the following table provides a detailed breakdown of tools and techniques applied across the key core cloud security domains, organized for clarity and focus:

Vulnerability management		
Category	**Tools**	**Key audit techniques**
Vulnerability scanners	AWS Inspector, Azure Defender VA, GCP Security Scanner, Qualys, Tenable, OpenVAS	Scan coverage validation Configuration and scheduling audits Managing false positives/negatives
Asset inventory tools	Cloud consoles, CMDBs, CSPMs	Inventory accuracy audits Tagging and classification reviews
Patch management	AWS SSM Patch Manager, Azure Update Management, third-party tools	Policy review for patch SLAs Patch deployment verification and rollback testing
Configuration management	Terraform, CloudFormation, Azure ARM, Ansible, Chef, Puppet	Secure baseline enforcement audits Configuration drift detection

Vulnerability management		
Category	**Tools**	**Key audit techniques**
Pen testing / Red teaming	N/A (Method-based)	Review of test scope and findings Validation of remediation and re-testing of vulnerabilities
Threat intelligence integration	Threat intel feeds and platforms	Incorporation of real-time threat data into vulnerability prioritization
Reporting and documentation review	VM platforms, SIEMs, custom tools	Review of KPIs like MTTR and vulnerability aging Completeness and accuracy of reports and remediation tracking

Table 10.11: Tools and technologies for auditing vulnerability management

In continuation, the following table provides a detailed breakdown of tools and techniques applied across the key core cloud security domains, organized for clarity and focus:

Incident response		
Category	**Tools**	**Key audit techniques**
Incident response plan (IRP)	Documentation-based	IR plan alignment with cloud threats Role clarity and escalation workflows CSP engagement procedures
Logging and monitoring	AWS CloudTrail, CloudWatch, VPC Flow Logs, Azure Monitor, GCP Logging, SIEMs, CDR, NDR, EDR	Coverage of all critical log sources Retention compliance checks Alerting efficiency
SIEM / SOAR platforms	Splunk, Azure Sentinel, IBM QRadar, SOAR tools	Detection rule audits- Playbook effectiveness reviews Integration checks with cloud logs
Forensic capabilities	Cloud-native snapshotting, forensic kits, third-party DFIR tools	Evidence collection and chain-of-custody process validation Availability of forensic expertise
IR testing and training	Tabletop exercises, simulated IR drills	Exercise documentation and outcome review Lessons learned integration into IRP
Containment and recovery	Backup tools, cloud firewall controls, and account disablement methods	Procedure validation for containment, eradication, and restoration Backup usability in recovery contexts
Shared responsibility understanding	IRP documentation	Escalation matrix with CSPs Clarification of organization vs. CSP responsibility for each cloud service model

Table 10.12: Tools and technologies for auditing IR

By applying a structured audit methodology, leveraging the right tools, and aligning them with proven techniques, organizations can holistically assess and enhance their cloud security posture across all critical domains.

Common audit observations

This section outlines frequently identified issues during cloud security audits, grouped by core security domains. Addressing these observations proactively strengthens an organization's cloud security posture and improves compliance.

Data security

Audits of data security in the cloud often uncover issues related to data protection, classification, and handling. The details are as follows:

- **Inadequate data classification and tagging**: Sensitive data such as PII, PHI, or financial records is not consistently identified or tagged across storage services, hindering security control implementation and increasing the risk of exposure or regulatory non-compliance.

- **Misconfigured storage permissions:** Publicly accessible or overly permissive storage (e.g., S3 buckets, Azure containers) can lead to unauthorized data access, breaches, or loss.

- **Insufficient encryption at rest:** Weak or absent encryption for stored data, along with poor key management, exposes sensitive information if storage is compromised.

- **Weak or missing encryption in transit:** Use of outdated protocols or unencrypted data transfer increases the risk of interception during transmission.

- **Inadequate DLP**: Poorly configured or missing DLP controls allow sensitive data to be exfiltrated or shared inappropriately.

- **Insufficient data backup and recovery**: Lack of regular, encrypted backups and untested recovery procedures leads to potential data loss and business disruption.

- **Poor key management practices**: Weak practices such as hardcoded keys, lack of rotation, or default cloud-managed keys increase the risk of key compromise and data exposure.

- **Lack of data activity monitoring:** Insufficient logging and monitoring of access to sensitive data hinders the ability to detect or investigate unauthorized activities.

Identity and access management

IAM is a cornerstone of cloud security, and audits frequently reveal gaps in how identities and access are managed. The details are as follows:

- **Overly permissive IAM roles and policies:** Excessive permissions (e.g., use of wildcards) increase risk exposure if accounts are compromised.

- **Lack of MFA enforcement:** Missing or weak MFA, especially for privileged accounts, makes organizations vulnerable to credential theft.

- **Dormant or orphaned accounts:** Inactive or legacy accounts retain access and can be exploited if credentials are weak or compromised.

- **Inadequate PAM**: Shared accounts and a lack of monitoring for privileged users reduce accountability and increase insider threat risk.

- **Weak password policies:** Insufficient enforcement of complexity, rotation, or history makes credentials easy to compromise.

- **Insufficient IAM policy review and attestation**: Infrequent access reviews result in privilege creep and outdated permissions.

- **Insecure use of root/global administrator accounts**: Routine use of root or global admin accounts without strong controls risks full environment compromise.

- **Lack of centralized identity management or federation**: Disparate identity stores or misconfigured federation cause inconsistent policy enforcement and management challenges.

- **Misconfigured service principal/service account permissions:** Overprivileged service accounts with long-lived credentials create security gaps if compromised.

Vulnerability management

Effective vulnerability management is crucial for reducing the attack surface in the cloud. Audits often find process and execution gaps. The details are as follows:

- **Incomplete asset inventory**: Missing or outdated inventories allow unmanaged resources and *shadow IT*, increasing vulnerability exposure.

- **Infrequent or incomplete vulnerability scanning**: Lack of regular or comprehensive scanning delays detection of known vulnerabilities.

- **Ineffective vulnerability prioritization**: Risk is misjudged by relying solely on CVSS scores without considering business impact or exploitability.

- **Slow or inconsistent patch management**: Manual, delayed, or poorly tested patching processes leave systems exposed to known threats.

- **Misconfigured cloud services and resources**: Insecure defaults or exposed services create unnecessary attack surfaces.

- **Lack of container image security scanning**: Unscanned or outdated container images introduce vulnerabilities into production environments.

- **Insufficient web application security testing**: Lack of routine testing for OWASP Top 10 and other vulnerabilities exposes applications to exploitation.

- **Poor third-party software management**: Failure to track or patch open-source or third-party components introduces known vulnerabilities into the environment.

Incident response

The ability to respond effectively to security incidents is critical. Audits often find weaknesses in preparedness and execution. The details are as follows:

- **Lack of a documented and tested cloud-specific IR plan**: Generic or untested plans hinder effective response in cloud-specific scenarios, prolonging incident impact.

- **Insufficient logging and monitoring for incident detection**: Missing or inadequate logs and alerting mechanisms delay detection and limit forensic capabilities.

- **Inadequate incident detection and analysis capabilities**: Lack of appropriate tools or trained personnel results in undetected or misclassified incidents.

- **Poorly defined roles and responsibilities for IR**: Unclear roles and communication processes cause confusion during response efforts.

- **Lack of forensic readiness in the cloud**: Missing procedures for evidence collection complicate investigations and hinder root cause analysis.

- **Ineffective containment, eradication, and recovery procedures**: Absence of defined recovery actions increases downtime and risk of reinfection.

- **Failure to leverage cloud provider IR capabilities**: Unawareness of CSP support options leads to missed opportunities for assistance during incidents.

- **Insufficient post-incident analysis and lessons learned**: Lack of structured reviews prevents organizational learning and long-term improvements.

By understanding and addressing these common security audit findings, organizations can take targeted actions to reduce cloud-related risks, enhance operational resilience, and ensure regulatory compliance.

Conclusion

This chapter explored the comprehensive auditing of cloud security controls, emphasizing key domains such as data protection, IAM, vulnerability management, incident response, and the assessment of CSPs' security postures. It detailed the essential tools and techniques required to conduct effective, in-depth audits tailored to the dynamic and shared-responsibility nature of cloud environments, ensuring organizations can identify risks, enforce compliance, and enhance their overall security posture.

In the next chapter, we will discuss auditing governance and data privacy in the cloud, including data residency, data encryption, and privacy-by-design principles. It emphasizes compliance with national and international regulations.

Points to remember

- Cloud security audits differ significantly from traditional on-premises audits due to the dynamic, automated, and abstract nature of cloud environments.

- Before exploring the specific methods used in auditing cloud security, it's crucial to first understand the broader context, namely, the common risks associated with cloud environments.

- Establishing a clear audit scope ensures focus and alignment with business objectives, legal obligations, and technological realities.

- The audit must establish a clear understanding of the shared responsibility model with the CSP(s).

- Performing a data security audit in the cloud requires a nuanced approach that acknowledges the shared responsibilities and dynamic nature of cloud environments.

- In cloud environments, IAM is the cornerstone of security, controlling who (identities) can do what (permissions) on which resources.

- When a CASB is implemented, IAM audits extend beyond just reviewing native cloud controls.

- Ensure all cloud resources (VMs, containers, serverless functions, databases, etc.) are accurately discovered and continuously inventoried to avoid blind spots for ensuring effective audit of vulnerability management.

- Auditing the organization's cloud IR capability is vital to ensure it can respond effectively to security events.

- A thorough cloud security audit should include an assessment of the CSP's own security posture, viewed through the lens of the shared responsibility model.

- Finally, auditors should be aware of common audit observations, to ensure prioritizing high-risk areas and ensuring that critical vulnerabilities are not overlooked.

Multiple choice questions

1. **Which of the following is the most critical reason for enforcing proper data classification and tagging in cloud environments during a security audit?**

   a. To reduce the cost of cloud storage

   b. To improve cloud resource naming conventions

   c. To ensure sensitive data is handled appropriately

   d. To enable faster deployment of cloud applications

2. **During a cloud IAM audit, which finding is MOST indicative of poor access control hygiene?**

   a. Use of strong password policies

   b. Regular role-based access reviews

   c. Use of wildcard permissions in IAM policies

   d. Centralized identity federation

3. **Why is container image scanning important in cloud-based environments?**

   a. To reduce container build time

   b. To ensure container portability across regions

   c. To detect known vulnerabilities before deployment

   d. To improve application load balancing

4. **Which AWS service is most appropriate for auditing user activity during a cloud security incident response?**

   a. Amazon GuardDuty

   b. AWS Shield

   c. AWS CloudTrail

   d. AWS Inspector

5. **Which of the following is the most effective method for assessing CSP's security posture?**

   a. Conducting vulnerability scans on CSP-managed resources

   b. Reviewing the CSP's third-party certifications and compliance reports (e.g., ISO 27001, SOC 2)

   c. Implementing your own security monitoring tools on the CSP's infrastructure

   d. Relying solely on the CSP's marketing materials and security claims

Answers

1	c
2	c
3	c
4	c
5	b

Join our Discord space

Join our Discord workspace for latest updates, offers, tech happenings around the world, new releases, and sessions with the authors:

https://discord.bpbonline.com

CHAPTER 11

Auditing Cloud Governance and Privacy

Introduction

As organizations increasingly migrate their operations and data to cloud environments, ensuring proper governance and maintaining data privacy become critical responsibilities. Cloud computing introduces new layers of complexity and risk, from multi-tenant infrastructures to global data transfers and dynamic access control models.

Auditing cloud governance and privacy involves systematically evaluating how cloud services are managed, secured, and aligned with internal policies and regulatory requirements. It ensures that an organization maintains visibility, control, and compliance over its data and operations in the cloud.

We have discussed GRC in the cloud in *Chapter 4, GRC in Cloud,* which laid a critical foundation.

That foundational understanding highlighted that while establishing GRC principles is vital, the *governance* component, comprising the system of rules, practices, and processes by which cloud resources are directed and controlled, is paramount to achieving strategic objectives, managing risks effectively, and ensuring sustained compliance. While the previous discussion touched upon the role of auditors in the broader GRC implementation, the sheer criticality and distinct challenges of cloud governance warrant a more focused and in-depth examination.

Further discussion on *auditing cloud governance* is therefore necessary to move beyond the *what* and *why* of cloud governance, and to concentrate on the *how* specifically, how organizations can obtain assurance that their cloud governance structures are not only well-designed but also operating effectively.

Structure

This chapter covers the following topics:

- Assessing policies and procedures
- Governance structures in multi-cloud
- Privacy laws and regulations impacting cloud
- Auditing data privacy in cloud
- Tools and techniques
- Case studies

Objectives

This chapter focuses on auditing governance and data privacy in the cloud, including data residency, data encryption, and privacy-by-design principles. It emphasizes compliance with national and international regulations.

Assessing policies and procedures

Auditing cloud governance begins with a thorough assessment of the organization's established policies and procedures. This evaluation aims to determine if these documented guidelines are comprehensive, clearly defined, consistently implemented, and effectively enforced. Key areas of focus during this assessment include:

- **Policy clarity and comprehensiveness:** Auditors should assess whether cloud governance policies are not only clear and comprehensive but also well-coordinated across departments such as technology, privacy, cybersecurity, and compliance. effective governance requires that policies collectively address all critical domains, including data security, access control, resource management, cost efficiency, regulatory compliance, and incident response. Each policy should be clearly written, easily accessible, and understandable to all relevant stakeholders. Additionally, auditors should evaluate whether roles and responsibilities related to cloud activities are explicitly defined and consistently communicated across departmental boundaries, ensuring there are no gaps, overlaps, or ambiguities in accountability.

- **Procedure effectiveness:** Beyond well-defined policies, auditors should scrutinize the documented procedures for implementing these policies. This involves assessing if the procedures are practical, up-to-date, and align with industry best practices and relevant regulatory frameworks. For example, procedures for provisioning new cloud resources, managing user access, or responding to a security breach should be detailed and actionable.

- **Alignment with business objectives and risk appetite:** The auditors should assess whether the cloud governance policies directly support the organization's strategic goals and reflect its defined risk appetite. Auditors should assess whether the governance framework effectively mitigates identified cloud-related risks without unduly hindering business agility or innovation.

- **Change management processes:** The cloud environment is dynamic, with frequent updates and new service offerings. Auditors should review the change management processes related to cloud governance. This includes how policies and procedures are updated, communicated, and how changes to the cloud infrastructure itself are governed and tracked.

- **Training and awareness:** Effective governance relies on personnel understanding their roles and responsibilities. Auditors should assess the adequacy of training programs designed to educate employees on cloud governance policies and procedures. This includes evaluating the frequency of training and methods for verifying comprehension.

- **Monitoring and enforcement:** Policies and procedures are only effective if they are consistently monitored and enforced. Auditors should examine the mechanisms in place to track compliance with governance directives. This includes reviewing automated compliance checks, regular internal audits, and the processes for addressing non-compliance and policy violations.

- **Documentation and record keeping:** Comprehensive documentation of governance policies, procedures, roles, responsibilities, and audit trails is crucial. Auditors should assess the quality and completeness of this documentation, ensuring it provides a clear picture of the governance framework and its operation over time.

The assessment process should typically involve reviewing documentation, interviewing key personnel (including cloud administrators, security teams, legal and compliance officers, and business unit leaders), and observing processes in action. The findings from this assessment will identify gaps, weaknesses, and areas for improvement in the organization's cloud governance posture.

Governance structures in multi-cloud

The adoption of multi-cloud strategies, where organizations utilize services from multiple **cloud service providers** (**CSPs**), introduces additional layers of complexity to governance. Establishing effective governance structures in such environments is paramount to maintaining control, security, and cost-efficiency.

Key considerations for governance in multi-cloud environments include:

- **Centralized vs. federated governance models:** Organizations must decide on the most appropriate governance model. A centralized model enforces a common set of policies and controls across all cloud platforms, typically managed by a central IT or cloud governance team. This approach promotes consistency but can sometimes be less flexible. A federated model allows for some degree of autonomy for individual business units or cloud environments while still adhering to overarching organizational policies. This can offer greater agility but requires strong coordination and oversight to avoid inconsistencies and security gaps. Often, a hybrid approach that combines elements of both is adopted.

- **Policy abstraction and harmonization:** Different CSPs have unique service offerings, APIs, and security controls. A significant challenge is creating a unified governance framework that can be consistently applied across disparate cloud environments. This often involves abstracting policies to a higher level and then translating them into the specific configurations and controls applicable to each CSP. Tools that provide a common control plane across multiple clouds can be invaluable here.

- **Identity and access management (IAM):** Managing user identities and access privileges consistently across multiple clouds is critical. Organizations need robust IAM strategies that can integrate with different CSP identity systems or utilize third-party identity providers to ensure least privilege access and centralized control over user accounts.

- **Security and compliance consistency:** Maintaining a consistent security posture and meeting compliance requirements across various cloud platforms requires a unified approach. This includes standardizing security controls, monitoring tools, and reporting mechanisms wherever possible. Automation plays a key role in enforcing security policies consistently across different cloud environments.

- **Cost management and optimization:** Tracking and optimizing costs in a multi-cloud environment can be challenging due to varying pricing models and service consumption patterns. Effective governance includes establishing clear cost allocation methodologies, implementing showback or chargeback mechanisms, and utilizing multi-cloud cost management tools to identify and eliminate wasteful spending.

- **Data governance and portability:** Ensuring data security, privacy, and sovereignty across multiple clouds requires careful planning. Governance policies must address data classification, encryption standards, data residency requirements, and data transfer mechanisms between different cloud environments. The ability to port data and applications between clouds without significant re-engineering is also a key governance consideration for avoiding vendor lock-in.

- **Interoperability and integration:** Governance structures need to facilitate interoperability and integration between services running on different clouds and with on-premises systems. This involves defining standards for APIs, data formats, and communication protocols.

- **Skills and expertise:** Managing governance in a multi-cloud environment requires a skilled workforce proficient in the specific technologies and nuances of each CSP being used. Governance structures should address training and skill development to ensure the team can effectively oversee the diverse cloud landscape.

Auditing governance in a multi-cloud setup involves assessing the effectiveness of these strategies in managing the inherent complexities. Auditors should look for evidence of a cohesive governance framework that spans all cloud environments, ensuring consistent policy enforcement, risk management, and compliance.

Privacy laws and regulations impacting cloud

Before dwelling further, let us look at what data privacy is. Data privacy, or information privacy, is the individual's right to control their personal information, how it is collected, stored, and used. It emphasizes respecting personal choices, complying with data protection laws, and handling sensitive data responsibly and lawfully. At its core, data privacy ensures the confidentiality and autonomy of individuals over their own data.

The rapid adoption of cloud computing has brought immense benefits but also significant challenges, particularly concerning data privacy. As organizations increasingly migrate sensitive data to the cloud, they become subject to a complex web of international and regional privacy laws, regulations, and standards. This landscape places a critical responsibility on the auditors to ensure that cloud environments and practices adhere to these stringent requirements, safeguarding personal data and maintaining legal compliance.

Evolving regulatory and standards landscape

Numerous privacy laws, regulations, and globally recognized standards dictate how organizations must handle personal data and secure information systems in the cloud. With the global rise in data privacy concerns and legislation, auditors need a comprehensive understanding of these frameworks to effectively assess compliance and best practices. Auditors play a critical role in evaluating whether organizations handle personal data in compliance with applicable laws and best practices. While regulations are mandatory, several global standards and best practices provide frameworks for achieving and demonstrating robust cloud security and privacy. Auditors often use these as benchmarks. This requires a thorough understanding of both regulatory requirements and global privacy standards, discussed as follows:

- **General Data Protection Regulation (GDPR) – EU:** GDPR remains a global benchmark, emphasizing lawful processing, transparency, accountability, and the rights of data subjects. Where applicable, auditors should evaluate compliance with key provisions such as data protection by design and default, breach notification protocols, and the appointment of **data protection officers** (**DPOs**).

- **NIST privacy framework:** Offers a risk-based, voluntary framework for managing privacy risks, emphasizing outcomes and flexible implementation. Auditors can use it to evaluate how organizations identify, manage, and reduce privacy risks.

- **ISO/IEC 27701:** An extension of ISO/IEC 27001 and 27002, this standard provides a framework for implementing a **Privacy Information Management System** (**PIMS**), supporting compliance with GDPR and other global privacy laws.

- **ISO/IEC 27018:** Focused on protecting personal data in cloud environments, ISO 27018 establishes controls for public CSPs. Auditors should consider this when assessing privacy safeguards in outsourced or cloud-hosted environments.

- **Health Insurance Portability and Accountability Act (HIPAA):** Governs the privacy and security of **Protected Health Information** (**PHI**). Mandates administrative, physical, and technical safeguards in the jurisdiction of the United States. When PHI is stored or processed in the cloud, both healthcare providers (Covered Entities) and their CSPs (Business Associates) must comply with HIPAA. Auditors evaluate the implementation of safeguards, **Business Associate Agreements** (**BAAs**), risk analyses, and breach notification procedures.

- **HITRUST CSF:** Widely used in healthcare and other regulated sectors, the HITRUST Common Security Framework integrates multiple standards (including HIPAA, ISO, NIST, and GDPR). Auditors may rely on HITRUST certification as evidence of privacy and security control maturity, particularly in the U.S. healthcare context.

- **SOC 2 reports:** Particularly relevant for cloud services, these reports, based on the AICPA's Trust Services Criteria (security, availability, processing integrity, confidentiality, and privacy), provide assurance on the design and operating effectiveness of a service organization's controls. Auditors heavily rely on SOC 2 Type II reports from CSPs as part of their due diligence.

- **Local and national laws:** Auditors must reference jurisdiction-specific privacy laws, which may vary widely in terms of scope, enforcement, and terminology. Local legal counsel, legal departments within the organizations, or regulatory guidance may be necessary to ensure comprehensive assessments.

Adherence to these regulations, any applicable standards, and best practices can significantly help organizations meet the requirements of various privacy laws and demonstrate a strong commitment to data protection in the cloud. Auditors should always ensure to assess privacy practices in the context of both global standards and the applicable national or local legal frameworks. Regulatory environments evolve, and jurisdiction-specific nuances (e.g., sectoral regulations, data localization laws, or enforcement thresholds) can significantly impact compliance obligations.

Impact on cloud environments

Privacy laws and standards profoundly affect how organizations manage data in the cloud:

- **Data sovereignty and localization:** Many regulations impose restrictions on cross-border data transfers and may require data to be stored and/or processed within specific geographic locations. This has significant implications for cloud architecture, CSP selection, and contractual agreements. Auditors must verify that data residency and transfer mechanisms comply with these rules.

- **Shared responsibility model:** In the cloud, security and compliance are shared responsibilities between the CSP and the customer. Auditors need to clearly understand this division of responsibility for the specific cloud services being used (IaaS, PaaS, SaaS) to assess controls effectively. For example, the CSP is typically responsible for the security *of* the cloud, while the customer is responsible for security *in* the cloud (e.g., data, applications, access management).

- **Data lifecycle management:** Regulations mandate how personal data is collected, used, stored, retained, and disposed of. Cloud environments must have mechanisms to support these requirements, including data discovery, classification, secure deletion, and data retention policies. Auditors examine these processes.

- **Security controls:** Privacy laws and standards necessitate robust technical and organizational security measures, including:

    - **Encryption:** Protecting data at rest and in transit.

    - **Access controls:** Implementing principles like least privilege and **multi-factor authentication (MFA)**.

    - **Vulnerability management and patching:** Regularly identifying and remediating security flaws.

    - **Logging and monitoring:** Detecting and responding to security incidents and suspicious activities.

    - **Incident response and breach notification:** Having well-defined plans to manage data breaches and notify relevant authorities and individuals within mandated timelines.

- **Privacy-by-design and by default:** Regulations and best practices increasingly emphasize embedding privacy considerations into the design and architecture of systems and processes from the outset. Auditors may look for evidence of these principles in cloud deployments.

- **Third-party risk management:** Organizations are often responsible for the data processing activities of their cloud providers and other third-party vendors. Due diligence, contractual safeguards (like DPAs), and ongoing monitoring of CSPs are critical. Auditors review the vendor management processes, often leveraging CSP certifications and attestations (e.g., ISO 27001, SOC 2).

Privacy laws, regulations, and global standards are fundamental drivers of how organizations must manage data and secure systems in the cloud. The auditors play an indispensable role in providing assurance that these requirements are met. By conducting thorough, risk-based audits focused on data protection, security controls, and adherence to relevant frameworks, auditors help organizations mitigate risks, avoid costly penalties, build trust with customers, and harness the benefits of cloud computing responsibly and securely. As cloud adoption continues to grow, the expertise and diligence of auditors will become even more critical in navigating the intricate intersection of technology, privacy, and security.

Auditing data privacy in cloud

As organizations increasingly migrate their operations to the cloud, safeguarding data privacy has become a mission-critical priority. The decentralized, scalable nature of cloud environments introduces a new layer of complexity to privacy audits, requiring a deep understanding of shared responsibilities, ever-evolving regulations, and sophisticated audit methodologies. This section offers a detailed roadmap for effectively auditing data privacy in cloud environments.

Key challenges and considerations

Auditing cloud-based data privacy differs significantly from traditional on-premises assessments. Understanding these distinct challenges, discussed as follows, is essential to designing an effective audit framework:

- **Shared responsibility model:** Cloud security and privacy are jointly managed by CSPs and their customers. Typically, CSPs secure the infrastructure, while customers are responsible for securing data, applications, and configurations within the cloud. Clearly delineating these roles is crucial. Any ambiguity can result in critical control gaps and vulnerabilities.

- **Complexity of cloud environments:** Modern cloud ecosystems often involve multiple CSPs (e.g., AWS, Azure, Google Cloud), hybrid architectures, and a multitude of services. This complexity makes it difficult to maintain full visibility over configurations, data flows, and access controls.

- **Rapidly changing infrastructure:** The elastic nature of the cloud means resources are continuously provisioned and decommissioned. These rapid changes heighten the risk of misconfigurations and complicate efforts to maintain accurate inventories of assets and data.

- **Limited transparency:** CSPs typically operate as black boxes, limiting customer visibility into backend infrastructure and security controls. This opacity can hinder effective auditing and increase the risk of undetected compliance breaches.

- **Regulatory landscape:** Cloud deployments must comply with a patchwork of data privacy regulations depending on the geography, industry, and type of data involved. From GDPR and CCPA to HIPAA and ISO standards, navigating these diverse obligations is resource-intensive and requires ongoing vigilance.

- **Data sovereignty concerns:** Where data is stored and processed can significantly impact compliance. Cloud environments often distribute data across multiple jurisdictions, complicating adherence to local data residency laws.

- **Third-party risk:** Integrating third-party SaaS applications and services introduces additional privacy risks. Auditing must extend beyond the primary cloud environment to assess the privacy practices of all connected vendors.

Best practices for data privacy audits

A comprehensive audit strategy should incorporate the following best practices:

- **Define clear audit objectives and scope:** Establish audit goals, identify all cloud services in use, categorize the types of data handled, and map applicable regulatory requirements.

- **Assess CSP capabilities**: Review the provider's certifications (e.g., SOC 2, HITRUST, ISO 27018, ISO 27701), security features, and SLAs. Understand which controls are provided and what your organization must manage.

- **Review policies and procedures:** Audit internal documentation such as privacy policies, data processing agreements, incident response plans, and training materials to ensure alignment with legal and industry standards.

- **Assess data discovery and classification:** Assess how sensitive data, such as **Personally Identifiable Information** (**PII**) or PHI, is discovered and classified, and whether it is based on sensitivity and regulatory requirements.

- **Evaluate access controls:** Audit IAM policies. Enforce least-privilege access principles and ensure the use of MFA.

- **Verify encryption standards**: Ensure encryption is enforced for data both at rest and in transit. Review key management practices, including generation, storage, rotation, and access control.

- **Evaluate network security:** Audit firewall rules, segmentation strategies, and intrusion detection/prevention systems to guard against unauthorized access.

- **Test incident response readiness:** Ensure incident response plans are cloud-aware, regularly tested, and include procedures for privacy breach detection, containment, recovery, and reporting.

- **Verify continuous monitoring and logging**: Assess whether tools are deployed for real-time monitoring and centralized log collection, and whether adequate use cases related to privacy have been designed and implemented for privacy enforcement. SIEM platforms can assist in log analysis and alerting on anomalies or potential privacy breaches.

- **Evaluate vulnerability assessments:** Assess if scans and penetration tests are performed regularly and to identify and remediate privacy weaknesses in applications, configurations, and infrastructure.

- **Audit third-party programs:** Review privacy policies, contractual commitments, and certifications of third-party service providers with data access.

- **Privacy awareness:** Ensure ongoing employee training on privacy protection responsibilities and best practices in a cloud context.

- **Evaluate internal audit effectiveness**: Verify the effectiveness of periodic internal reviews to identify issues proactively and whether timely corrective actions are being identified and implemented.

Focus areas for cloud privacy audits

Auditors should emphasize the following focus areas during the cloud privacy audits to ensure that their evaluations are structured, effective, and risk-based, especially in complex domains like cloud privacy:

- **Privacy governance and accountability:** Assess whether the organization has established a comprehensive privacy governance framework. This includes the presence of designated privacy leadership, employee training programs, clear roles and responsibilities, and well-documented privacy policies aligned with applicable regulations and standards.

- **Personal data lifecycle management:** Evaluate how personal data is managed throughout its lifecycle in the cloud, from collection and processing to storage, sharing, retention, and secure disposal. Ensure data minimization, purpose limitation, and transparency principles are upheld at each stage.

- **Privacy and data protection impact assessments (PIAs/DPIAs):** Verify that PIAs or DPIAs are systematically conducted for processing activities likely to pose significant privacy risks. Confirm that these assessments are reviewed regularly and integrated into the organization's risk management and change management processes.

- **Technical and organizational security measures:** Examine the effectiveness of implemented security controls, including encryption, IAM, intrusion detection, and audit logging. Confirm that these controls are continuously monitored, tested, and updated to address evolving threats.

- **Third-party and CSP oversight:** Review how the organization manages privacy and security risks associated with cloud vendors and third-party processors. This includes evaluating contractual safeguards, conducting due diligence, and ensuring ongoing oversight through risk assessments and compliance audits.

- **Data subject rights fulfillment:** Determine whether the organization has implemented accessible, reliable mechanisms for individuals to exercise their data protection rights (e.g., access, rectification, erasure, data portability). Verify that these requests are handled within legal timeframes and supported by appropriate verification procedures.

Auditing data privacy in the cloud is not a one-time activity; it is a continuous process requiring strategic planning, rigorous control testing, and ongoing vigilance. By understanding cloud-specific privacy risks, adopting best practices, and utilizing the right tools, organizations can not only maintain compliance but also build a strong foundation of trust with customers, partners, and regulators.

Tools and techniques

Auditing privacy in the cloud is a critical undertaking for organizations to ensure compliance with data protection regulations, safeguard sensitive information, and maintain user trust. This process involves a combination of specialized tools and robust techniques to assess how cloud environments and associated services handle personal data. The landscape of cloud privacy auditing continues to evolve, driven by increasingly complex cloud architectures and a growing body of privacy legislation worldwide.

Key techniques for auditing privacy

Several established and emerging techniques are employed to effectively audit privacy in cloud environments:

- **Data discovery and classification:** The foundational step involves identifying where sensitive data resides within the cloud infrastructure. This includes structured and unstructured data across various cloud services (IaaS, PaaS, SaaS). Techniques include automated data discovery scans, metadata analysis, and content inspection to classify data based on its sensitivity and applicable privacy regulations.

- **Data flow mapping and analysis:** Understanding how personal data moves into, through, and out of the cloud is crucial. This technique involves creating comprehensive data flow diagrams that illustrate data paths, processing points, storage locations, and third-party integrations. Analyzing these flows helps identify potential privacy risks, such as unauthorized access, insecure transfers, or excessive data retention.

- **PIAs/DPIAs:** These systematic processes are designed to identify, analyze, and mitigate privacy risks associated with new or significantly changed cloud projects or systems that process personal data. They involve evaluating the necessity and proportionality of data processing, assessing potential threats to data subjects' rights, and implementing appropriate controls.

- **Compliance audits against regulatory frameworks:** This involves assessing the cloud environment and related processes against specific privacy regulations and standards. Auditors use checklists, conduct interviews, review documentation, and perform technical tests to verify adherence to requirements such as consent management, data subject rights fulfillment, data security measures, and breach notification procedures. Common frameworks include ISO 27701 (PIMS), SOC 2 Type II with a focus on privacy criteria, and industry-specific regulations.

- **Security controls assessment:** Privacy and security are intrinsically linked. This technique focuses on evaluating the effectiveness of security controls implemented in the cloud to protect personal data. This includes assessing IAM configurations, encryption mechanisms (in transit and at rest), network security, vulnerability management, and incident response capabilities.

- **Penetration testing and vulnerability scanning:** Ethical hacking techniques are used to simulate attacks on cloud environments to identify vulnerabilities that could lead to privacy breaches. Vulnerability scanning tools automatically probe systems for known weaknesses. These activities help uncover potential unauthorized access points or data exfiltration routes.

- **Configuration audits:** Misconfigurations in cloud services are a leading cause of data breaches. This technique involves regularly reviewing and auditing the configurations of cloud resources (e.g., storage buckets, databases, virtual machines) to ensure they align with security and privacy best practices and organizational policies.

- **Log review and analysis:** Analyzing audit logs from cloud services, applications, and security tools provides valuable insights into data access patterns, system activities, and potential security incidents. This helps detect anomalous behavior, unauthorized access attempts, or policy violations that could impact privacy.

- **Third-party vendor risk management:** Organizations often rely on third-party cloud providers and sub-processors. Auditing techniques must extend to assessing the privacy practices and contractual obligations of these vendors to ensure they meet the required privacy standards. This includes reviewing their certifications, audit reports, and data processing agreements.

- **Privacy-enhancing technologies (PETs) assessment:** Where implemented, the effectiveness of PETs such as homomorphic encryption, differential privacy, or zero-knowledge proofs in protecting data privacy needs to be audited.

- **Contractual and policy review:** This involves scrutinizing contracts with CSPs and internal privacy policies to ensure they adequately address data ownership, data processing responsibilities, data residency, breach notification, and audit rights.

Key tools for auditing privacy

A variety of tools support the aforementioned techniques, as discussed as follows:

- **Data discovery and classification tools:** These tools automate the process of finding and categorizing sensitive data across cloud repositories. Examples include native cloud provider tools (e.g., Amazon Macie, Google Cloud Data Loss Prevention API, Microsoft Purview) and third-party solutions (e.g., Varonis, OneTrust DataDiscovery).

- **Security information and event management (SIEM) Systems:** SIEM tools collect, correlate, and analyze log data from various cloud sources to detect security threats and potential privacy incidents. Examples include Splunk, IBM QRadar, Microsoft Sentinel, and Elastic Stack.

- **Cloud security posture management (CSPM) tools:** CSPM solutions continuously monitor cloud environments for misconfigurations, compliance violations, and security risks. They provide dashboards and automated remediation capabilities. Examples include *Palo Alto Networks Prisma Cloud, CrowdStrike Falcon Horizon, Wiz,* and *Orca Security*.

- **Cloud access security brokers (CASBs):** CASBs serve as intermediaries between users and cloud services, helping to enforce security and privacy policies, monitor user activity, and safeguard sensitive data. They offer capabilities like DLP, threat protection, and identity management. Examples include *Netskope, Zscaler,* and *Microsoft Defender* for cloud apps.

- **Vulnerability scanners and penetration testing tools:** These tools help identify security weaknesses in cloud infrastructure and applications. Examples include *Nessus, Qualys, Metasploit,* and *Burp Suite*, often adapted for cloud environments.

- **IAM auditing tools:** Tools that help review and audit IAM policies, user permissions, and access patterns to ensure the principle of least privilege is enforced. Cloud providers offer native IAM services with auditing capabilities, and third-party tools can provide more advanced analytics.

- **DLP tools:** DLP solutions monitor and control the flow of sensitive data to prevent unauthorized exfiltration from the cloud. They can identify sensitive content in transit or at rest and apply policies to block or encrypt it. These are often integrated within CASBs, email security gateways, or endpoint protection platforms, and offered by cloud providers.

- **GRC platforms:** These platforms help automate and manage the compliance auditing process against various privacy regulations. They provide frameworks, controls mapping, evidence collection, and reporting capabilities. Examples include *OneTrust, Archer, ServiceNow GRC,* and *LogicManager*.

- **PET platforms and libraries:** While PETs themselves are techniques, specific software libraries and platforms facilitate their implementation and, by extension, their auditability. For instance, libraries for homomorphic encryption or differential privacy.

- **Log management and analysis tools:** Beyond SIEMs, dedicated log management tools can be used for in-depth analysis of specific logs relevant to privacy events.

- **Forensic tools:** In the event of a suspected privacy breach, cloud forensic tools help in collecting and analyzing digital evidence from cloud environments.

In conclusion, auditing privacy in the cloud is an ongoing and multifaceted endeavor. It necessitates a combination of robust methodologies, specialized tools, and a deep understanding of both privacy principles and cloud technologies. By strategically employing these tools and techniques, organizations can effectively manage privacy risks, demonstrate accountability, and build trust with their users in the ever-expanding cloud landscape.

Case studies

Understanding how cloud governance failures and data privacy breaches provide valuable lessons for organizations. While specific company names involved in these case studies are often not publicly detailed due to sensitivities, general scenarios and anonymized examples highlight common pitfalls. Note that the company names mentioned in these case studies are purely fictitious and used solely for illustrative purposes.

Case study on governance failures

Let us look at a scenario, *uncontrolled cloud sprawl and data exposure at a rapidly growing tech startup,* to understand the impact of governance failures. The lessons learned can help auditors strengthen their audit frameworks, identify gaps in governance implementation, and provide more informed recommendations to mitigate risks.

Background

A fast-growing tech startup, *InnovateFast Inc.*, embraced a cloud-first strategy to support its rapid development and scaling needs. Different development teams were given significant autonomy to provision cloud resources across multiple CSPs to foster innovation and speed to market.

Governance gaps

While analyzing a breach, the following gaps in governance were observed:

- **Lack of centralized oversight:** *InnovateFast* lacked a dedicated cloud governance body or a clearly defined set of enterprise-wide cloud policies. Individual teams made independent decisions regarding resource provisioning, security configurations, and data storage.

- **Inconsistent security configurations:** Without standardized security baselines, development teams configured security groups, access controls, and encryption settings inconsistently across different cloud instances and services. Some S3 buckets and databases were inadvertently left publicly accessible or had overly permissive access rules.

- **Shadow IT and unmanaged resources:** Developers frequently experimented with new cloud services without informing a central IT or security team. This led to a proliferation of unmanaged and unmonitored shadow IT resources, increasing the attack surface.

- **Absence of cost management practices:** With no centralized tracking or accountability for cloud spending, costs spiraled out of control. Teams often over-provision resources or leave unused instances running, leading to significant financial waste.

- **Insufficient data classification and protection:** Sensitive customer data was sometimes stored in development or test environments without adequate protection or anonymization, driven by the pressure to accelerate development cycles.

- **Inadequate audit trails and monitoring:** Due to the decentralized approach and lack of standardized logging, it was difficult to track who made what changes, identify misconfigurations, or detect suspicious activities across the multi-cloud environment.

Failure and its consequences

A security researcher discovered a publicly accessible database containing sensitive customer information, including PII and transaction details. The breach was traced back to a misconfigured cloud database set up by a development team for a temporary project and subsequently forgotten.

Upon conducting a deeper investigation into the breach, the following consequences were identified:

- **Data breach and reputational damage:** The exposure of customer data led to significant reputational damage, loss of customer trust, and negative media coverage.

- **Regulatory fines and legal action:** InnovateFast faced substantial fines from data protection authorities for non-compliance with regulations like GDPR and CCPA. They also faced potential lawsuits from affected customers.

- **Financial loss:** Beyond the fines, the company incurred significant costs related to forensic investigations, incident response, customer notifications, credit monitoring services for affected individuals, and lost business.

- **Operational disruption:** The incident response and remediation efforts consumed significant time and resources, diverting attention from core product development and innovation.

- **Loss of investor confidence:** The governance failure and subsequent data breach negatively impacted investor confidence and could have affected future funding rounds.

Lessons learned from the case

This case underscores the critical importance of proactive and robust cloud governance, even for agile and fast-moving organizations. Key takeaways include:

- **Establish centralized governance early:** Implement a cloud governance framework with clear policies, roles, and responsibilities from the outset, even if it is lightweight and evolves over time.

- **Enforce standardized security baselines:** Define and enforce minimum security configurations for all cloud resources. Utilize automation to check for compliance.

- **Implement strong IAM:** Control who can access what resources using the principle of least privilege.

- **Promote visibility and control over cloud resources:** Use tools and processes to discover, monitor, and manage all cloud assets, including those in development and test environments.

- **Integrate security into DevOps (DevSecOps):** Embed security considerations throughout the development lifecycle, rather than treating it as an afterthought.

- **Implement robust data governance:** Classify data, define data protection requirements, and ensure appropriate security controls are applied based on sensitivity.

- **Monitor cloud spending:** Implement cost management practices and tools to track and optimize cloud expenditure.

- **Regular audits and assessments:** Conduct periodic audits of cloud governance policies, procedures, and controls to identify and remediate weaknesses.

By understanding the potential pitfalls through such case studies, organizations can better appreciate the necessity of investing in and continuously improving their cloud governance frameworks. Auditing plays a crucial role in this continuous improvement cycle, providing the necessary checks and balances to ensure that cloud environments are managed responsibly and securely.

Case study on privacy breaches

Let us look at a scenario, *unsecured patient data exposure at a healthcare SaaS provider*, to understand the impact of privacy breaches. For auditors, analyzing such incidents provides valuable insights into where controls may break down, what red flags to look for during assessments, and how to evaluate the effectiveness of data protection measures. The lessons learned can help auditors strengthen their audit frameworks, identify gaps in privacy and security controls, and provide more informed recommendations to mitigate risks.

Background

HealthRecord Solutions (HRS) was a mid-sized SaaS provider offering electronic health record (EHR) management systems to small and medium-sized clinics. To ensure scalability and rapid deployment for its clients, HRS built its entire platform on a leading public cloud provider. Their system stored vast amounts of sensitive patient data, including medical histories, personal identification details, insurance information, and treatment notes, data explicitly protected under regulations like HIPAA (in the US) and GDPR (if serving European clients). HRS was known for its feature-rich platform but was operating with a relatively small IT and security team due to budget constraints, prioritizing feature development over comprehensive security and privacy overhauls.

The privacy breach at HRS occurred over several months and was multi-faceted, stemming from a combination of misconfigurations and inadequate security practices, as discussed as follows:

- **Misconfigured cloud storage (object storage)**: A primary development team at HRS utilized cloud object storage buckets for storing backups of patient databases and logs containing sensitive patient information. Due to a misconfiguration during setup, one of these large storage buckets was inadvertently set to publicly readable. While not directly browsable without knowing the exact URLs, the data was accessible to anyone who could guess or discover the bucket's name and file paths.

- **Weak access controls on development databases**: To expedite development and testing, copies of production patient data (intended to be anonymized but often were not fully or correctly) were used in development and staging environments hosted in the cloud. These non-production databases often had weak or default credentials, and network access rules were overly permissive, allowing broader access than necessary.

- **Compromised developer credentials**: An attacker, through a phishing campaign targeting HRS developers, managed to obtain valid credentials for one of HRS's cloud management accounts. This account, while not having full administrative privileges, had sufficient permissions to list storage buckets and access certain database management services.

- **Lack of data minimization and encryption at rest for certain datasets**: While production databases had encryption at rest enabled, some auxiliary data stores and older backups in the misconfigured bucket were not encrypted. Furthermore, the development teams often copied more data than was strictly necessary for their tasks, increasing the potential impact of any exposure.

- **Insufficient monitoring and alerting**: HRS had basic logging enabled but lacked sophisticated monitoring tools or alerts specifically configured to detect unusual access patterns to their cloud storage or anomalous activity within their development environments. The public accessibility of the storage bucket went unnoticed for an extended period.

Failures and consequences

An external security researcher eventually discovered the publicly accessible storage bucket through automated scanning tools that look for common misconfigurations. Separately, the compromised developer credentials allowed the attacker to explore other parts of the cloud environment, identifying and exfiltrating data from poorly secured development databases.

The following consequences were identified upon conducting a deeper investigation of the privacy breach:

- **Significant patient privacy violations**: Tens of thousands of patients had their sensitive health information exposed, leading to potential identity theft, fraud, and personal distress.

- **Regulatory investigations and severe fines**: HRS faced immediate investigation by regulatory bodies (e.g., the Office for Civil Rights for HIPAA violations). The potential fines were substantial, running into millions of dollars due to the sensitivity of the data and the number of affected individuals.

- **Loss of customer trust and business**: Clinics using HRS's EHR system lost trust in the platform's ability to protect patient data. Many clients terminated their contracts, leading to a significant loss of revenue and market share.

- **Reputational catastrophe**: The breach became public knowledge, severely damaging HRS's reputation within the healthcare industry and with the general public. Rebuilding that trust would be a long and arduous process.

- **Legal costs and lawsuits**: HRS faced numerous class-action lawsuits from affected patients, leading to extensive legal fees and potential settlement costs.

- **Operational disruption and remediation costs**: The company had to dedicate significant resources to investigating the breach, notifying affected individuals and regulators, remediating the security vulnerabilities, and implementing new security measures. This diverted resources from product development and customer support.

- **Impact on business viability**: The combined financial impact of fines, legal costs, lost business, and remediation efforts put the long-term viability of HRS in jeopardy.

Lessons learned

This case study of HRS underscores critical lessons for any organization handling sensitive data, especially PII and PHI, in the cloud:

- **Prioritize data governance and classification**: Implement a robust data governance framework. Know what sensitive data you have, where it resides (including non-production environments), who has access to it, and how it's protected throughout its lifecycle.

- **Embed privacy and security by design**: Security and privacy must be integral to system architecture and development processes from the start, not an afterthought. Implement secure defaults for all cloud services.

- **Implement strong IAM and least privilege**: Enforce granular access controls based on the principle of least privilege. Ensure MFA is mandated for all accounts, especially those with access to sensitive data or management consoles.

- **Continuous configuration monitoring and auditing**: Regularly audit cloud configurations using both manual reviews and automated tools to detect and remediate misconfigurations (e.g., public storage, weak passwords, overly permissive network rules) promptly.

- **Secure non-production environments**: Treat data in development, testing, and staging environments with appropriate security measures. Use properly anonymized or synthetic data whenever possible. If production data must be used, ensure it receives the same level of protection.

- **Comprehensive employee training**: Conduct regular and effective training on data security best practices, privacy regulations, phishing awareness, and secure coding.

- **Robust encryption**: Encrypt sensitive data both at rest (in databases, storage) and in transit. Manage encryption keys securely.

- **Develop and test incident response plans**: Have a well-defined incident response plan specifically for cloud security and privacy breaches. Test it regularly.

- **Invest in security tools**: Utilize appropriate security tools for the cloud, such as CSPM, DLP, and advanced threat detection solutions.

- **Vendor risk management**: Thoroughly vet the security practices of any third-party vendors or tools that will interact with your cloud environment or data.

The HRS incident serves as a stark reminder that the convenience and scalability of the cloud come with significant responsibilities regarding data privacy. A proactive, defense-in-depth approach to security and governance is essential to prevent devastating privacy breaches.

Conclusion

This chapter explored the auditing of cloud governance and data privacy, with a focus on key areas such as data residency, encryption, and the implementation of privacy-by-design principles, while highlighting the importance of ensuring compliance with both national and international regulatory frameworks.

The upcoming chapter will provide guidance on auditing CSPs, covering third-party risk management, **service level agreements (SLAs)**, and the shared responsibility model. It includes key metrics to measure CSP compliance and performance.

Points to remember

- Auditing cloud governance begins with a thorough assessment of the organization's established policies and procedures.

- Establishing effective governance structures in multi-cloud environments is paramount to maintaining control, security, and cost-efficiency.

- Many regulations impose restrictions on cross-border data transfers and may require data to be stored and/or processed within specific geographic locations.

- Regulations and best practices increasingly emphasize *privacy-by-design and by default*, i.e., embedding privacy considerations into the design and architecture of systems and processes from the outset.

- The decentralized, scalable nature of cloud environments introduces a new layer of complexity to privacy audits, requiring a deep understanding of shared responsibilities, ever-evolving regulations, and sophisticated audit methodologies.

- Auditing data privacy in the cloud is not a one-time activity; it is a continuous process requiring strategic planning, rigorous control testing, and ongoing vigilance.

- Auditing privacy necessitates a combination of robust methodologies, specialized tools, and a deep understanding of both privacy principles and cloud technologies.

Multiple choice questions

1. **Which of the following is the most important reason for auditors to evaluate cloud governance during a cloud audit?**

    a. To verify that cloud services are using the latest technology

    b. To ensure the organization receives cost-effective cloud subscriptions

    c. To ensure cloud governance policies align with business objectives and risk appetite

    d. To confirm that employees prefer using cloud applications over on-premise systems

2. **Which of the following best distinguishes a federated governance model from a centralized governance model in cloud environments?**

    a. A federated model eliminates the need for governance altogether

    b. A centralized model allows each business unit to create its own policies independently

    c. A federated model allows for some degree of autonomy for individual business units

    d. A centralized model typically results in inconsistent compliance across the organization

3. **What is the primary purpose of the HITRUST Common Security Framework (CSF) in healthcare and related industries?**

    a. To replace all other cybersecurity frameworks with a single federal standard

    b. To provide a certifiable framework that harmonizes multiple security, privacy, and regulatory requirements

    c. To ensure that only large healthcare organizations can achieve compliance

    d. To regulate the pricing of healthcare IT services

4. **Which of the following is a key challenge when auditing data privacy in cloud environments?**

    a. Lack of internet connectivity in cloud platforms

    b. Excessive on-premise storage requirements

    c. Limited visibility into CSP data handling practices

    d. Incompatibility of cloud systems with encryption technologies

5. **What is the primary objective of conducting a privacy impact assessment (PIA)?**

    a. To assess the market value of personal data

    b. To analyze how an organization can profit from user data

    c. To identify and mitigate privacy risks in data processing activities

    d. To determine employee satisfaction with data handling procedures

Answers

1	c
2	c
3	b
4	c
5	c

Join our Discord space

Join our Discord workspace for latest updates, offers, tech happenings around the world, new releases, and sessions with the authors:

https://discord.bpbonline.com

CHAPTER 12
Auditing Cloud Service Providers

Introduction

Auditing **cloud service providers** (**CSPs**) is essential for organizations to ensure compliance, data security, service availability, and alignment with regulatory and business requirements. Given the shared responsibility model inherent in cloud computing, due diligence in evaluating and continuously monitoring CSPs is a critical component of enterprise risk management.

This chapter provides guidance on auditing CSPs, covering **third-party risk management** (**TPRM**), **service level agreements** (**SLAs**), and the shared responsibility model. It includes key metrics to measure CSP compliance and performance.

Structure

This chapter covers the following topics:

- Cloud service agreements and contracts
- Auditing CSP's certifications
- Auditing CSPs
- Key metrics to review

Objectives

By the end of this chapter, readers will gain a clear understanding of how to effectively audit CSPs. The chapter explores critical areas such as TPRM, SLAs and the shared responsibility model. It also introduces essential metrics for evaluating CSP compliance and performance.

Cloud service agreements and contracts

The migration to cloud services presents a paradigm shift for organizations, offering scalability, efficiency, and innovation. However, this transition also introduces new complexities and risks, particularly concerning the contractual agreements that govern these relationships. From an auditor's perspective, a thorough understanding of CSAs and contracts is paramount to ensuring data integrity, security, compliance, and effective governance. These legally binding documents outline the terms and conditions between a CSP and its customer, and auditors play a critical role in scrutinizing them to protect their organization's interests.

CSAs and contracts serve as the foundation of the relationship between a cloud consumer and a provider. These documents define the legal, technical, and operational framework for services delivered.

Key audit focus areas in CSAs

Auditors must dissect CSAs with a meticulous eye, focusing on several critical areas:

- **Data security and privacy:** This is often the foremost concern. Auditors need to verify clauses related to data ownership, data location (residency and sovereignty), encryption (in transit and at rest), access controls (including multi-factor authentication and least privilege principles), and data segregation. The agreement should clearly define the CSP's responsibilities for protecting sensitive data and outline procedures for data breach notifications and investigations.

- **SLAs:** SLAs define the expected level of service, including uptime guarantees, performance metrics (e.g., response times, processing speeds), and availability. Auditors must assess whether these SLAs are clearly defined, measurable, and aligned with business requirements. Crucially, the SLA should also detail remedies or penalties for non-compliance, such as service credits.

- **Compliance and regulatory requirements:** CSAs must address adherence to relevant industry-specific regulations (e.g., HIPAA for healthcare, PCI DSS for payment card industry, GDPR for data protection in Europe, SOX for financial reporting). Auditors need to ensure the CSP can provide evidence of compliance through certifications (e.g., ISO 27001, SOC 2 Type II reports) and that the agreement facilitates the organization's own compliance obligations.

- **Right to audit and transparency:** A critical clause for auditors is the *right to audit*. This provision grants the customer (or their appointed auditor) the ability to assess the CSP's controls and adherence to the agreement. Auditors should examine the scope of these rights, including the frequency of audits, methodologies allowed (e.g., penetration testing, vulnerability assessments), and access to relevant documentation and personnel. While direct audits of a CSP's data center might be limited, the agreement should provide for access to third-party audit reports (like SOC 2).

- **Business continuity and disaster recovery (BCDR):** The CSA should clearly delineate the CSP's BCDR capabilities and responsibilities. Auditors must review provisions related to data backup frequency, **recovery time objectives** (**RTOs**), **recovery point objectives** (**RPOs**), and the provider's disaster recovery testing procedures. Understanding the shared responsibilities for BCDR is crucial.

- **Data ownership, portability, and exit strategy:** Clarity on data ownership is non-negotiable. The agreement must explicitly state that the customer retains ownership of their data. Furthermore, auditors should scrutinize clauses related to data portability, the ability to retrieve data in a usable format if the organization decides to switch providers or terminate the service. A well-defined exit strategy, including data extraction procedures and timelines, is essential to avoid vendor lock-in.

- **Indemnification and limitation of liability:** These clauses address how liability is apportioned in case of breaches, service failures, or other issues. Auditors, often in conjunction with legal counsel, need to assess the fairness and adequacy of these provisions, ensuring the organization is not unduly exposed to risk.

- **Change management:** Cloud environments are dynamic. The CSA should outline the process for how the CSP will notify customers of changes to services, infrastructure, or security controls, and what rights the customer has in response to these changes.

- **Confidentiality and intellectual property:** Provisions protecting the confidentiality of the customer's data and respecting intellectual property rights are fundamental and require careful review.

Auditor's role in the CSA lifecycle

The auditor's involvement should not be limited to a post-contract review. Ideally, the internal auditors should participate throughout the CSA lifecycle, as follows:

- **Pre-contract due diligence:** Before an agreement is signed, auditors can help assess the CSP's security posture, review their standard contract terms, and identify potential risks.

- **Contract negotiation:** While legal teams lead negotiations, auditors can provide valuable input on technical and security-related clauses to ensure they meet the organization's control objectives.

- **Ongoing monitoring and review:** After the contract is in place, auditors are responsible for continuously monitoring the CSP's compliance with the agreed-upon terms, often through the review of performance reports, security attestations, and by exercising audit rights where applicable.

- **Contract renewal or termination:** Auditors play a key role in evaluating the CSP's performance and the continued suitability of the CSA when it's time for renewal. In case of termination, they oversee the secure extraction and deletion of data.

Challenges for auditors

Auditing CSAs in the cloud environment presents unique challenges, as discussed hereunder:

- **Limited visibility and control:** Organizations often have less direct control and visibility over the infrastructure and processes of the CSP compared to on-premises solutions.

- **Shared responsibility model:** Understanding and auditing the demarcation of responsibilities between the CSP and the customer for security and compliance can be complex.

- **Zero-day exploits:** A zero-day exploit targets a vulnerability that is unknown to the software vendor or CSP, meaning no patch or mitigation is available. Audits rely on assessing known risks and mitigation plans. Zero-day exploits are, by definition, unknown, which makes risk quantification impossible. Additionally, zero-day exploits may fall into a gray area in the shared responsibility model, where it is unclear who is liable or responsible for damage.

- **Black-box AI/ML services:** These are AI/ML systems (like recommendation engines, fraud detection models, etc.) whose inner workings are opaque or inaccessible to users. Without transparency, it is difficult for auditors to determine how decisions are made, which hinders compliance checks (e.g., GDPR's *right to explanation*) and to assess whether the models are free from bias or ethical concerns.

- **Standardized agreements:** Many CSPs offer standardized agreements with limited room for negotiation, requiring auditors to carefully assess if the standard terms adequately address the organization's risk appetite.

- **Rapid technological changes:** The fast pace of innovation in cloud services means that CSAs and the associated risks need to be continually reassessed.

- **Global data flows and jurisdictional complexity:** Data may be stored and processed in multiple jurisdictions, each with its own set of laws and regulations, adding layers of complexity to compliance.

In summary, as organizations continue to rely on CSPs to manage their data and critical operations, the thorough examination of CSAs becomes a cornerstone of effective auditing. By applying a diligent, risk-focused approach and scrutinizing key contractual elements, auditors play a vital role in safeguarding organizational assets, ensuring regulatory compliance, and enabling secure, strategic cloud adoption. Their oversight helps bridge the gap between innovation and governance, ensuring that the promises of the cloud are delivered without compromising security or accountability.

Auditors should ensure the contract aligns with organizational policy, compliance needs, and industry best practices.

Auditing CSP's certifications

CSPs often possess third-party certifications that attest to their security and compliance posture. These certifications should be verified and assessed for scope and relevance.

Auditing a CSP's security certifications is a critical step in due diligence and ongoing vendor risk management. It is not enough to simply see a list of logos on a CSP's website; organizations must understand the scope, relevance, and implications of these certifications. Effectively auditing these certifications ensures that the CSP's security practices align with the organization's own security and compliance requirements.

Landscape of CSP certifications

CSPs often hold a variety of global and industry-specific certifications to demonstrate their commitment to security and data protection.

Some of the most common and important ones include:

- **ISO/IEC 27001, 27017, 27018:** ISO/IEC 27001 is a globally recognized standard that defines the requirements for establishing, implementing, maintaining, and continually improving an **information security management system** (**ISMS**). A CSP certified under ISO 27001 demonstrates a systematic and risk-based approach to managing sensitive organizational and customer information, supported by a comprehensive set of security controls.

  During an audit, it is essential to review the **Statement of Applicability (SoA)**, which outlines the specific controls chosen by the CSP, those that have been excluded, and the justification for any exclusions. This document provides critical insight into how the organization tailors its security practices to meet its unique risk environment.

  To further strengthen cloud-specific and privacy-related assurances:

  o **ISO/IEC 27017** extends ISO 27001 by offering additional guidelines for information security controls applicable to cloud services. It addresses responsibilities shared between CSPs and customers and clarifies best practices for cloud-specific threats.

- o **ISO/IEC 27018** complements this by focusing on the protection of **Personally Identifiable Information** (**PII**) in public cloud environments, providing principles for handling personal data in line with privacy regulations.

Together, these standards form a robust framework for evaluating the security and privacy posture of cloud services, and their presence in a CSP's certification scope adds significant assurance regarding the provider's commitment to safeguarding information in the cloud.

- **ISO 22301**: It is the international standard for **business continuity management systems** (**BCMS**), and for a CSP, it demonstrates the ability to maintain and quickly recover critical cloud services during disruptions, ensuring resilience, availability, and trust for customers.

- **System and organization controls 2 (SOC 2):** Developed by the **American Institute of CPAs** (**AICPA**), SOC 2 reports on a CSP's controls relevant to one or more Trust Services Criteria: Security, Availability, Processing Integrity, Confidentiality, and Privacy.

  - o **Type I reports** assess the design of controls at a specific point in time.

  - o **Type II reports** assess the operational effectiveness of controls over a period (usually 6-12 months). **Type II reports are generally preferred** as they provide greater assurance. Pay close attention to any **exceptions** noted by the auditor.

- **Federal Risk and Authorization Management Program (FedRAMP):** This is a U.S. government-wide program that provides a standardized approach to security assessment, authorization, and continuous monitoring for cloud products and services. If the organization is a contractor handling federal data, this is mandatory. The **authorization level (Low, Moderate, High)** is a key consideration.

- **Cloud Security Alliance Security, Trust, Assurance, and Risk (CSA STA):** This program offers a multi-layered approach to cloud security assurance.

  - o **Level 1: Self-assessment:** Based on the **Consensus Assessments Initiative Questionnaire** (**CAIQ**).

  - o **Level 2: Third-party audit:** Builds on standards like ISO 27001 or SOC 2, tailored for cloud environments.

  - o **Level 3: Continuous monitoring:** The highest level, demonstrating ongoing security posture management.

- **Payment Card Industry-Data Security Standard (PCI-DSS):** Essential for CSPs that store, process, or transmit cardholder data. Ensure the CSP's certification aligns with the services the organization intends to use for handling such data.

- **Health Insurance Portability and Accountability Act (HIPAA):** U.S. healthcare providers and related entities must ensure their CSPs can support HIPAA compliance for **Protected Health Information (PHI)**. The CSP should be willing to sign a **business associate agreement (BAA)**.

Key steps in auditing CSP certifications

Auditing CSP certifications involves more than just collecting certificates. Here is a practical and systematic approach:

- **Identify requirements:** Before looking at CSP certifications, understand the organization's specific security needs, industry regulations (e.g., GDPR, CCPA, HIPAA), and data sensitivity levels. This will help in determining which certifications are most relevant.

- **Review documentation:** Ask the CSP for their latest certification documents and audit reports or other recognized compliance attestations (e.g., SOC 2 Type II report, ISO 27001 certificate, and SoA). Confirm that the reports are current and cover all relevant services and geographic regions used by the organization. Independent validation strengthens assurance that the CSP's controls are not only documented but also effectively implemented and regularly assessed.

- **Scope and validity**: Ensure the certification explicitly covers the specific services, data centers, and geographic regions relevant to the organization's usage. In some instances, certifications may only apply to certain segments of a CSP's operations, and not necessarily to the services the organization is consuming. Verify the validity period of the certification and confirm that it is current and up to date.

- **Analyze audit reports in detail:**
    o For SOC 2 reports, carefully read the auditor's opinion, the description of the system, and any identified exceptions or misconfigurations. Understand the implications of these exceptions for the organization's risk posture.
    o For ISO 27001, review the SoA to understand which controls are in place and why any might be excluded.

- **Understand the shared responsibility model:** Certifications cover the CSP's infrastructure and services, but the organization is still responsible for securing what they build *on* the cloud (e.g., applications, data access controls, user configurations). Clarify where the CSP's responsibility ends and the customer's begins.

- **Assess the auditor's reputation:** Consider the reputation and experience of the third-party auditing firm that issued the certification.

- **Look for continuous monitoring evidence:** For mature cloud environments, especially those with CSA STAR Level 3, inquire about their continuous monitoring practices. Security is not a one-time event.

- **Ask questions:** Auditors should not hesitate to ask the CSP clarifying questions about their certifications, audit findings, or security practices. Their willingness and ability to provide clear, transparent answers can be telling.

- **Confirm alignment with regulations:** During the audit of a CSP's certifications, it is critical to ensure that the certifications held by the provider align with the applicable regulatory and compliance requirements relevant to the organization and industry. Misalignment may lead to compliance gaps or increased risk exposure. Confirming this alignment ensures that the CSP can support the organization's governance, risk, and compliance objectives.

- **Consider contractual obligations:** Ensure that the CSP's contractual agreements reflect their security commitments and include provisions for notifying of security incidents or significant changes to their security posture.

While certifications are valuable indicators, they are not a silver bullet. A holistic approach to evaluating CSP security should also include:

- Reviewing the CSP's security policies and practices directly.

- Understanding their incident response and disaster recovery capabilities.

- Assessing their data privacy and data residency options.

- Seeking peer reviews and industry reputation.

By diligently auditing a CSP's security certifications, organizations can gain greater confidence in their cloud provider's ability to protect sensitive data and maintain operational resilience, ultimately supporting their own security and compliance objectives.

Auditing CSPs

In an era of ubiquitous cloud adoption, organizations increasingly rely on CSPs for critical business functions, data storage, and processing. While offering significant benefits in scalability, efficiency, and innovation, this reliance introduces complex risks. Effectively auditing CSPs has therefore become a non-negotiable component of an audit engagement. It provides necessary assurance that sensitive data and critical operations housed within external cloud environments are adequately protected and compliant with regulatory and organizational standards.

Third-party risk management

Third-party breaches, including those involving CSPs, are a leading cause of significant financial and reputational damage for organizations. The shared responsibility model dictates that while CSPs are responsible for the security *of* the cloud, their customers are responsible for security *in* the cloud. Auditing CSP's TPRM program allows organizations to:

- **Validate security posture:** Verify that the CSP's stated security controls and practices are effectively implemented and align with the organization's risk appetite and compliance requirements.

- **Ensure regulatory compliance:** Demonstrate due diligence to regulators and stakeholders by ensuring that both the organization and its CSPs adhere to relevant industry-specific and data protection regulations.

- **Identify and mitigate risks:** Proactively identify potential vulnerabilities, misconfigurations, or gaps in the CSP's environment that could expose the organization to threats such as data breaches, service disruptions, or compliance failures.

- **Enforce contractual obligations:** Ensure the CSP is meeting the security, availability, and confidentiality requirements outlined in SLAs and contracts.

- **Enhance visibility and control:** Gain a clearer understanding of the CSP's operational environment, sub-processor dependencies (fourth-party risks), and incident response capabilities.

- **Build trust and transparency:** Foster a more transparent and accountable relationship with the CSP through regular assessments and open communication about risk.

Engaging CSPs introduces a broad spectrum of risks, including cybersecurity, operational, regulatory, and strategic, that must be proactively managed through effective TPRM and rigorous auditing.

Let us discuss the common risks that are typical in these scenarios:

- **Cybersecurity threats**, such as data breaches, denial-of-service attacks, and malware infiltration, are among the most prominent risks. Mitigation relies on enforcing robust security controls within the CSP, supported by contractual obligations, penetration testing, continuous monitoring, and scheduled audits to validate their effectiveness.

- **Operational risks**, including service outages, data loss, or disruptions underscore the need for comprehensive BCDR plans. Auditors must ensure the CSP provides clear SLAs for availability and transparency around redundancy and failover mechanisms.

- **Compliance and regulatory exposure** can arise from non-adherence to applicable regulations and standards. Organizations must validate the CSP's certifications, confirm contractual clauses address compliance requirements, and ensure data residency, sovereignty, and audit rights are adequately covered.

- **Reputational damage** may result from CSP-related incidents or unethical practices. TPRM should include assessments of the CSP's public trust, incident response transparency, and legal protections through well-defined contractual terms.

- **Financial risks**, arising out of breaches, downtime, or provider insolvency, necessitate an evaluation of the CSP's financial health, insurance provisions, and liability definitions within the contractual framework.

- **Strategic misalignment and vendor lock-in** can hinder long-term agility. Risk mitigation involves ensuring alignment between CSP services and business objectives, establishing flexible contracts, and defining clear exit strategies to avoid dependency.

- **Geopolitical considerations**, such as the legal and political stability of regions hosting data centers, must be factored into risk assessments, particularly when dealing with cross-border data flows.

- **Limited visibility and control** over cloud-hosted systems can impair oversight. Auditors should confirm that CSPs offer comprehensive reporting, support for extended monitoring tools, and unambiguous audit rights.

- **Fourth-party risks**, introduced by CSP subcontractors and sub-processors, require attention to the CSP's own TPRM practices. This includes contractual notification requirements, approval mechanisms for sub-processors, and scrutiny of the criticality and risk posture of downstream vendors.

Tools and techniques for auditing TPRM

Leveraging appropriate tools and techniques can streamline and enhance the effectiveness of CSP TPRM audits:

- **Vendor risk management (VRM) platforms**: Software solutions to automate and manage the TPRM lifecycle, including onboarding, risk assessments, due diligence, contract management, and continuous monitoring.

- **Continuous monitoring**: Continuous auditing in TPRM leverages automated tools and real-time techniques to monitor third-party activities and compliance with contractual, regulatory, and security standards. Key tools include vulnerability management and security assessment tools (e.g., *tenable.io, Qualys, Rapid7* etc.), GRC platforms (e.g., *Archer* or *ServiceNow*), and SIEM solutions (e.g., *Splunk, IBM QRadar, Microsoft Sentinel*) that provide ongoing visibility into vendor behavior. Techniques such as API-based data integration, automated control testing, continuous vulnerability scanning, and AI-driven anomaly detection enable organizations to proactively identify and address emerging risks. These tools support a shift from point-in-time assessments to a dynamic, risk-based monitoring approach, improving resilience and accountability in third-party ecosystems.

- **Security ratings services**: Provide objective, data-driven scores of a CSP's security posture based on externally observable data.

- **Questionnaires**: The SIG Questionnaire developed and maintained by Shared Assessments, a non-profit organization and CAIQ with STAR Registry developed by Cloud Security Alliance are foundational tools in third-party risk assessments, promoting standardization, transparency, and scalability. They support continuous auditing by enabling structured, repeatable evaluations of vendor controls and by integrating with broader risk monitoring processes, especially in cloud and hybrid environments.

- **Automated questionnaires**: Streamline the distribution, collection, and analysis of security questionnaires.

- **CSPM tools**: Help identify and remediate misconfigurations and compliance risks in cloud environments (often used by the customer to manage their side of the shared responsibility model, but insights can inform CSP discussions).

- **Threat intelligence platforms**: Provide insights into the threat landscape relevant to the CSP and the services they provide.

- **DLP tools**: Can help monitor and control sensitive data movement to and from cloud environments.

- **Identity and access management (IAM) solutions**: Crucial for managing access to cloud resources based on the principle of least privilege.

- **Penetration testing and vulnerability scanning tools**: Used to actively test the security of cloud environments (often with CSP coordination and approval).

Evaluating CSP's supply chain

While direct audits of sub-contractors are rarely feasible for an end-customer, auditors can (and should) evaluate how well the CSP manages these superscript th-party risks.

This involves the following:

- **Due diligence:** Conducting due diligence during CSP selection and onboarding is a critical component of TPRM. Key due diligence activities include the following:

  o **TPRM program:** Review the CSP's TPRM program for its critical suppliers. Look for evidence of a mature program that includes due diligence, contractual requirements, and ongoing monitoring of its own vendors.

  o **Sub-contractor management:** Review specifically how they identify, assess, and monitor critical sub-contractors. Do they flow down security and compliance requirements to them?

  o **Identify critical sub-contractors:** For services that are heavily reliant on specific sub-contractors (e.g., a particular data center provider for a specific region), try to get visibility into who these are.

- **Contractual agreements with the CSP:** Establishing robust contractual agreements with CSPs is essential in TPRM to clearly define responsibilities, expectations, and legal protections. Contracts should address key areas such as:

  o **Right to information/audit:** While a direct audit of sub-contractors is unlikely, the organization's contract with the CSP should ideally include clauses requiring them to provide assurance regarding the security practices of their critical sub-contractors.

- **Notification of sub-contractor changes:** Require the CSP to notify of any changes to critical sub-contractors involved in delivering the service and potentially grant approval rights.

- **Flow-down of obligations:** The contract should stipulate that the CSP imposes security, confidentiality, and compliance obligations on its sub-contractors that are at least as stringent as those imposed on the CSP itself.

- **Liability for sub-contractor failures:** Clarify the CSP's liability in the event of a breach or service disruption caused by one of its sub-contractors.

- **Reviewing CSP's certifications/attestations:** As part of TPRM, reviewing a CSP's certifications and attestations is a key step in validating their security and compliance posture:

  - **SOC 2 reports:** A CSP's SOC 2 report may include controls related to its vendor management program. Look for details on how they assess and manage risks from their own suppliers.

  - **ISO 27001 certification:** An ISO 27001-certified CSP should have processes for managing information security in its supply chain.

  - **Industry-specific certifications:** Certifications like HITRUST may also incorporate aspects of supply chain risk management.

- **Ongoing monitoring and communication:** Ongoing monitoring and communication are vital components of TPRM to ensure that CSPs continue to meet contractual, security, and compliance obligations throughout the relationship.

  This includes:

  - **Regular reviews:** During periodic reviews with CSP, include questions about their supply chain risk management practices and any significant changes or incidents involving their key sub-contractors.

  - **Incident response plans:** Understand how the CSP's incident response plan incorporates incidents originating from their supply chain. How would they notify if a subcontractor breach affects the organization's data or service?

  - **Threat intelligence:** Monitor threat intelligence feeds for reports of compromises or vulnerabilities affecting known major technology suppliers, as these could indirectly impact the CSP.

- **Focus on the CSP's resilience and security posture**: Evaluating a CSP's overall resilience and security posture is a critical element of TPRM.

Key focus areas include:

- o Ultimately, a strong indicator of a well-managed supply chain is the CSP's own robust security posture and demonstrated resilience. If the CSP has mature security practices, it is more likely that they apply similar rigor to their own vendor selection and management.

- o Assess their ability to mitigate and recover from disruptions, regardless of whether the root cause is internal or within their supply chain.

Auditing CSPs is not a one-time checkbox activity but an ongoing, integral part of a dynamic TPRM program. The risks associated with a CSP do not just reside within their immediate infrastructure and operations; they extend down their supply chain to their own vendors and subcontractors (often referred to as n superscript th-parties or fourth-party risks). The *trust but verify* approach, extended to the nth-party level where possible, is crucial in today's interconnected digital landscape.

Service level agreements

Auditing SLAs is crucial for ensuring that the cloud services received by the organization meet performance, availability, security, and compliance requirements as contractually agreed. It involves systematically reviewing and verifying that the CSP is adhering to the promises made in the SLA. This process helps in identifying discrepancies, managing risks, optimizing costs, and maintaining a healthy and transparent relationship between the CSP and the customer.

SLAs form the contractual backbone between a CSP and its customers. These documents outline the specific terms of service, including performance metrics, availability guarantees, security responsibilities, and remedies for non-compliance. However, simply having an SLA in place is not enough. Auditing SLAs is a critical process that ensures these agreements are being met and that the cloud services align with business needs and expectations.

Importance of auditing SLAs

Auditing SLAs offers several key benefits, discussed as follows:

- **Verification of service delivery:** It confirms that the CSP is delivering the agreed-upon levels of service regarding uptime, performance, and support.

- **Risk management:** Identifies potential risks associated with non-compliance, such as data loss, security breaches, or service disruptions, allowing for proactive mitigation.

- **Cost optimization:** Ensures that the organization is getting the expected value and can help identify if the organization is over-provisioned or if penalties for SLA breaches are due.

- **Compliance and governance:** Helps meet regulatory and internal governance requirements by demonstrating due diligence in vendor management.

- **Improved vendor relationship:** Fosters transparency and accountability, leading to a stronger, more collaborative relationship with the CSP.

- **Informed decision-making:** Provides data-driven insights to make informed decisions about service continuation, migration, or negotiation of SLA terms.

Key components to audit

When auditing SLAs, focus should be on the specific commitments made by the provider. Common areas to be assessed by auditors include:

- **Availability (Uptime):** Verify the CSP's reported uptime against actual service availability. Understand how downtime is defined and measured (e.g., scheduled maintenance exclusions).

- **Performance:** Assess whether the application and infrastructure performance meet the defined thresholds. This may involve using monitoring tools to collect independent data.

- **Security and compliance:** Review the CSP's compliance certifications, audit reports, security policies, and incident response plans. Verify that data handling and protection measures align with the SLA and relevant regulations.

- **Data management:** Confirm that backup and recovery procedures are in place and tested. Verify that data is stored in agreed-upon geographical locations.

- **Support and incident response:** Evaluate the timeliness and effectiveness of the CSP's support services. Review incident logs and resolution pathways.

- **Penalties and remedies:** Understand the process for claiming remedies and ensure it's clearly defined and actionable. Track instances of non-compliance and the application of penalties.

Audit tools

Tools that can aid in auditing SLAs include the following:

- Cloud provider's own monitoring dashboards and reporting tools (e.g., AWS CloudWatch, Azure Monitor, Google Cloud Monitoring)
- Third-party cloud monitoring and observability platforms
- **Security information and event management** (**SIEM**) systems
- Compliance management software

Challenges in auditing SLAs

Auditing SLAs presents several challenges. Variability in reporting practices and the CSP's willingness to share detailed audit data further complicate effective oversight. Despite these obstacles, regular SLA reviews are essential to ensure accountability and alignment with business and regulatory expectations.

Let us look at some of the challenges in auditing SLAs:

- **Lack of transparency:** Some CSPs may provide limited visibility into their operations and performance data, making independent verification difficult.

- **Complexity of cloud environments:** Multi-cloud and hybrid cloud architectures can complicate monitoring and data collection.

- **Standardized vs. customized SLAs:** Standard SLAs offered by major CSPs may be non-negotiable and difficult to audit against specific, unique requirements. Custom SLAs, while more tailored, can be complex to manage.

- **Defining and measuring metrics:** Ambiguity in how metrics are defined or measured in the SLA can lead to disputes.

- **Shared responsibility model:** Understanding the division of responsibilities between the CSP and the customer is crucial, as the audit scope needs to reflect this.

- **Resource intensive:** Conducting thorough audits requires time, expertise, and potentially specialized tools.

- **Vendor resistance:** CSPs might be hesitant to provide access to certain data or systems for auditing purposes, citing security or proprietary concerns.

By diligently auditing SLAs, organizations can gain greater control over their cloud investments, mitigate risks, and ensure that their cloud services effectively support their business objectives. It is an ongoing process that demands attention to detail, clear communication, and a proactive approach to vendor management.

Shared responsibilities

Auditing shared responsibilities in cloud environments is a crucial aspect. Effective auditing requires a clear understanding of this shared responsibility model, documented roles, and verification that both parties are fulfilling their obligations. Without proper oversight, gaps in shared responsibilities can lead to security vulnerabilities and compliance failures, making regular audits essential for risk mitigation and accountability.

Effective auditing provides clarity and accountability by ensuring both parties understand and adhere to their respective roles. This not only helps manage risk and identify potential security or compliance gaps but also supports regulatory alignment, vendor performance evaluation, and clearly defined incident response procedures. By formally reviewing how responsibilities are assigned and fulfilled, organizations can better mitigate risks arising from assumptions, oversights, or unaddressed areas in the shared responsibility model.

Areas of focus in auditing shared responsibilities

Now, let us discuss the key areas the auditor should focus on while auditing the shared responsibilities:

- **Contractual agreements**: Audits should begin by reviewing formal agreements such as contracts, terms of service, and SLAs to ensure responsibilities are explicitly defined. Clear responsibility matrices (e.g., RACI charts) can help delineate who is accountable for specific tasks. Additionally, third-party attestations such as SOC 2 or ISO/IEC 27001 reports provide valuable insight into the CSP's control environment and the scope of their responsibilities.

- **CSP responsibilities**: Though direct access to a CSP's internal systems may be limited, auditors can still assess the CSP's obligations through available documentation and third-party reports. Focus areas include data center security, infrastructure protection (compute, storage, and networking), virtualization safeguards, personnel vetting and training, and the CSP's incident detection and response capabilities.

- **Customer responsibilities**: The customer is typically responsible for securing their own data, applications, and configurations. Audits should verify the implementation of strong IAM, proper data protection mechanisms (e.g., encryption, DLP), application and operating system security, network segmentation, and effective logging, monitoring, and configuration management. Ensuring the principle of least privilege, timely patching, and continuous monitoring are especially important in this domain.

- **Shared controls and integration points**: Certain areas require collaboration between the CSP and the customer. These include federated IAM systems, security event monitoring interfaces, API security, and disaster recovery capabilities. Auditors should examine how responsibilities are coordinated across these shared controls, ensuring both parties contribute effectively to the overall security posture.

Challenges in auditing shared responsibilities

Despite its importance, auditing shared responsibilities presents notable challenges. The complexity of cloud environments, particularly in PaaS or hybrid models, can blur lines of accountability. CSPs may limit transparency, requiring reliance on third-party audit reports instead of direct evidence. Additionally, the dynamic nature of cloud services means that configurations and responsibilities can shift frequently, making it difficult to maintain a current audit perspective.

Skill gaps within audit teams may also hinder effectiveness, as cloud-specific expertise is often required to interpret controls and architectures accurately. Furthermore, limitations imposed by CSP contracts, such as the absence of *right to audit* clauses, can restrict an organization's ability to verify provider compliance directly.

Auditing shared responsibilities in cloud environments is not solely about assessing the CSP's controls; it is equally about ensuring the organization is upholding its own obligations.

A comprehensive audit approach must combine a clear understanding of the shared responsibility model with thorough documentation review, stakeholder engagement, and risk-based evaluation of both external and internal controls. By doing so, organizations can maintain a resilient, secure, and compliant cloud posture while strengthening their overall TPRM strategy.

Business continuity and disaster recovery

The ubiquitous nature of CSP's operations underscores the critical importance of robust BCDR capabilities at the CSP level. For organizations entrusting their data and services to these providers, a thorough audit of the CSP's BCDR preparedness is not just a best practice, but a fundamental requirement for managing risk and ensuring their own operational resilience.

Auditing a CSP's BCDR framework involves a comprehensive evaluation of their ability to maintain service availability, protect data integrity, and recover operations effectively in the face of disruptions. These disruptions can range from natural disasters and power outages to cyberattacks and human error. A well-structured audit provides assurance that the CSP can meet its contractual obligations and safeguard customer interests even under duress.

Key areas of auditing BCDR

A comprehensive audit of a CSP's BCDR capabilities should delve into several critical domains discussed as follows:

- **BCDR strategy and policies:** Scrutinize the existence, clarity, and completeness of the CSP's documented BCDR strategy and supporting policies. These should align with industry standards (e.g., ISO 22301, NIST SP 800-34) and clearly define roles, responsibilities, and communication protocols.

- **Risk management integration:** Verify that BCDR planning is an integral part of the CSP's overall risk management framework. This includes regular risk assessments specific to business continuity threats.

- **Compliance and certifications:** Assess the CSP's adherence to relevant regulatory requirements and industry certifications (e.g., SOC 2 Type 2 with a focus on the Availability Trust Service Principle, ISO 22301, which provides a framework for ensuring the continuity of their services, even during disruptions). These certifications often provide a baseline level of assurance.

- **Criticality assessment:** Review the **business impact analysis (BIA)** to evaluate the CSP's process for identifying critical business processes, applications, and underlying infrastructure that support their services to customers.

- **Recovery objectives:** Verify the definition and documentation of **recovery time objectives (RTOs)** and **recovery point objectives (RPOs)** for critical services. These should be clearly communicated to customers, often within SLAs.

- **BCDR plans and procedures:** Review the BCDR plans for completeness, including activation criteria, detailed recovery procedures for various scenarios, and return-to-normal processes.

- **Data backup and replication:** Assess the robustness of data backup and replication strategies, including frequency, storage locations (geographic redundancy), encryption of backups, and procedures for data restoration.

- **Failover mechanisms:** Understand the CSP's failover capabilities, whether manual or automated, and the infrastructure supporting these mechanisms (e.g., redundant data centers, availability zones).

- **Communication plan:** Evaluate the internal and external communication plans during a disaster. This includes how customers will be notified of incidents, provided with status updates, and informed of recovery progress.

- **Testing:** Verify that the CSP conducts regular BCDR tests and exercises, including different types like tabletop exercises, walkthroughs, simulations, and full failover tests.

- **Test documentation:** Review test plans, execution records, and post-test analysis reports. Look for evidence that identified weaknesses are addressed through corrective actions.

- **Customer involvement (if applicable):** For some services, especially IaaS or PaaS, determine if and how customers can participate in or observe BCDR tests relevant to their specific environments.

- **Infrastructure redundancy:** Assess the physical and logical redundancy built into the CSP's infrastructure, including power, cooling, network connectivity, and server hardware.

- **Geographic distribution of infrastructure:** Verify that critical infrastructure and data are distributed across geographically separate locations to mitigate regional disasters.

- **Security in BCDR:** Evaluate the measures in place to maintain security during a disruptive event and throughout the recovery process.

- **Shared responsibility:** Ensure a clear understanding and documentation of the shared responsibility model for BCDR. This outlines which aspects are managed by the CSP and which are the customer's responsibility (particularly relevant for IaaS and PaaS models).

- **BCDR support:** Assess the tools, capabilities, and guidance the CSP provides to help customers implement their own BCDR strategies within the cloud environment.

- **Incident response:** Evaluate how the BCDR plan integrates with the CSP's overall incident response plan to ensure a coordinated and effective response to disruptive events.

- **SLAs:** Review SLAs for specific commitments related to availability, RTOs, and RPOs. Assess the remedies or compensation offered if these SLAs are not met during a disaster.

Challenges in auditing BCDR

The following are some of the challenges:

- **Limited transparency:** CSPs may be hesitant to share highly detailed information about their infrastructure and BCDR plans due to security and proprietary concerns.

- **Complexity of cloud environments:** The dynamic and complex nature of cloud architectures can make it challenging to fully grasp all interdependencies.

- **Shared responsibility ambiguity:** Misunderstandings or lack of clarity in the shared responsibility model can lead to gaps in overall BCDR preparedness.

- **Reliance on CSP attestations:** Organizations often have to rely heavily on CSP-provided documentation and third-party audit reports rather than direct, in-depth testing.

- **Scale and scope:** The sheer scale of some CSP operations can make a comprehensive audit a significant undertaking.

Auditing a CSP's BCDR capabilities is a critical due diligence activity. It provides organizations with the necessary assurance that their chosen provider is adequately prepared to handle disruptive events, thereby safeguarding their own data, applications, and ultimately, their business operations.

While challenges exist, a well-planned audit focusing on governance, planning, testing, infrastructure, and clear articulation of responsibilities can significantly mitigate risks. By fostering a transparent dialogue with CSPs and leveraging industry best practices and standards, organizations can build greater trust and ensure the resilience of their cloud-dependent services in an unpredictable world.

Key metrics to review

Auditing a CSP is crucial for ensuring they meet contractual obligations, regulatory requirements, security best practices, and performance expectations. Effective audits rely on well-defined metrics.

Here are some of the key metrics to measure CSP compliance, security, and performance.

Security metrics

Reviewing a CSP's security metrics is essential to evaluate whether the provider upholds robust protections for customer data and infrastructure, and the following table discusses some of the key security metrics to be reviewed:

Category	Metric	Importance
Identity and access management	Effectiveness of access control mechanisms	Prevents unauthorized access to sensitive systems and data
Incident response	Efficiency and effectiveness of incident response	Measures ability to handle incidents promptly and minimize impact
Vulnerability management and patching	Proactiveness in identifying and remediating vulnerabilities	Reduces attack surface and likelihood of exploitation
Log management and security monitoring	Comprehensiveness of logging and monitoring	Critical for detecting, investigating, and responding to incidents
Data encryption and key management	Strength and management of encryption	Protects confidentiality and integrity of data
Network security	Effectiveness of network defenses	Protects network infrastructure and limits incident impact
Threat detection and prevention	Effectiveness of proactive threat defenses	Enhances defense against known and emerging threats
Security configuration management	Adherence to secure configuration baselines	Reduces vulnerabilities from insecure configurations

Table 12.1: Security metrics

Compliance metrics

Auditing compliance metrics involves assessing the CSP's adherence to relevant standards and regulations, certification status, etc. The following table details certain key compliance metrics that should be reviewed by an auditor:

Category	Metric	Importance
Adherence to applicable regulations	Compliance with regulations	Ensures information is managed in accordance with the regulatory requirements
Adherence to standards and certifications	Status of certifications	Demonstrates commitment to best practices
Change management	Adherence to formal change control	Controls changes to reduce risk of disruptions
Business continuity and disaster recovery (BCDR)	Preparedness and recoverability	Ensures availability and data integrity in disasters
Security awareness and training	Effectiveness of security training	Addresses human risk in security posture

Table 12.2: Compliance metrics

Performance metrics

Now, let us discuss the performance metrics that should be reviewed by an auditor in the following table. Evaluating performance metrics such as service availability, latency, throughput, and resource scalability helps determine whether the CSP consistently meets its SLAs and supports the operational needs of its clients.

Category	Metric	Importance
Availability and uptime	Availability of operational service time	Direct impact on business operations
Latency and response time	Speed and responsiveness	Affects user experience and performance
Scalability and elasticity	Ability to scale resources	Ensures efficient handling of workload fluctuations
Throughput and bandwidth	Data transfer capacity	Essential for large and fast data transfers
Resource utilization	Efficiency of consumption	Affects cost, performance, and planning
Customer support	Support responsiveness and effectiveness	Enables timely and effective customer support

Table 12.3: Performance metrics

Selecting the right metrics depends on the specific services being audited, contractual agreements, and the regulatory landscape. A combination of these security, compliance, and performance metrics will provide a comprehensive view of the CSP's posture, enabling organizations to make informed decisions, manage risks, and ensure value from their cloud investments. Regular audits using these metrics are key to maintaining a strong governance framework over cloud services.

Conclusion

Auditing CSPs is an ongoing process that goes beyond reviewing documentation. It involves active verification of controls, performance, and compliance. By understanding cloud contracts, assessing certifications, evaluating critical service aspects, and monitoring key metrics, organizations can mitigate cloud-related risks and build a more secure, resilient, and transparent cloud strategy.

The upcoming chapter explores the use of automation tools in cloud auditing, such as **continuous control monitoring (CCM)** and **security information and event management (SIEM)** tools.

Points to remember

- Given the shared responsibility model inherent in cloud computing, due diligence in evaluating and continuously monitoring CSPs is a critical component of enterprise risk management.

- A thorough understanding of Cloud Service Agreements and contracts is paramount to ensuring data integrity, security, compliance, and effective governance.

- Auditing a CSP's security certifications is a critical step in due diligence and ongoing vendor risk management.

- Auditing CSPs is an ongoing, integral part of a dynamic TPRM program.

- When auditing SLAs, focus should be on the specific commitments made by the provider.

- By diligently auditing SLAs, organizations can gain greater control over their cloud investments, mitigate risks, and ensure that their cloud services effectively support their business objectives.

- Effective auditing of the shared responsibility model provides clarity and accountability by ensuring both parties understand and adhere to their respective roles.

- Auditing shared responsibilities in cloud environments is not solely about assessing the CSP's controls; it is equally about ensuring the organization is upholding its own obligations.

- Auditing a CSP's BCDR capabilities is a critical due diligence activity.

- For organizations entrusting their data and services to a CSP, a thorough audit of the CSP's BCDR preparedness is not just a best practice, but a fundamental requirement for managing risk and ensuring their own operational resilience.

Multiple choice questions

1. **A key element of most cloud service agreements is the shared responsibility model. What does this model describe?**

    a. Joint ownership of cloud provider assets

    b. Division of responsibilities between CSP and the customer

    c. Equal cost-sharing for data breaches

    d. Shared use of on-premises infrastructure

2. **Which of the following would not typically be covered in a standard cloud service agreement?**

    a. Data ownership and portability

    b. Customer support response times

    c. Terms of software licensing for third-party tools

    d. The customer's employee dress code policy

3. **When auditing a CSP, which of the following certifications would best demonstrate that the provider follows internationally recognized information security management practices?**

    a. NIST-CSF

    b. ISO 31000

    c. ISO 27001

    d. ISO 22301

4. **In the context of TPRM, which risk is most associated with using a CSP?**

    a. Direct control over the CSP's hiring process

    b. Loss of data due to poor endpoint device maintenance

    c. Loss of visibility and control over hosted systems and data

    d. Inability to access cloud APIs for development

5. **During an audit of a CSP, which of the following metrics is most relevant for evaluating the provider's service performance?**

    a. Number of employees working remotely

    b. Monthly uptime percentage

    c. Office energy consumption

    d. Total number of social media followers

Answers

1	b
2	d
3	c
4	c
5	b

Join our Discord space

Join our Discord workspace for latest updates, offers, tech happenings around the world, new releases, and sessions with the authors:

https://discord.bpbonline.com

CHAPTER 13

Automating Cloud Auditing

Introduction

As organizations increasingly adopt cloud services, maintaining visibility, security, and compliance becomes more complex. Automating cloud auditing is the practice of using software tools and scripts to continuously monitor cloud resources, configurations, and activities to ensure they meet organizational and regulatory standards without relying solely on manual checks.

This automation enables real-time auditing of critical elements like user access, data storage, network configurations, and compliance posture across platforms such as **Amazon Web Services** (**AWS**), Azure, and Google Cloud. By automating audits, businesses can quickly detect misconfigurations, enforce security policies, generate compliance reports, and respond to threats, thereby improving efficiency, accuracy, and security.

This chapter explores the importance of automation in cloud auditing, the use of automation tools in cloud auditing, such as cloud native tools, and third-party cloud audit automation tools.

Structure

This chapter covers the following topics:

- Importance of automation in cloud auditing
- Benefits and challenges of automation in cloud auditing
- Automating compliance assessments
- Best practices for implementing automated auditing
- Tools and techniques

Objectives

By the end of this chapter, readers will have a clear understanding of the core concepts behind automating cloud auditing and why it plays a vital role in enhancing security, ensuring continuous compliance, and boosting operational efficiency in cloud environments. They will also learn how automated auditing enables scalability across complex, multi-cloud infrastructures while ensuring consistent application of governance policies. Additionally, the chapter will highlight how centralized visibility and real-time alerts help organizations detect and resolve issues faster, making it easier to meet regulatory requirements with greater accuracy and efficiency.

Importance of automation in cloud auditing

Cloud computing offers unprecedented scalability, flexibility, and speed, allowing organizations to innovate rapidly. However, this dynamic environment also brings complexity and volatility that traditional, manual auditing methods struggle to manage. Ensuring strong security, continuous compliance, and sound governance in the cloud requires a shift toward automation, which is no longer optional but essential.

The following table illustrates why it is important to automate cloud auditing by comparing the limitations of manual auditing and how automation helps with various cloud auditing challenges:

Challenge	Limitations of manual auditing	How automation helps
Scale and complexity	Thousands to millions of resources across regions are impossible to audit manually.	Systematically scans entire environments quickly and thoroughly, ensuring complete coverage.
Dynamic, ephemeral infrastructure	Constant resource creation and change make point-in-time audits obsolete.	Enables continuous monitoring and near real-time detection of non-compliant changes.
Consistency and accuracy	Results vary between auditors; manual checks are error-prone and inconsistent.	Applies predefined policies uniformly, reducing human error and ensuring repeatable, reliable results.

Challenge	Limitations of manual auditing	How automation helps
Speed and efficiency	Slow, labour-intensive audits delay issue detection and remediation.	Delivers rapid feedback, allowing for faster identification and correction of vulnerabilities.
Continuous compliance	Periodic audits fail to meet the need for ongoing regulatory compliance.	Continuously assesses configurations against compliance standards and auto-generates audit evidence.
Security posture enhancement	Misconfigurations and overlooked vulnerabilities are common and risky.	Continuously scans for security risks and enforces best practices throughout the development lifecycle.
Resource optimization	Skilled professionals waste time on repetitive, manual tasks.	Frees up experts to focus on strategic risk management and control design.

Table 13.1: Importance of automating cloud auditing

Benefits and challenges of automation

Automating cloud auditing represents a compelling opportunity for organizations to strengthen their security posture, streamline compliance workflows, and boost operational efficiency. However, realizing these benefits requires navigating a range of complexities. A balanced understanding of both the advantages and the inherent challenges is essential for any organization aiming to modernize its audit processes through automation.

Benefits of automating cloud auditing

Automating the audit process in a cloud environment offers a multitude of benefits that can transform a traditionally manual and time-consuming task into a strategic advantage. The following points highlight the key benefits of cloud audit automation:

- **Continuous security and compliance**: One of the most transformative benefits of automation is the shift from periodic, point-in-time audits to continuous monitoring and compliance. Automated tools can relentlessly scan cloud configurations, user activities, and network traffic for anomalies and policy violations, delivering real-time alerts and enabling rapid remediation. This proactive approach significantly reduces the window of exposure to security threats.

- **Greater accuracy and minimized human error**: Manual audits are susceptible to oversight and inconsistencies, potentially leaving vulnerabilities undetected. Automation addresses this by executing predefined checks with consistent precision, ensuring that audit results are comprehensive, repeatable, and free from manual lapses. This level of accuracy provides greater confidence in risk assessments and compliance status.

- **Scalability and operational efficiency**: Cloud environments are dynamic by design, often scaling up and down in response to demand. Manual audit methods struggle to keep pace with this fluidity. Automated solutions, however, adapt effortlessly, continuously auditing newly provisioned resources and decommissioned assets. By automating routine checks and data gathering, skilled security professionals can focus on higher-value activities such as threat analysis and strategic security planning.

- **Enhanced reporting and audit readiness**: Automation excels at generating detailed, up-to-date reports that provide actionable insights for internal stakeholders and facilitate external compliance assessments. This automated documentation creates a clear, traceable audit trail that simplifies regulatory reporting and demonstrates compliance with industry standards and legal requirements.

- **Cost efficiency over time**: Although adopting automation involves upfront investments in tools and expertise, the long-term savings can be significant. By reducing the labor-intensive nature of audits and minimizing costly incidents through early detection, organizations can lower operational expenses and protect their reputation from the fallout of preventable security breaches.

Challenges and addressing complexities

Despite the compelling benefits, organizations must be prepared to address several challenges when implementing automated cloud auditing, described as follows:

- **Managing diverse and complex cloud architectures**: Modern organizations often operate across multi-cloud and hybrid environments, each with distinct services, APIs, and security frameworks. Developing a unified automated auditing strategy that seamlessly spans these heterogeneous platforms demands deep technical knowledge and carefully customized automation scripts.

- **Navigating the shared responsibility model**: Cloud security responsibilities are divided between the provider and the customer, a nuance that can complicate automated auditing. Tools must be properly configured to monitor only the aspects within the customer's control, avoiding overlaps with the provider's domain and ensuring that compliance checks remain accurate and relevant.

- **Adapting to constant change**: The cloud's inherent flexibility means resources are frequently provisioned, reconfigured, or terminated. Automated audit systems must be robust and adaptive enough to track these changes in real-time, preventing false positives and ensuring that critical security issues are not overlooked amidst constant flux.

- **Integration complexities and skills shortages**: Integrating automated auditing tools with existing security ecosystems, such as **security information and event management** (**SIEM**) platforms, ticketing systems, and incident response workflows, can be technically demanding. Furthermore, successful deployment requires skilled personnel to select, implement, and maintain these tools. Many organizations face a talent gap in this specialized area, which can hinder effective automation.

- **Upfront investment and tool selection**: While automation can yield substantial long-term savings, the initial costs for commercial tools and skilled implementation can be high. Open-source alternatives may lower licensing expenses but typically require greater in-house expertise to deploy and manage. Choosing a solution that aligns with an organization's unique cloud footprint, compliance requirements, and budget constraints is a critical yet challenging decision.

Automating cloud auditing is a powerful strategy to elevate security, ensure continuous compliance, and maximize resource efficiency. However, its success depends on a clear understanding of the evolving cloud landscape, thoughtful integration with existing systems, investment in the right tools, and the development of in-house expertise. By anticipating and addressing these challenges, organizations can unlock the full potential of automated auditing and thus transform it from a routine obligation into a strategic advantage.

Role of auditors

Automation transforms how audits are conducted, but it does not eliminate the need for skilled auditors. Instead, it elevates their role from performing repetitive checks to providing strategic oversight, expert judgment, and continuous improvement.

Here is how auditors add value in an automated cloud auditing environment:

- **Designing and configuring automated controls**: Auditors play a critical role in selecting the right automated tools and defining what controls should be automated. They determine which compliance requirements, security policies, and organizational standards need to be continuously monitored and ensure that automation aligns with regulatory expectations.

- **Validating and testing automation tools**: Even the best automation tools require human oversight to ensure accuracy and reliability. Auditors validate that automated scripts and configurations produce correct results, do not generate excessive false positives or negatives, and adapt appropriately as the cloud environment evolves.

- **Interpreting and contextualizing results**: Automated tools generate vast amounts of data and alerts. Auditors analyze this information, interpret findings within the organization's risk context, and differentiate between critical issues and low-risk deviations. This human judgment ensures that automation supports well-informed risk management decisions.

- **Investigating anomalies and incidents**: When automation flags potential threats, misconfigurations, or compliance breaches, auditors investigate these alerts to confirm their validity, assess their impact, and coordinate remediation. Their expertise is vital for incident response and root cause analysis.

- **Providing assurance and communicating with stakeholders**: Auditors are responsible for communicating audit outcomes to stakeholders, regulators, and external auditors. They translate technical findings into clear, actionable insights and demonstrate how automated processes meet regulatory and governance requirements.

- **Maintaining and improving audit processes**: Cloud environments and compliance frameworks continually evolve. Auditors ensure that automated controls stay current by reviewing and updating them as needed. They also refine audit processes based on lessons learned and emerging best practices.

- **Advising on governance and risk management**: Beyond technical checks, auditors guide the organization on improving overall governance, policy design, and security practices. They use insights gained from automated audits to identify trends, systemic issues, and opportunities to strengthen controls across the organization.

Automation enhances the efficiency, scope, and frequency of cloud audits but does not replace the professional judgment, critical thinking, and domain expertise of auditors. Instead, it enables them to shift from repetitive manual tasks to higher-value activities by designing better controls, interpreting complex results, advising on risk, and helping the organization maintain robust, adaptive cloud security and compliance programs.

Automating compliance assessments

In today's digital-first world, operating in the cloud is no longer optional; it is an operational imperative. Yet with this transformation comes a critical responsibility, that is, maintaining continuous compliance with an increasingly complex landscape of regulations and various industry-specific standards. Traditional manual compliance checks, performed periodically and dependent on spreadsheets and screenshots, fall dramatically short of what is needed to secure dynamic, rapidly changing cloud environments. The answer lies in automation, which shifts compliance from a reactive, periodic task to a continuous, integrated, and proactive discipline.

Automated cloud compliance assessments leverage specialized tools and workflows to continuously monitor, verify, and document the organization's cloud environment against a defined set of security and regulatory controls. This evolution from occasional spot checks to real-time, automated validation is essential for maintaining a strong and defensible compliance posture.

Now, let us look at why manual compliance assessments fail in the cloud. The main issue is speed. Manual assessments provide static snapshots of an environment that can change minute by minute. Cloud resources are created, modified, and decommissioned dynamically, and by the time a manual audit concludes, their results are often outdated. This mismatch leads to persistent risk exposure, as misconfigurations can go unnoticed for weeks or months; high operational costs and audit fatigue, as teams spend countless hours gathering evidence; inconsistent results prone to human error; and an inability to scale manual efforts as the cloud footprint expands.

Core elements of automated compliance

A robust automated compliance program rests on several critical pillars, detailed as follows:

- **Compliance as Code (CaC)**: This foundational practice involves expressing compliance policies as version-controlled code. These codified rules can be tested, automatically enforced, and easily updated. For example, a policy could dictate that no cloud storage bucket can be publicly accessible or that all databases must have encryption enabled at rest. Common CSP-native services include AWS CloudFormation, Checkov, Terrascan, AWS Config, and Azure Policy.

- **Continuous monitoring and real-time alerting**: Automation relies on tools that continuously assess cloud resources by tapping into CSP APIs (AWS, Azure, Google Cloud, etc.) and comparing configurations to code-defined policies. Any deviation from the compliant state generates an immediate alert, enabling faster detection and response. Examples of continuous monitoring and alerting services offered by major CSPs include AWS CloudWatch, Azure Monitor, AWS Config, Defender for Cloud, and Google Cloud Security Command Center.

- **Automated evidence collection**: Proving compliance during audits is often a painful, manual exercise. Automated tools streamline this by continuously collecting and storing evidence such as configuration snapshots, change logs, and activity histories, complete with timestamps and integrity checks. When an audit is due, evidence can be compiled into detailed reports instantly, saving substantial time and effort. Representative CSP services for automated evidence collection include AWS CloudTrail, S3 Object Lock, AWS Audit Manager, Azure Compliance Manager, Azure Log Analytics, and GCP Assured Workloads.

- **Guided remediation and automatic enforcement**: Advanced automation does not stop at detection. It provides clear remediation guidance for engineering teams and, in mature setups, can enforce policies automatically. For instance, the system might revoke an overly permissive firewall rule or quarantine a non-compliant virtual machine without manual intervention. CSP-native remediation and automatic enforcement tools include AWS Lambda, Azure Functions, Google Cloud Functions, Azure Policy (Deny), AWS Systems Manager Automation, and Azure Sentinel Playbooks.

Roadmap for implementing automated compliance

Successfully transitioning to automated compliance requires a thoughtful, phased rollout as described here:

- **Define the control universe:** Begin by mapping all applicable regulations and internal security standards, then translate these into specific, measurable controls tailored to the cloud environment. For example, a GDPR mandate for *data protection by design* might become explicit requirements such as mandatory encryption for all databases and strict **identity and access management (IAM)** role definitions based on least privilege.

- **Select the right tools:** Choose tools that align with the environment and compliance objectives. Look for multi-cloud visibility, pre-built frameworks for common standards (CIS Benchmarks, NIST, PCI DSS), customization capabilities for organization-specific policies, and seamless integration with CI/CD pipelines, SIEMs, and ticketing systems.

- **Establish visibility:** Deploy the selected tool in read-only mode to map cloud assets and assess the current compliance status. This step provides a data-backed baseline and typically reveals misconfigurations that should be addressed first.

- **Enable continuous monitoring and alerting:** Once visibility is established, activate continuous monitoring and configure real-time alerts. Integrate these alerts into existing workflows and tools, such as Slack, Jira, or PagerDuty, to ensure issues are addressed promptly rather than accumulating unnoticed.

- **Automate remediation and embed compliance in the pipeline:** In the final stage, integrate compliance checks directly into CI/CD processes to prevent non-compliant resources from being deployed. Simultaneously, implement automated remediation for well-understood, low-risk issues, such as automatically disabling public access for new storage buckets or enforcing multi-factor authentication for user accounts.

By following this roadmap, organizations can shift from inefficient, reactive audits to a modern, intelligent compliance framework. Automated cloud compliance transforms compliance from a burdensome obligation into a continuous safeguard that helps maintain security, audit readiness, and resilience as the cloud ecosystem expands.

Best practices for implementation

Automating cloud auditing has become a vital practice for organizations committed to maintaining a strong security posture and continuous compliance in today's dynamic cloud landscape. However, simply deploying a tool is not enough. Success depends on a strategic, well-planned implementation that aligns with business objectives and adapts as the environment evolves.

The following best practices provide a roadmap for building an effective and sustainable automated cloud auditing program, in a phased manner as depicted in *Figure 13.1*:

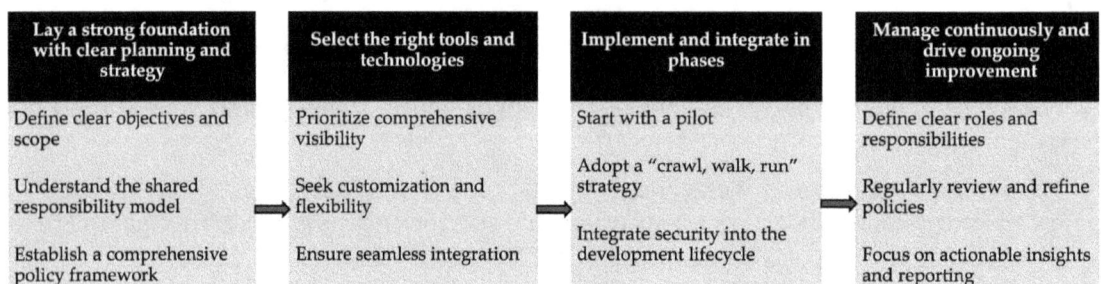

Lay a strong foundation with clear planning and strategy	Select the right tools and technologies	Implement and integrate in phases	Manage continuously and drive ongoing improvement
Define clear objectives and scope	Prioritize comprehensive visibility	Start with a pilot	Define clear roles and responsibilities
Understand the shared responsibility model	Seek customization and flexibility	Adopt a "crawl, walk, run" strategy	Regularly review and refine policies
Establish a comprehensive policy framework	Ensure seamless integration	Integrate security into the development lifecycle	Focus on actionable insights and reporting

Figure 13.1: Implementing best practices for automated cloud auditing

The explanations are as follows:

- **Lay a strong foundation with clear planning and strategy**: Before implementing any tool or automation script, establish a solid groundwork to ensure that the efforts deliver meaningful value and meet regulatory obligations.

- **Define clear objectives and scope:** Begin by articulating exactly what needs to be achieved, such as whether the goal is to detect security vulnerabilities, maintain compliance with all applicable regulations, optimize costs, or address all these objectives. Clearly define the audit's scope, indicating whether it will cover the entire multi-cloud landscape, specific environments, or critical business units. Clarity at this stage shapes every decision that follows.

- **Understand the shared responsibility model:** A deep understanding of the shared responsibility model for each CSP is essential. Automated audits must focus on elements within organizational control, including data, applications, IAM policies, and network configurations, rather than areas managed by the provider's underlying infrastructure.

- **Establish a comprehensive policy framework:** Auditing requires a clearly defined baseline. Develop clear, well-documented security and compliance policies aligned with the specific cloud environment and industry requirements. These policies form the foundation against which automation tools validate configurations and monitor activities.

- **Select the right tools and technologies:** The market offers a wide range of tools claiming to deliver automated cloud auditing, but selecting the appropriate solution is critical for success.

- **Prioritize comprehensive visibility:** Choose tools that provide end-to-end visibility across all cloud platforms, whether AWS, Azure, Google Cloud, or others. Ensure coverage of all relevant services and resources and leverage unified dashboards to maintain a clear, real-time view of the security posture.

- **Seek customization and flexibility:** Pre-configured policies offer a solid starting point, but each organization has unique compliance requirements and risk profiles. Ensure selected tools allow customization of checks, creation of new rules, and adaptation of policies as needs evolve.

- **Ensure seamless integration:** Auditing solutions should integrate smoothly within existing workflows. Favor tools with robust API support and out-of-the-box integrations with CI/CD pipelines, SIEM platforms, ticketing systems like Jira, or collaboration tools such as Slack. Integration accelerates remediation and streamlines response to detected issues.

- **Implement and integrate in phases:** Avoid risks associated with a rushed, organization-wide rollout. A phased approach minimizes disruption and allows for process refinement.

- **Start with a pilot:** Initiate automation within a non-critical environment or with a limited set of controls. Use this pilot to evaluate tool capabilities, fine-tune policies, and identify gaps without impacting production workloads.

- **Adopt a crawl, walk, run strategy:** Begin with the *crawl* phase by focusing on discovery and mapping cloud assets while identifying misconfigurations. Transition to the *walk* phase by implementing continuous monitoring and automated alerting, ensuring alerts reach the appropriate teams for manual resolution. Conclude with the *run* phase by enabling automated remediation for low-risk, repetitive issues, such as revoking public access to storage buckets or enforcing multi-factor authentication for user accounts.

- **Integrate security into the development lifecycle:** Embed automated security checks within the CI/CD pipeline to identify vulnerabilities early in the development cycle, reducing risk and lowering remediation costs compared to post-deployment detection.

- **Manage continuously and drive ongoing improvement:** Automation is not a *set-and-forget* solution; sustained governance is vital for long-term success.

- **Define clear roles and responsibilities:** Assign accountability for monitoring alerts, investigating findings, and updating audit policies. Clear ownership ensures prompt responses and prevents issues from being overlooked.

- **Regularly review and refine policies:** As cloud technologies and threats evolve, revisit and update audit rules, policies, and automation logic to address new services, emerging risks, and shifting compliance obligations.

- **Focus on actionable insights and reporting:** Automated systems generate vast amounts of data that can be translated into clear, actionable insights. Create tailored dashboards and reports for various audiences, from high-level executive summaries to technical details for engineering teams. Monitor trends and key metrics over time to demonstrate progress and validate the return on investment in automation.

By applying these best practices, organizations can progress beyond a reactive, checklist-driven approach and establish an automated cloud auditing program that acts as a dynamic, intelligent layer of defense. When implemented thoughtfully, automated auditing provides continuous assurance that cloud environments remain secure, compliant, and resilient, thus empowering teams to stay ahead of evolving threats and regulatory demands.

Tools and techniques

Automating cloud auditing is crucial for maintaining security, ensuring compliance, and managing the dynamic nature of cloud environments. It involves a combination of specialized tools and techniques that help organizations continuously monitor, assess, and report on their cloud posture. In this section, we will look at an overview of key tools and techniques.

Tools for cloud audit automation

Several categories of tools are instrumental in automating cloud audits as described in the following table:

Category	Description	Features	Examples
Cloud Security Posture Management (CSPM) tools	Identify and remediate misconfigurations and compliance risks in cloud environments.	Visibility into cloud assets, continuous compliance monitoring (CIS Benchmarks, NIST, PCI DSS, HIPAA, GDPR), automated remediation, and threat detection.	Microsoft Defender for Cloud, Wiz, Check Point CloudGuard, Palo Alto Networks Prisma Cloud, Sysdig Secure
Infrastructure as Code (IaC) scanning tools	Analyze IaC templates (Terraform, AWS CloudFormation, Azure Resource Manager) for vulnerabilities and compliance issues before deployment.	Static analysis of IaC files, CI/CD pipeline integration, policy enforcement, and detection of insecure configurations.	Checkov, Terrascan, TFLint, KICS, tfsec, Snyk IaC
Automated cloud compliance and reporting tools	Collect evidence, manage audit data, and generate compliance reports for regulatory and internal standards.	Pre-built frameworks for regulations, automated evidence collection, customizable controls, and audit-ready reporting.	AWS Audit Manager, Jatheon Cloud, various GRC platforms with cloud modules
Native cloud provider tools	Built-in tools from cloud providers to support auditing and compliance.	Logging and monitoring (AWS CloudTrail, Azure Monitor, Google Cloud Logging), configuration management (AWS Config, Azure Policy), and IAM services.	AWS (CloudTrail, Config, IAM, Security Hub, GuardDuty); Microsoft Azure (Monitor, Policy, Sentinel, Defender for Cloud); Google Cloud (Cloud Logging, Cloud Monitoring, Security Command Center)
SIEM systems	Aggregate, correlate, and analyze log data to detect security incidents and compliance violations.	Log aggregation, real-time alerting, threat detection, incident response, and compliance reporting.	Splunk, IBM QRadar, Microsoft Sentinel, Exabeam
Configuration management tools	Automate configuration and enforce desired states for cloud resources to maintain compliance.	Desired state configuration, automated enforcement, and drift detection.	Ansible, Chef, Puppet, SaltStack

Table 13.2: Tools for cloud audit automation

Techniques for automating cloud auditing

Alongside the tools discussed previously, specific techniques are employed to enhance cloud audit automation, as discussed in the following table:

Technique	Description	How it works
Continuous auditing	An ongoing process of collecting audit evidence and indicators in near real-time or at frequent intervals, enabling a proactive approach rather than point-in-time audits.	Automated tools continuously monitor cloud configurations, user activities, data access, and compliance controls, triggering alerts for deviations or potential issues.
Policy as Code (PaC)	Defines policies and compliance requirements in a codified, machine-readable format, enabling automated enforcement and validation across the cloud environment.	Policies are written as code (e.g., using Open Policy Agent, Cloud Custodian, or native policy engines) and integrated into deployment pipelines and monitoring systems.
AI and **machine learning (ML)**	Enhances audit automation by identifying complex patterns, anomalies, and risks that traditional rule-based systems may miss.	ML algorithms analyze large audit datasets to detect unusual behavior, predict threats, automate risk assessment, and improve fraud detection efficiency.
Automated evidence collection and analysis	Focuses on automatically gathering data from cloud services and analyzing it against predefined audit criteria.	Scripts and specialized tools connect to cloud provider APIs to extract relevant data, which is processed and correlated to identify compliance gaps or security issues.
Integration with DevOps	Embeds security and audit checks directly into the CI/CD pipeline to ensure compliance and security throughout the software development lifecycle.	IaC scanning, vulnerability assessments, and compliance checks are automated as part of the build and deployment processes.
Automated reporting and remediation	Automates the generation of compliance reports and can trigger remediation actions for identified issues.	CSPM and compliance tools provide dashboards for real-time visibility and features to generate auditor-ready reports or automatically execute remediation workflows.

Table 13.3: Techniques for automating cloud auditing

By leveraging these tools and techniques, organizations can significantly improve the efficiency, accuracy, and coverage of their cloud auditing processes, leading to a stronger security posture and more reliable compliance.

Conclusion

This chapter discussed how organizations can achieve continuous security and compliance at scale, reduce operational overhead, and stay resilient in the face of evolving threats and regulatory demands by embracing automation in cloud auditing. Leveraging the right tools, techniques, and strategies transforms auditing from a reactive task into a proactive, intelligent process that safeguards cloud environments and supports sustainable growth.

In the next chapter, we will discuss emerging trends in cloud auditing, such as AI and ML-driven audits, cloud supply chain security, and the evolving regulatory landscape.

Points to remember

- Establish what needs to be monitored and ensure alignment with applicable regulatory frameworks or internal security policies.

- Map key assets, including virtual machines, databases, storage buckets, and sensitive data; categorize them based on risk levels and compliance priorities.

- Activate built-in cloud tools such as AWS CloudTrail, Azure Monitor, or Google Cloud Audit Logs to automatically record activities, API calls, and configuration changes.

- Develop and deploy security and compliance policies as code to maintain uniform enforcement across development, staging, and production environments.

- Schedule regular compliance and audit reports, automate report creation, and distribute them to relevant stakeholders to demonstrate regulatory adherence.

- Integrate audit tools with issue tracking or service management platforms such as Jira or ServiceNow to create, assign, and track remediation tasks automatically.

- Conduct periodic reviews and testing of automated compliance checks to ensure effectiveness and alignment with evolving standards and cloud service updates.

- Document all automated audit workflows, compliance rules, and policy changes thoroughly and maintain versioned evidence and logs to support regulatory inspections.

Multiple choice questions

1. **Which of the following is a primary benefit of automating cloud auditing?**
    a. Reduces the need for regular compliance reporting
    b. Eliminates the need for security policies
    c. Enables continuous monitoring and faster detection of misconfigurations
    d. Replaces all manual IT operations

2. **What is a key responsibility of auditors when working with automated cloud auditing systems?**

   a. Designing the cloud infrastructure architecture

   b. Developing all automation scripts from scratch

   c. Validating and testing automation tools

   d. Managing the day-to-day operations of cloud servers

3. **Which statement best describes the purpose of automating cloud compliance assessments?**

   a. To eliminate the need for any human oversight in the compliance process

   b. Continuous monitoring and real-time alerting

   c. To manually check each cloud resource for compliance on a scheduled basis

   d. To replace compliance standards with custom organizational policies only

4. **Which of the following is considered a best practice when implementing automation in cloud auditing?**

   a. Deploy automation tools across the entire organization immediately, without testing

   b. Rely solely on pre-configured policies without customization

   c. Start with a pilot project and adopt a phased "crawl, walk, run" strategy

   d. Disable alerts to reduce unnecessary notifications

5. **When interpreting results from an automated cloud auditing tool, what should be done to ensure effective remediation?**

   a. Treat all alerts as equally critical and resolve them in the order received

   b. Ignore low-risk findings to focus only on high-severity threats

   c. Disable reporting features to reduce the volume of audit data

   d. Contextualize findings based on business impact and prioritize actions accordingly

Answers

1	c
2	c
3	b
4	c
5	d

CHAPTER 14

Emerging Trends in Cloud Auditing

Introduction

As organizations increasingly migrate their operations to cloud environments, cloud auditing is undergoing a significant transformation to keep pace with new technological, security, and compliance challenges. A major trend is the adoption of **artificial intelligence** (**AI**) and **machine learning** (**ML**) to enhance audit processes. Additionally, blockchain technology is emerging as a promising tool in the cloud auditing landscape. By providing a decentralized, tamper-evident ledger, blockchain enhances the integrity and transparency of audit trails, making it easier to verify data authenticity and detect unauthorized changes. Together, these trends are redefining how organizations approach trust, accountability, and risk management in an increasingly complex cloud ecosystem. The shift toward **Zero Trust architecture** (**ZTA**) is also reshaping cloud auditing practices. In a zero-trust model, no user or device is automatically trusted, even within the organization's network perimeter. At the same time, the regulatory landscape is evolving rapidly, with stricter and more diverse requirements emerging worldwide. Auditors are expected to navigate a growing maze of local, national, and industry-specific compliance demands, often in multi-cloud and hybrid environments. Finally, continuous auditing and compliance-as-code are becoming industry norms, enabling organizations to proactively monitor compliance in real time rather than relying on periodic reviews. These trends are collectively pushing cloud auditing toward a more dynamic, intelligent, and risk-aware future.

This chapter discusses emerging trends in cloud auditing, such as AI and ML-driven audits, cloud supply chain security, and the evolving regulatory landscape.

Structure

This chapter covers the following topics:

- Emerging trends in cloud auditing
- Auditing in multi-cloud and hybrid cloud environments
- AI and ML in cloud security and auditing
- Blockchain in cloud auditing
- ZTA in cloud auditing
- Evolving regulatory landscape

Objectives

By the end of this chapter, the readers will be able to understand the emerging trends in cloud auditing that equip professionals with the knowledge and skills needed to effectively assess, secure, and ensure compliance within increasingly dynamic and complex cloud environments.

Emerging trends in cloud auditing

The ongoing shift to the cloud has fundamentally transformed the information technology landscape and, with it, the practice of auditing. Traditional point-in-time audits have become inadequate for dynamic, complex, and rapidly scaling cloud environments. In response, a new model of continuous, automated, and intelligent auditing is emerging to provide real-time assurance, strengthen security, and maintain compliance in an increasingly regulated digital landscape. *Figure 14.1* depicts key trends emerging in the field of cloud auditing:

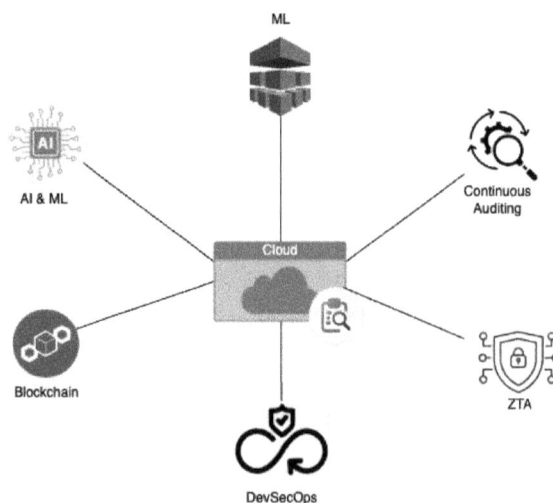

Figure 14.1: Emerging trends in cloud auditing

This evolution goes beyond adopting new tools; it represents a fundamental change in mindset. Cloud auditing is transitioning from a reactive, compliance-oriented activity to a proactive, risk-driven discipline integrated throughout the cloud lifecycle. Let us now look at the key trends driving this transformation.

Multi-cloud and hybrid cloud complexity

Most organizations now operate in a mix of on-premises, multi-cloud, and hybrid environments, creating challenges such as fragmented visibility and inconsistent controls. To address this complexity, keep the following in mind:

- **Unified auditing platforms:** Organizations are adopting platforms that provide centralized oversight across multiple cloud providers.

- **Standardized control frameworks:** Common frameworks ensure consistent application of controls regardless of provider or environment.

- **Robust data governance:** Strong policies for data classification and governance ensure protection and compliance even when data spans multiple locations.

AI and ML

AI and ML are introducing advanced capabilities to cloud auditing by providing predictive analytics and intelligent automation, as detailed here:

- **Enhanced threat detection:** AI-driven analytics detect abnormal behavior, such as unauthorized access or data leaks. For example, Azure OpenAI Service can analyze over 1TB of AWS CloudTrail logs to uncover novel attack patterns.

- **Automated risk assessment:** ML models analyze large data sets to pinpoint and prioritize vulnerabilities and control weaknesses. E.g., Google Chronicle can automatically assess risk by correlating millions of events to highlight misconfigured resources, such as publicly exposed GCP storage buckets, and prioritize them based on potential business impact and exploitability.

- **Automated compliance mapping:** AI assists in aligning controls with various regulations (e.g., GDPR, HIPAA, PCI DSS) and generating audit-ready reports. E.g., Microsoft Purview or AWS Audit Manager use ML to scan cloud infrastructure and automatically map configurations to compliance frameworks like GDPR, HIPAA, and PCI DSS, generating audit-ready evidence and flagging control gaps without manual intervention.

- **Policy analysis with NLP:** NLP can review and compare policies and standards to identify gaps and ensure alignment with cloud configurations. Amazon Comprehend or IBM Watson NLP can parse and compare organizational security policies against standards like NIST 800-53.

Blockchain

Blockchain technology is gaining traction as a way to strengthen trust and transparency in cloud auditing, and the key aspects are as follows:

- **Immutable audit trails:** Blockchain provides tamper-evident, time-stamped records, enabling auditors to verify that logs and transactions have not been altered. For example, IBM Hyperledger Fabric can be used to store time-stamped access logs from a multi-cloud environment, enabling auditors to verify that no unauthorized modifications have occurred.

- **Decentralized verification:** Auditors can rely on distributed consensus mechanisms to validate data integrity across multiple nodes, reducing the risk of single points of failure. For instance, a Quorum-based private Ethereum network can be deployed across multiple cloud regions to cross-verify audit events and make it nearly impossible for a rogue actor to manipulate records undetected.

- **Enhanced accountability:** Smart contracts and transparent ledgers help enforce compliance automatically and create an auditable chain of custody for sensitive operations. For example, using Chainlink smart contracts on a permissioned blockchain, an organization can automatically log and validate each data access request against a GDPR-compliant rule set, ensuring an auditable and enforceable chain of custody for sensitive personal data.

Zero trust architecture

Zero trust principles, *never trust, always verify*, are becoming central to cloud security and impact how audits are conducted, and the key aspects are as follows:

- **Continuous verification:** Audits now emphasize the effectiveness of ongoing authentication and authorization mechanisms for all users and devices.

- **Micro-segmentation:** Auditors evaluate how workloads are isolated to limit lateral movement by potential attackers.

- **Identity and access management (IAM):** Robust IAM practices and the principle of least privilege are now core audit focal points in a zero-trust model.

Continuous auditing and monitoring

A major development is the shift from periodic audits to continuous, real-time monitoring. Annual or occasional audits cannot keep pace with the constant changes in cloud environments, where resources are provisioned or decommissioned within minutes.

Continuous auditing employs automation to maintain an up-to-date view of security and compliance status, including the following:

- **Real-time configuration monitoring:** Ongoing scans to detect misconfigurations and deviations from security standards.

- **Automated evidence collection:** Continuous gathering of logs and configuration data, reducing manual workload for audit teams.

- **Continuous controls monitoring (CCM):** Ongoing verification that security controls are properly implemented and functioning as intended.

This continuous approach enables timely detection and remediation of issues, preventing surprises during formal audits.

DevSecOps

The rise of DevOps has increased the speed of development and deployment. To keep up, security and compliance must be embedded directly into the development process, a principle known as DevSecOps, and the key aspects are as follows:

- **Automated security in CI/CD:** Security and compliance checks are integrated into the continuous integration and delivery pipeline, enabling early detection of issues.

- **Infrastructure as Code (IaC) scanning:** Audits extend to the code that defines infrastructure, ensuring security and compliance before resources are deployed.

- **Proactive controls:** By embedding checks early, auditing shifts from reactive checks to proactive prevention.

Emerging trends in cloud auditing are reshaping how organizations secure and validate their cloud environments. Identity-centric auditing, using tools like Azure's **Privileged Identity Management** (**PIM**) and Netflix's RepoKid, focuses on monitoring and enforcing least-privilege access dynamically. Confidential computing audits, enabled by solutions like Google's Confidential Space, ensure sensitive data remains protected even during processing, enhancing trust in multi-tenant cloud models. Meanwhile, chaos engineering for audit testing, through platforms like GCP's Attack Path Simulation and MITRE's ATLAS techniques, allows organizations to proactively test resilience and uncover hidden vulnerabilities. Additionally, quantum-resistant audit logs are emerging as a future-proofing strategy to safeguard audit trails against potential quantum decryption threats, reinforcing long-term data integrity and compliance.

To sum it up, the future of cloud auditing is intelligent, automated, and continuous. As organizations place more critical workloads and data in the cloud, the role of auditing is expanding from a backward-looking compliance check to a forward-looking risk management function. By adopting these trends, organizations can strengthen security, maintain compliance, and build resilient, trustworthy cloud environments.

Auditing in multi-cloud and hybrid cloud environments

The era of single-provider cloud dominance is over. Today, organizations are strategically embracing multi-cloud (using services from multiple public cloud providers like AWS, Azure, and Google Cloud) and hybrid cloud (a mix of private, on-premise infrastructure and public clouds) architectures. This shift is driven by a desire for best-of-breed services, cost optimization, improved resilience, and avoidance of vendor lock-in. However, this distributed, heterogeneous landscape introduces a new frontier of complexity for governance, risk, and compliance, making auditing more challenging and more critical than ever before.

As businesses navigate this new paradigm, traditional auditing methods are proving inadequate. A new set of trends and technologies is emerging to provide the visibility, automation, and continuous assurance required to effectively audit these complex ecosystems.

Auditing a single cloud is difficult enough, and extending that to multiple providers and on-premise systems creates a host of new challenges as follows:

- **Fragmented visibility:** Each cloud provider has its own unique set of tools, interfaces, and security configurations. This lack of standardization creates blind spots, making it nearly impossible for auditors to gain a single, unified view of the organization's security posture.

- **Inconsistent controls and policies:** A security policy implemented in AWS may not translate directly to Azure or GCP. This inconsistency can lead to misconfigurations and security gaps, significantly expanding the attack surface.

- **Data governance and sovereignty:** With data spread across different geographical regions and providers, ensuring compliance with regulations like GDPR, HIPAA, and various data residency laws becomes a logistical and legal nightmare.

- **Complex identity and access management (IAM):** Managing user identities, roles, and permissions across multiple platforms is a major hurdle. Over-privileged accounts and inconsistent access controls are common vulnerabilities that auditors must scrutinize.

- **Shared responsibility model:** The shared responsibility model, which defines the security obligations of the cloud provider versus the customer, is now multiplied and varied across each platform, creating ambiguity and increasing the risk of unaddressed security gaps.

To combat these challenges, the field of cloud auditing is rapidly evolving. The following trends are at the forefront of this transformation, moving organizations from a reactive, periodic audit cycle to a proactive, continuous state of compliance:

- **Unified visibility through centralized platforms:** The most significant trend is the move towards a single pane of glass for security and compliance. **Cloud Security**

Posture Management (CSPM) tools and the more advanced **Cloud-Native Application Protection Platforms (CNAPP)** are becoming indispensable. These platforms connect to all of an organization's cloud environments (public and private) to:

- o Provide a centralized inventory of all cloud assets.

- o Continuously monitor for misconfigurations against established security benchmarks (like CIS controls) and regulatory frameworks.

- o Visualize complex network paths and access permissions.

- **Automation as a necessity:** Manual, evidence-gathering audits are no longer feasible in dynamic cloud environments. Automation is the key to managing complexity at scale, and can be achieved by the following:

  - o **Policy as Code (PaC)**: Frameworks like **Open Policy Agent (OPA)** allow teams to define security and compliance rules as code. These policies can be automatically enforced across different cloud environments, ensuring consistency.

  - o **Automated evidence collection**: Tools like AWS Audit Manager automate the collection of evidence required for audits. They continuously gather data related to resource configurations and user activity, mapping it directly to the requirements of specific compliance frameworks like PCI DSS or SOC 2.

  - o **Automated remediation**: Advanced CSPM and CNAPP solutions can automatically remediate certain misconfigurations, such as closing a publicly exposed storage bucket, reducing the window of risk.

- **Continuous, real-time compliance:** The *snapshot-in-time* annual audit is being replaced by a model of continuous assurance. Instead of discovering issues during a formal audit, organizations are leveraging technology to monitor their compliance posture in real-time. This allows for the immediate detection and remediation of compliance drifts, ensuring the organization is always audit-ready.

- **AI and ML for smarter audits:** AI and ML are being integrated into auditing tools to move beyond simple configuration checks.

  - o **Anomaly detection:** AI algorithms can analyze vast amounts of log data and user behavior to identify suspicious activities that might indicate a threat, which a human auditor could easily miss.

  - o **Predictive risk analysis**: By analyzing trends and patterns, AI can help predict where future vulnerabilities are most likely to emerge, allowing auditors to focus their efforts on high-risk areas.

  - o **FinOps and cost anomaly detection:** An adjacent but critical audit function, AI-powered tools can detect unusual spending patterns across clouds, identifying potential resource misuse or compromise.

- **Rise of ZTA:** The principle of *never trust, always verify* is perfectly suited for complex multi-cloud and hybrid environments. A zero-trust approach mandates that no entity, whether inside or outside the network, is trusted by default. For auditors, this means verifying that:

  o Strong authentication is required for every user and service.

  o The principle of least privilege is strictly enforced across all platforms.

  o Network micro-segmentation is used to prevent lateral movement in the event of a breach.

Moving to a multi-cloud or hybrid cloud architecture is a strategic business decision; securing and auditing it must be a strategic imperative. The future of auditing in this new landscape is not about checklists and manual reviews. It is about embracing a unified, automated, and intelligent approach. By leveraging centralized platforms, continuous monitoring, and a zero-trust mindset, organizations can tame the complexity of their distributed environments, turning the challenge of auditing into a strategic advantage that fosters trust, security, and sustained compliance.

AI and ML in cloud security and auditing

AI and ML are fundamentally transforming cloud security and auditing. By automating complex tasks, accelerating threat detection, and delivering deeper, actionable insights, these technologies enable organizations to shift from reactive defenses to proactive, adaptive security strategies in today's dynamic cloud ecosystems.

AI/ML in cloud security

AI and ML algorithms process vast streams of data generated by cloud environments, detecting and responding to threats in real time, far beyond the speed and scale achievable by human analysts alone. The following approaches show how AI/ML can be used to improve cloud security:

- **Intelligent threat detection and prevention:** ML models, leveraging algorithms such as random forests or support vector machines, are trained on extensive datasets comprising both benign and malicious traffic. These models learn to recognize patterns indicative of threats like malware, phishing, and **distributed denial-of-service (DDoS)** attacks. For example, an ML-based system can detect subtle deviations in network behavior that traditional rule-based systems often overlook, enabling immediate threat identification and automated containment of malicious activity.

- **Vulnerability management:** AI continuously scans cloud infrastructures, application codebases, and runtime environments to detect vulnerabilities. By correlating insights from internal scans, public vulnerability feeds, and contextual risk factors, AI systems prioritize vulnerabilities by potential impact and exploitability. This risk-driven approach helps security teams remediate the most critical flaws first, strengthening overall cloud resilience.

- **Identity and access management (IAM):** ML-driven **User and Entity Behavior Analytics (UEBA)** establishes behavioral baselines for each user and system entity, covering typical login patterns, access times, and resource usage. Anomalies, such as an employee logging in from an unusual location at an atypical time and downloading large datasets, are flagged as potential indicators of compromise. Such scenarios are quantified by assigning a dynamic risk score, where greater deviation from normal behavior elevates the risk score.

- **Automated incident response:** When a threat is detected, AI-powered response systems can autonomously execute containment actions. For instance, if a virtual machine exhibits signs of compromise, the system can isolate it from the network, capture forensic snapshots for further investigation, and alert the security team, thus minimizing damage and response time.

AI/ML in cloud auditing

Auditing complex, ever-changing cloud environments is challenging. AI and ML simplify and enhance this process, ensuring continuous compliance and more effective risk oversight. The following are some of the key aspects of AI/ML in auditing the cloud:

- **Continuous compliance automation:** AI tools continuously monitor cloud configurations against regulatory frameworks. Unlike periodic manual audits, these systems maintain an always-on compliance posture, immediately flagging configuration drifts or policy violations and leveraging automated remediation & self-healing to correct issues proactively. They can also suggest remediation steps and auto-generate evidence reports for auditors.

- **Log analysis and anomaly detection:** Cloud operations generate immense volumes of log data. Manually analyzing these logs is infeasible, but ML algorithms excel at detecting anomalies within them. By learning what constitutes normal log activity, they can instantly highlight suspicious or abnormal log entries that may indicate security incidents, operational faults, or compliance breaches.

- **Dynamic risk assessment:** Predictive compliance and risk scoring leverages AI to assess threats in real time. AI models enable more accurate, real-time risk assessments by analyzing threats, known vulnerabilities, and their potential business impact. For example, an AI system can calculate the probability of asset compromise based on factors like configuration weaknesses, exposure level, and evolving threat intelligence. This empowers auditors to prioritize high-risk areas efficiently.

- **Automated evidence collection and reporting:** During an audit, AI can rapidly aggregate the necessary evidence from diverse cloud services and generate audit-ready reports tailored to specific compliance standards. This significantly reduces the manual workload and accelerates the overall audit process.

Benefits and challenges

Integrating AI and ML into cloud security and auditing brings substantial benefits: improved accuracy in threat detection, faster incident response, real-time compliance monitoring, and reduced operational overhead. By automating routine tasks, security teams can focus on strategic defense initiatives and continuous improvement.

While AI and ML bring powerful capabilities to cloud security, they also introduce several important challenges:

- **Data dependency**: The effectiveness of AI systems depends heavily on the quality, diversity, and completeness of training data. Poor or biased datasets can lead to inaccurate predictions, blind spots, or missed threats.

- **Lack of transparency**: Many AI models, particularly deep learning systems, operate as *black boxes*, making their decision-making difficult to interpret. This raises concerns around trust, explainability, and accountability.

- **Adversarial attacks**: Threat actors can manipulate input data in subtle ways to deceive AI models, resulting in incorrect classifications or security blind spots. This remains a fast-evolving risk area requiring ongoing research and defense strategies.

- **Privacy and legal risks**: The use of personal or sensitive data in training or inference processes raises significant privacy concerns and legal implications, especially under regulations like GDPR, CCPA, and others. Ensuring compliance and responsible data handling is critical.

- **Data drift and quality issues**: Over time, data patterns can change (data drift), reducing the accuracy and reliability of AI models. Without continuous monitoring and retraining, models may degrade in performance, leading to outdated or incorrect security insights.

AI and ML are redefining how organizations secure and audit their cloud environments. By enabling intelligent threat detection, automated response, and continuous compliance, they empower businesses to build more robust and resilient cloud infrastructures. As cloud adoption and complexity continue to grow, the role of AI and ML in safeguarding these environments will become increasingly indispensable.

Blockchain in cloud auditing

Blockchain technology has the potential to fundamentally transform cloud auditing by delivering unparalleled levels of security, transparency, and data integrity. By harnessing its decentralized and tamper-resistant architecture, blockchain can address many of the limitations inherent in traditional cloud auditing methods, paving the way for more reliable, continuous, and trustworthy assurance.

Benefits of blockchain

Integrating blockchain into cloud auditing introduces a range of compelling benefits. At its foundation, blockchain operates as a decentralized and immutable ledger. Every transaction, configuration change, or data access event within the cloud can be recorded as an encrypted block, securely linked to its predecessor. This creates a tamper-evident, chronological audit trail, making unauthorized alterations virtually impossible and ensuring the integrity and authenticity of audit logs.

Moreover, blockchain's inherent transparency allows all authorized stakeholders, including auditors, cloud customers, and service providers, to access a shared, real-time view of the audit trail. This shared visibility reduces information asymmetry, builds trust, and enhances accountability across the entire cloud ecosystem.

In addition, smart contracts, which are self-executing code that enforce predefined rules, can automate critical aspects of the audit process. For instance, a smart contract can automatically monitor for unauthorized data access attempts or policy violations, triggering alerts or enforcement actions when predefined conditions are met. This automation reduces reliance on manual oversight, minimizes human error, and accelerates incident detection and response.

Challenges

Despite its promise, deploying blockchain in cloud auditing is not without challenges. Scalability is a significant concern: cloud environments generate a vast volume of transactions and events, and a blockchain network must be capable of processing this high throughput efficiently, without introducing latency or performance bottlenecks.

Integration with existing cloud infrastructure and legacy audit tools also presents a complex hurdle. Organizations would need to invest in specialized expertise, updated architectures, and robust governance frameworks to deploy and manage blockchain-based audit systems effectively.

Cost is another critical consideration. Setting up and maintaining a secure, resilient blockchain network can be resource-intensive, potentially offsetting some of the operational efficiencies gained. Additionally, while blockchain's transparency is a major advantage for auditability, it must be balanced with the need to protect sensitive or confidential information on-chain, necessitating advanced cryptographic techniques such as zero-knowledge proofs or privacy-preserving consensus mechanisms.

Emerging applications

Although large-scale public implementations of blockchain for cloud auditing are still emerging, its use in adjacent domains provides valuable proof points. In supply chain management, for example, blockchain ensures an immutable record of a product's journey from origin to consumer, a concept that can be directly applied to tracking data flows and lifecycle events in cloud environments. Similarly, blockchain's role in safeguarding electronic health records demonstrates its capability to handle highly sensitive information while ensuring compliance and auditability.

Looking ahead, the convergence of blockchain and AI holds immense potential for the next generation of cloud auditing. AI can analyze the verifiable, tamper-proof data stored on blockchains to detect anomalies, uncover patterns indicative of emerging threats, and even autonomously initiate remediation workflows. This synergy promises to usher in an era of intelligent, self-healing, and continuously verified cloud assurance.

To sum it up, blockchain stands poised to elevate the standards of trust, integrity, and automation in cloud auditing. As adoption matures and technical challenges are addressed, organizations that embrace this technology will be better equipped to deliver auditable, resilient, and transparent cloud services in an increasingly complex digital landscape.

ZTA in cloud auditing

The traditional defense-in-depth approach to security is no longer sufficient in today's perimeter-less cloud environments. Instead, ZTA has become the new security paradigm, built on a simple yet powerful principle: *Never trust, always verify*. For cloud auditing, this represents a seismic shift. The focus is no longer on validating the strength of the perimeter but on scrutinizing the intricate web of continuous verification mechanisms that now define an organization's security posture. Within the context of emerging auditing trends, Zero Trust does not just add a new layer to audit; it fundamentally redefines its scope and methodology.

ZTA assumes breaches will happen and enforces a policy where no user or device is trusted by default, regardless of its network location. This forces auditors to move beyond static, point-in-time assessments and embrace a more dynamic and continuous approach to verification. The audit is no longer about checking if a firewall is configured correctly once a year; it is about continuously assessing the systems that grant, monitor, and revoke access in real time.

The foundational pillars of ZTA have emerged as primary points of emphasis for modern cloud auditors, explained as follows:

- **Identity as the primary control plane:** In a zero-trust world, identity is the new perimeter. Auditors must now perform deep-dive assessments of IAM systems. This goes beyond checking password policies. The audit must now validate the implementation and effectiveness of **multi-factor authentication** (**MFA**), the enforcement of least-privilege access on a just-in-time basis, and the continuous monitoring of user behavior for anomalies.

- **Micro-segmentation and the blast radius:** Zero trust relies on breaking down the network into small, isolated segments to limit the lateral movement of attackers. Auditors must now verify that these micro-segments are effectively implemented and enforced. This involves examining **network access control lists** (**NACLs**), security groups, and service mesh configurations to ensure that traffic is restricted based on a strict need-to-know basis. The key audit question becomes, *if one segment is breached, how effectively is the blast radius contained?*

- **Continuous monitoring and real-time response:** The *always verify* mantra of Zero Trust is powered by continuous monitoring. Auditors must assess the organization's ability to detect and respond to threats in real-time. This includes evaluating the configuration and effectiveness of **security information and event management** (**SIEM**) systems, threat intelligence feeds, and automated response playbooks. The audit trail is no longer a historical record but a live feed of security events and responses.

Zero trust and emerging auditing trends

The principles of Zero Trust are not just a new subject for audit, but they are a catalyst for the adoption of emerging auditing trends that are better suited to the dynamic nature of the cloud. We will now review the emerging trends in auditing brought about by ZTA, as follows:

- **Continuous auditing and compliance:** Zero trust demands a state of continuous compliance. This aligns perfectly with the move towards continuous auditing, where automated tools constantly monitor the cloud environment for deviations from security policies and regulatory requirements. An auditor's role shifts from periodic testing to reviewing the effectiveness of these automated monitoring and remediation systems.

- **AI and automation in auditing:** The sheer volume of data generated by a ZTA that includes every access request, every device health check, and every network flow is impossible to audit manually. AI and ML are becoming essential tools for the auditor. AI-powered analytics can identify anomalous patterns in user behavior, detect sophisticated threats, and automate the assessment of security controls, allowing auditors to focus on higher-risk areas.

- **DevSecOps and the shift-left audit:** Zero trust principles are being embedded directly into the software development lifecycle through DevSecOps. Security is no longer an afterthought but an integral part of the development process. For auditors, this means shifting left as well. Audits will increasingly focus on the security of the CI/CD pipeline, the use of IaC scanning to enforce Zero Trust policies before deployment, and the secure management of secrets and credentials throughout the development process.

ZTA and regulatory landscape

The evolving regulatory landscape, with stringent requirements from regulations like the GDPR, DORA, and the EU AI Act, finds a powerful ally in Zero Trust. For auditors, a well-implemented ZTA can provide a strong foundation for demonstrating compliance, as detailed:

- **Demonstrating data protection by design:** By enforcing strict access controls and micro-segmentation, Zero Trust provides tangible evidence of *data protection by design and by default,* a key requirement of the GDPR.

- **Ensuring operational resilience:** The continuous monitoring and rapid response capabilities inherent in a Zero Trust model are critical for meeting the operational resilience mandates of regulations like DORA.

- **Building trust in AI systems:** As AI models are increasingly deployed in the cloud, a zero-trust approach can help secure the data pipelines and infrastructure that these systems rely on, providing a foundation of trust for AI governance.

ZTA is more than just a security model; it is a fundamental shift in how we approach trust in the digital world. For cloud auditors, it represents both a challenge and an opportunity. It challenges them to move beyond their traditional comfort zones and embrace new skills and technologies. However, it also provides them with a powerful framework to provide more meaningful and continuous assurance in an increasingly complex and hostile digital landscape. The auditor of the future will not just be checking boxes; they will be verifying trust in a world that has decided to trust nothing.

Evolving regulatory landscape

The ground beneath the world of cloud auditing is in constant motion. A wave of new and updated regulations, driven by a global push for data privacy, operational resilience, and ethical AI, is fundamentally reshaping the scope, complexity, and stakes of providing assurance over cloud environments. For auditors, keeping pace is no longer a matter of updating a checklist; it requires a deep understanding of a complex, multi-jurisdictional legal minefield and the technical mechanisms used to navigate it.

The evolving regulatory landscape is moving far beyond baseline security frameworks, demanding a more sophisticated and continuous approach to cloud auditing. Let us look at the key regulatory pressures forcing this evolution and their profound implications for auditors.

General Data Protection Regulation

The **General Data Protection Regulation (GDPR)** remains a dominant force, and its impact on cloud auditing has been supercharged by the *Schrems II* ruling from the Court of Justice of the European Union. This decision invalidated the EU-US Privacy Shield and clarified that **Standard Contractual Clauses (SCCs)** alone are not a *get out of jail free* card for international data transfers.

Now, let us look at the implications of GDPR for cloud auditing as follows:

- **Scrutinizing supplementary measures:** The auditor's job has shifted from simply verifying the existence of SCCs to critically assessing the supplementary measures implemented to protect data from foreign government surveillance. This is not a legal or contractual check; it is a technical one. Auditors must now seek evidence of robust, end-to-end encryption where the cloud customer, not the US-based provider, holds and manages the encryption keys.

- **Verifying transfer impact assessments (TIAs):** Organizations are now required to conduct and document TIAs for their data transfers. Auditors must review these assessments for thoroughness, ensuring the organization has realistically evaluated the risks and implemented tangible, technical safeguards to protect data processed in the cloud.

- **Auditing data intelligibility:** The key audit question has become, even if the cloud provider is compelled to hand over data, is that data intelligible? This pushes the audit focus towards cryptographic key management, data pseudonymization, and other advanced security techniques that render the data useless to unauthorized parties.

European Union's AI Act

The European Union's AI Act is a landmark regulation that introduces a risk-based framework for the design and deployment of AI. As AI and ML services are predominantly cloud-hosted, this act carves out an entirely new and challenging domain for cloud auditors.

The following are the key points that outline the implications of the EU AI Act on cloud auditing:

- **Risk-based audit scopes:** Auditors will need to understand the AI Act's risk classification (unacceptable, high, limited, minimal) and tailor their audit scope accordingly. For *high-risk* AI systems, which include common cloud use cases like credit scoring, recruitment software, and critical infrastructure management, a conformity assessment is mandatory before the system is put on the market and throughout its lifecycle.

- **Auditing transparency and human oversight:** The act mandates that high-risk AI systems be transparent and allow for human oversight. Auditors will need to test the mechanisms that fulfil these requirements. This includes examining the quality and relevance of the data used to train the models to check for bias, reviewing the technical documentation that providers must supply, and ensuring that deployers are properly informing end-users.

- **Traceability and explainability:** For the first time, auditors will be asked to verify the traceability of AI decision-making. This involves examining logs and records to understand how an AI model reached a particular conclusion, creating a new and complex audit trail to follow within the cloud environment. Auditors can leverage **Explainable AI (XAI)** to enhance traceability and explainability in AI-driven systems by providing clear, interpretable insights into how decisions are made. XAI helps auditors trace data flows, understand model behavior, and validate outcomes against regulatory or organizational standards. This transparency is crucial for identifying potential biases, ensuring accountability, and demonstrating compliance in increasingly complex AI-integrated environments.

DORA

The **Digital Operational Resilience Act (DORA)** is a specific and stringent regulation targeting the financial services sector in the EU. It recognizes that cloud providers have become critical third parties and imposes rigorous requirements to ensure the sector can withstand severe operational disruptions.

DORA strengthens the regulatory framework for ICT risk management, which has significant implications for cloud auditing as discussed here:

- **Expanded scope of ICT risk management:** DORA mandates a comprehensive and integrated ICT risk management framework. Auditors must now assess not just security controls but the entire resilience strategy, including the firm's ability to identify, protect, detect, respond, and recover from ICT-related incidents in the cloud.

- **Stringent third-party (Cloud) risk management:** Auditors are now required to perform deep dives into how a financial firm manages its cloud providers. This includes scrutinizing contracts for DORA-specific clauses, verifying the firm's process for vendor due diligence and ongoing monitoring, and assessing the exit strategies for critical cloud services.

- **Verifying advanced resilience testing:** DORA requires firms to conduct regular, advanced security testing. A key new requirement is **threat-led penetration testing (TLPT)**, where auditors must verify that firms are simulating real-world attack scenarios against their critical live production systems in the cloud.

Health Insurance Portability and Accountability Act

In the evolving regulatory landscape for cloud auditing, the **Health Insurance Portability and Accountability Act (HIPAA)** remains a foundational framework for protecting sensitive health information in cloud environments. It mandates strict controls around data privacy, security, and access, especially for covered entities and their cloud service providers.

HTI-1 Final Rule

This is specifically a comprehensive rule issued by the **Office of the National Coordinator for Health Information Technology (ONC)** that updates the certification program (Health Data, Technology, and Interoperability) for health IT systems, promotes algorithm transparency, and establishes standards for information sharing in healthcare further advances this landscape by emphasizing secure, standardized, and interoperable data sharing, while reinforcing anti-information blocking provisions. For cloud auditing, this underscores the need for transparent data practices, enhanced access controls, and the ability to demonstrate compliance with both security and interoperability requirements.

Data sovereignty

Underpinning all these trends is the growing wave of data sovereignty and localization laws. Nations from India to Brazil are enacting rules that dictate where their citizens' data can be stored and processed. This creates a significant compliance headache for global organizations using centralized cloud services, and the implications on auditing the cloud are as follows:

- **Verifying data residency:** The audit trail must now definitively prove where data resides at all times. This requires auditors to assess the technical controls used to enforce data residency, such as geo-fencing, region-specific resource deployment policies, and the configuration of content delivery networks.

- **Auditing the right to audit:** While many regulations grant a *right to audit*, exercising this on a major cloud service provider is often impractical. The audit focus, therefore, shifts to a critical evaluation of the provider's own compliance reports (e.g., SOC 2, ISO 27001). However, auditors must assess whether these generic reports adequately cover the specific, and often stricter, requirements of new regulations like DORA and the AI Act. This places a greater burden on auditing the customer's own vendor management and oversight processes.

- **A Unified, yet adapted, approach:** Auditors must now help organizations develop a unified compliance framework that can still be adapted to the specific, and sometimes conflicting, demands of different jurisdictions. This involves verifying that data is classified according to its risk and associated legal requirements, and that the appropriate controls are applied consistently, regardless of the cloud platform.

In this hyper-regulated, multi-cloud world, the role of the cloud auditor is more critical than ever. It has evolved from a historical compliance checker to a forward-looking advisor who must possess a hybrid of legal, technical, and risk management expertise. Success now depends on the ability to look past the paper policies and contractual clauses and to audit the technical reality of how data is protected, how resilience is ensured, and how intelligent systems are governed in the cloud.

Conclusion

This chapter discussed how emerging technologies like AI, ML, blockchain, and ZTA are transforming cloud auditing into a more intelligent, automated, and resilient practice. Combined with continuous monitoring and an evolving regulatory landscape, these innovations are equipping organizations to maintain trust, ensure compliance, and proactively manage risks in real time. By embracing these advancements, organizations can strengthen their security posture and build a foundation for sustainable cloud governance in an increasingly digital world. By adopting these emerging practices, auditors can enhance their effectiveness, ensure robust compliance, and support resilient cloud governance in an ever-evolving digital landscape.

Points to remember

- AI/ML algorithms analyze vast amounts of data in real-time that might indicate a threat, which a human auditor could easily miss.

- ML models can learn from historical data to predict potential vulnerabilities, compliance issues, and areas of high risk, enabling proactive mitigation.

- AI/ML facilitates continuous monitoring of cloud environments, allowing for real-time compliance checks and immediate flagging of non-compliance or security incidents.

- AI-powered systems can initiate automated responses to detected threats, such as isolating affected resources or applying patches, reducing response times.

- AI can extract and integrate relevant information from diverse sources, including unstructured data, improving the comprehensiveness of audit evidence.

- Automation of routine audit tasks frees up human auditors to focus on higher-value analysis and critical decision-making.

- ZTA fundamentally shifts security from perimeter-based models to a principle where no user, device, or application is implicitly trusted, regardless of its location.

- In ZTA, every access request is rigorously authenticated, authorized, and continuously validated based on context, ensuring least privilege access.

- ZTA requires continuous monitoring of user and device behavior for any anomalies, even after initial access is granted, to detect potential insider threats or compromised accounts.

- Zero trust relies on breaking down the network into small, isolated segments, limiting the *blast radius* of a breach if one occurs.

- The continuous verification and explicit authorization inherent in ZTA provide richer and more detailed audit trails, making it easier to track and understand access patterns and security events.

- Blockchain's decentralized and immutable ledger provides a tamper-proof record of transactions and events within cloud environments. This ensures the integrity and authenticity of audit evidence.

- By recording data access logs and other critical events on a blockchain, organizations can create a verifiable and unalterable history, reducing the risk of data manipulation.

- The distributed nature of blockchain can increase transparency in multi-cloud or hybrid cloud environments, enhancing trust among different stakeholders and auditors.

- Smart contracts can be used to automatically enforce compliance rules and policies, triggering actions or alerts when conditions are met or violated, further automating audit processes.

- Blockchain can streamline the verification of data and transactions, as the cryptographic linking of blocks inherently provides a high level of assurance.

Multiple choice questions

1. **Which of the following best describes a key emerging trend in cloud auditing?**

    a. Relying solely on manual, periodic audits to check compliance.

    b. Using AI and ML to automate threat detection and continuous compliance monitoring.

    c. Storing all audit logs in a single centralized database without encryption.

    d. Eliminating the need for any compliance checks due to increased cloud provider responsibility.

2. **In the context of modern cloud auditing, what is the primary purpose of implementing ZTA?**

    a. To allow unrestricted access to internal network resources

    b. To trust all users inside the organization's network by default

    c. To ensure that no user or device is trusted automatically

    d. To eliminate the need for encryption within cloud services

3. **Which technology enhances the integrity and transparency of cloud audit trails by providing a decentralized and tamper-evident ledger?**

    a. VPNs

    b. Blockchain

    c. AI/ML

    d. Zero trust architecture

4. **What does the term compliance-as-code refer to in modern cloud auditing practices?**

    a. Writing compliance reports manually

    b. Hard-coding compliance policies into the network hardware

    c. Embedding compliance requirements into automated deployment and configuration scripts

    d. Relying solely on periodic audits to check for compliance

5. **How do smart contracts contribute to automated cloud auditing?**

   a. They manually verify audit logs after every transaction

   b. They enable self-executing rules that trigger actions based on predefined conditions

   c. They encrypt all cloud data automatically

   d. They replace the need for compliance frameworks entirely

Answers

1	b
2	c
3	b
4	c
5	b

Join our Discord space

Join our Discord workspace for latest updates, offers, tech happenings around the world, new releases, and sessions with the authors:

https://discord.bpbonline.com

Index

www.ingramcontent.com/pod-product-compliance
Lightning Source LLC
Chambersburg PA
CBHW061804210326
41599CB00034B/6875